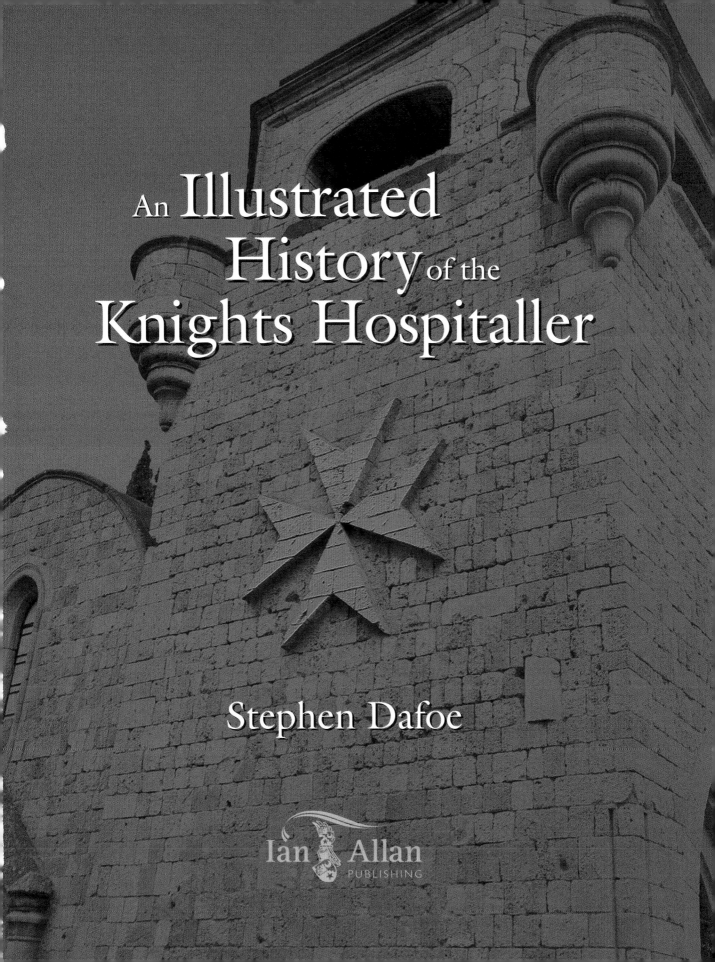

An Illustrated History of the Knights Hospitaller

Stephen Dafoe

Ian Allan
PUBLISHING

First published 2010

ISBN 978 07110 3497 6

Published by Ian Allan Publishing

an imprint of Ian Allan Publishing Ltd, Hersham, Surrey KT12 4RG.
Printed by Ian Allan Printing Ltd, Hersham, Surrey KT12 4RG.

Visit the Ian Allan Publishing website at www.ianallanpublishing.com

Captions without copyright are property of the author.

Contents

Acknowledgements

This book is dedicated to the memory of Cathy Chester, a friend whose energy and compassion was worthy of the Hospitallers and who, like the Templars, had her brightly burning flame extinguished while it still had so much light to give.

Writing a book is as easy for a writer as drawing a picture is for an artist. Unfortunately, this book called for words and images and, as I am more comfortable with a keyboard than a paintbrush, I needed help on the latter.

If you have flipped through this book you will see that it is divided into three sections, each chronicling one era of the Hospitallers' story. The wonderful illustrations of the knights in full gear were drawn by David Naughton Shires, a talented artist from Ireland. Another of his illustrations graces the back cover of the book, along with a digitally rendered Maltese cross created by another talented artist friend, Stephen McKim. Stephen also designed the cross on the front cover as well as the galleys and galleons used in many of the battle maps throughout the book. It is my job as a writer to make the Hospitallers' story come alive in a colourful manner, but chances are David and Stephen's work prompted you to pick the book up.

I'd also like to thank a few people who took photographs for me or allowed me to use photographs they had taken. My thanks go out to Doug Bewick for his pictures of Balantrodoch and Torphichen in Scotland, and to John Brunette and Mark Williams for the use of their Hospitaller re-enactment photographs.

As there is more to the creation of a book like this than merely words and pictures, I would like to thank my agent Fiona Spencer-Thomas for representing me and my editor Jay Slater for all the little tweaks and corrections that prevent me from looking like an idiot. And making the entire book look good is Matthew Wharmby, who took the pictures and prose and made them into the elegant-looking product you now hold in your hands.

I would be remiss if I did not thank Randy Williams and John Hayes for their continued friendship, support, and for dragging me out for a 'Three Amigos' lunch now and again; my wife Bonnie for putting up with me for these past fourteen years and past four or five books; and my readers who continue to read my work and encourage me to produce more.

Introduction

When Nick Grant of Ian Allan Publishing approached me a couple years ago with the idea of writing a companion book to my 2007 work *Nobly Born: An Illustrated History of the Knights Templar*, I was relieved and delighted. I was relieved that he wasn't asking me to write another book on the Templars and delighted that he thought a similar treatment of the Hospitallers was in order. For nearly two centuries the Templars and Hospitallers ran an almost parallel course, sharing the same victories, enduring the same defeats, and almost engaging in the same battles, when they were not at odds with one another. It seemed only fitting that the Hospitallers' story should stand side by side with that of the Templars. Sadly that has not been the case.

Despite expending the same efforts on behalf of Christendom that their armed co-religionists did, the Hospitallers have always played second fiddle to the Templars when it comes to having their story told. This is largely because of the tragic circumstances of the Templars' demise and the myths that evolved, crediting to the Order a variety of motives which the Templars themselves would have been repulsed by. As I wrote in the introduction to *Nobly Born*: 'There have been a number of books on the Templars in recent months, but what would seem to be missing are books that concentrate on the actual history of the Order, which is no less interesting than the speculative material and fictional accounts that have dominated the marketplace in recent years.' With respect to the Hospitallers there has been little of their story told, mythical or otherwise.

This is an unfortunate situation because where the Templars' story covers the years 1119 to 1314, that of the Hospitallers precedes and exceeds that of their white-mantled contemporaries by many years indeed. Unlike the Templars, who largely became stagnant after the fall of Acre in 1291, the Hospitallers were not content to remain on dry land, taking to the seas to conquer Rhodes in 1306. After capturing the island three years later, the Hospitallers would call Rhodes home until 1522 when the Ottoman Sultan Suleiman the Magnificent captured the island, sending the Hospitallers in search of a new home. But neither the growing power of the Ottoman Empire, the changing face of Christendom or the increase in wars between nations stopped the Hospitallers from fulfilling their dual role as crusaders and humanitarians. After the realisation that Rhodes was lost to them forever, the Order accepted Malta as a gift and remained on the island until the closing years of the French Revolution, when Napoleon Bonaparte succeeded where others had failed, and forced the Hospitallers to leave.

An Illustrated History of the Knights Hospitaller covers a seven and a half century period of time and traces the story of this remarkable Military Order over land and sea. As with *Nobly Born*, this book is not only a story about the Hospitallers themselves, but about the ever-changing world they lived in. On the 487th anniversary of the Hospitallers' eviction from Rhodes, it is my sincerest hope that this book will increase interest in a remarkable Order of knighthood who, despite every adversity thrown their way, continued to survive and continue to survive to this day, engaged in the same humble and important work their founders performed at Jerusalem – looking after the poor and sick.

Stephen Dafoe
1 January 2010 on the 487th anniversary of the Hospitallers' eviction from Rhodes

The Hospitallers' armour evolved over the years. Shown from left are depictions of how a battle-dressed Hospitaller would have looked circa 1250-1300, 1350-1400 and 1400-1450.
David Naughton Shires

Author's note

Although this book has been divided into sections entitled 'The Knights of Jerusalem', 'The Knights of Rhodes' and 'The Knights of Malta', I have used the terms Hospitallers, the Order and occasionally the Religion throughout the entirety of the book when referring to the subject collectively. Although the Order was known varyingly as the Knights of St John, Rhodes, Malta, etc., they never ceased in their original role as Hospitallers. Additionally, I have not included endnotes in this book, preferring to reference major sources in the body of the text. Although I have been as meticulous with my research in writing this book as I have in my previous heavily noted books, this book is not intended to be an academic treatment of the subject. That is not to say that I have not tried to be scholarly, but rather that, like *Nobly Born*, the book is intended to take a normally dry subject and make it accessible to a general readership. Whether you are a medieval history buff or casually interested in the subject, I hope you will enjoy the present volume.

CHAPTER 1

The Blessed Gerard

Unlike their monastic and military counterparts, the Knights Templar, the Hospitallers were not created as a result of the Crusades but rather were transformed by them. From their formation in AD1119, the Templars had a mandate of protecting pilgrims travelling to the Holy Land to view the sites sacred to their faith.

This protection, which was a necessity, included the frequent use of the sword and shield as the Templars patrolled the roads in and around the Holy City rescuing distressed pilgrims from Muslim aggression. However, in the decades prior to the Christian conquest of Jerusalem in 1099, the situation in Jerusalem was considerably different. Christian and

Above: **A Hospitaller knight circa 1259-1300 is shown in this original image by David Naughton Shires after a depiction of knights of the era found in the Grand Master's palace at Rhodes. In the closing years of the Crusader States era, the Hospitallers adopted a red surcoat with white cross. This change in statutes was introduced in 1259.**
David Naughton Shires

Left: **The Church of the Holy Sepulchre was originally built around AD325 by order of Emperor Constantine I. It had been erected over a pagan temple, but during the construction Constantine's mother is said to have discovered the True Cross on which Christ was crucified, as well as his tomb. The discovery popularised Christian pilgrimages to Jerusalem. Destroyed in AD1009 by Caliph Al-Hakim, it was rebuilt around 1027. It remains Christianity's most sacred site.**
Bigstock/ Bernhard Richter

St John Eleemon, shown in this sixteenth-century painting by Titian, is better known by the names St John the Merciful, St John the Almoner and St John the Almsgiver. Johannes Eleemon was a nobly born Cypriot who served as the Patriarch of Alexandria during the seventh century, but is best remembered for the acts of compassion and almsgiving that characterised his life.

Muslim lived in relative peace within their fortified walls. Although pilgrims still needed taking care of, that protection was largely in the form of food and shelter, as well as the minimal medical care then available. It is in this capacity that the Hospitallers emerged at a time when Jerusalem was under Muslim rule.

Pilgrimage had been popular within Christianity since the fourth century AD, when Emperor Constantine I ordered the construction of the Church of the Holy Sepulchre over the site of an old pagan temple dedicated to Aphrodite. It was during the excavation of the site that Constantine's mother Helena is alleged to have discovered the True Cross upon which Christ was crucified and the tomb in which he was buried. Whether the story is based in truth or an apocryphal tale to fit the purpose of the newly erected holy site, by the turn of the millennium the Christian faithful were travelling thousands of miles across harsh terrain to see and pray at the Church of the Holy Sepulchre.

As with any tourist destination, religious or secular, commerce is certain to make an appearance and the mixture of pilgrimage and business was common in Jerusalem, particularly among a group of merchants from Amalfi, a rich maritime city in the Kingdom of Naples whose trading history could be traced back to the sixth century. Amalfian merchants were well respected in Islamic ports and places, but had a special relationship with the Fatimids with whom they had traded in Egypt. As such, the Amalfian traders were always welcomed in Jerusalem while it was under Fatimid rule. In fact, with the exception of the Caliph Al-Hakim, who destroyed a number of Christian buildings, including the Church of the Holy Sepulchre and a hostel for pilgrims, in AD1009, Christians and Jews had both fared well during the Fatimid years between 969 and 1071.

Before the Fatimids were ejected from Jerusalem by the Seljuk Turks in 1071, the Amalfian merchants rebuilt the hospital that had been destroyed by Al-Hakim and constructed a second specifically for female travellers. Each of these hospitals, or xenodochium as they were called, was supported by its own church, one dedicated to St Mary Magdalene and the other to St John Eleemon, which were built after the completion of the hospitals. Additionally, the Amalfians ordered the construction of a church dedicated to the Virgin and called it Santa Maria ad Latinos to differentiate it from those Christian churches where eastern rituals and observances were performed. It was this complex of hostels and religious houses that would be the foundation stone of a religious Order that continues to this day engaged in the very work performed by its founders.

It is interesting that the male hospice was connected to the name of St John Eleemon, for the Hospitallers have long been associated with the headless and more famous St John the Baptist. However, it would seem that, at least prior to the Hospitallers' official recognition by the Holy See, it was St John Eleemon whom the founding caregivers were dedicated to. This makes for a fitting patron when one considers that St John Eleemon is better known by the names St John the Merciful, St John the Almoner or St John the Almsgiver. Johannes Eleemon was a nobly born Cypriot who served as the Patriarch of Alexandria during the seventh century. Although historically recognised for restoring the church in Alexandria, it is the acts of compassion and almsgiving that characterised his life that earned him his posthumous name John the Merciful.

The Seljuk Turks who wrested control of the Holy City from the Fatimids in 1071 were not as merciful as St John Eleemon or their Muslim predecessors in Jerusalem. Since defeating the Byzantine Christians at the Battle of Manzikert in August of 1071, the fledgling empire had made great ground. Upon adding Jerusalem to their territory, they greatly increased the jizya, a per capita tax levied on non-Muslim residents. Although pilgrims were still permitted to visit the city, they were not treated with the same courtesy that previous generations of pious travellers had received, and pilgrims travelling outside the city's walls were often treated poorly. It was under these conditions that the story of the founding of the Hospitallers began.

Around 1080, the name Brother Gerard becomes connected with the Order of St John. Little is known of the man who would be remembered in Hospitaller history as the Blessed Gerard. Even his alleged surname,

Tunc, often rendered as Thom or even Tongue, is highly questionable. In his 1994 book *The Knights of Malta*, H. J. A. Sire posits that Gerard's surname was developed by the seventeenth-century writer Anne de Nabirat, who discovered the words *Geraldus tunc* in a document. De Nabirat, perhaps not realising that *tunc* was the Latin word for then, assumed it to be the man's surname. Although Gerard's place of birth has been given as either Amalfi or Provence, there is nothing conclusive to establish if either suggestion is correct; likewise the circumstances of his arrival in Jerusalem. Major Whitworth Porter in his 1883 history of the Order suggests that Brother Gerard was inspired by the work of the Amalfian hospital:

'[Gerard] had undertaken the pilgrimage to the East in accordance with the prevailing custom of the times, and having been an eye-witness of the many charities administered by the hospital, he had abandoned all idea of returning to Europe, and devoted himself instead to the service of the institution. Here by his energy and zeal as well as by the general piety of his life, he gained so much influence that eventually he was appointed rector.'

St John the Baptist is shown here in this fragment of the Deësis (Entreaty) mosaic in the Hagia Sophia in Istanbul, Turkey. John is the saint connected to the Knights Hospitaller and among the Order's most sacred relics was what they believed to be his right hand. Some of the Order's seals also depicted the saint's severed head – an interesting icon, given that the Templars were accused of worshipping a head. *Bigstock/ Alexander Zotov*

The rectorship to which Porter refers is that of the hospital for men. At the same time an Italian woman named Agnes was said to have managed the hospital for women. It is important to understand that these hospitals were not a hospital in the sense with which we are familiar today, although they would have treated sickness and wounds to the best of their ability out of necessity. The facility's principal purpose was to offer a place of rest for travelling pilgrims, providing them with nourishment for their bodies from the kitchens and nourishment for their souls through the associated churches.

However, the Amalfians were not entirely altruistic in creating these hospitals. A considerable amount of their business during the apex of pilgrim travel to the Holy Land was transporting pious Europeans to the east. It was only good business to accommodate their passengers on their arrival at their destination, rather than leaving them to fend for themselves. Although we will never know how or why Brother Gerard became involved with the hospital dedicated to St John Eleemon, the fact that the Amalfian founders of the Jerusalem hospitals were not entirely philanthropic in their designs may suggest a greater likelihood that they would leave one of their own countrymen in charge of such an important part of their operations. But wherever Brother Gerard came from and why ever he joined the cause, his involvement allowed the institution to weather one of the greatest transitions the Holy City would ever endure: the capture of Jerusalem by Godfrey de Bouillon on 15 July 1099.

The great campaign that would become known as the First Crusade grew out of a church council held in Clermont, France, in 1095. Pope Urban II had united Christendom to deal with a number of matters, including the excommunication of the King of France, Philip I, for adultery. But there was also the matter of upholding the 'Treuga Dei' or Truce of God.

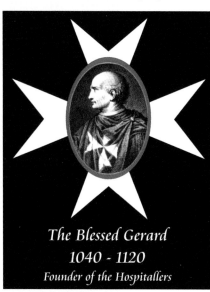

The Blessed Gerard, founder of the Hospitallers, is shown in this romantically depicted seventeenth century copper engraving by Laurent Cars.

Although the truce had been introduced in France a century earlier, it was the first of thirty decrees issued by the Council of Clermont. Feudalism had given rise to infighting among Christians, especially those of the knightly and noble classes, and the Truce of God was designed to put an end to this. It prohibited fighting from sunset on Wednesday until sunrise on Monday for the nobility; women, churchmen, labourers and merchants were forbidden from fighting at all times. However, if the Pope was unwilling to countenance fighting between Christians, he seemed to have no problem with them directing their hostilities towards a common foe. Following the regular ecclesiastical business of the council, Urban moved the proceedings to a large field outside the church where the council was held. It was here that he would give the speech which would move the Christian west to action against a common enemy in the east.

Although several accounts of Urban's speech exist, many of which were written by men who were actually in attendance, it is almost certain that all were written in retrospect after the Christian victory at Jerusalem in 1099. Among the first hand accounts is that of Fulcher of Chartres who was not only present at the Council of Clermont, but also participated in and chronicled the campaign from the front lines. As such, his may be regarded as being the most reliable. Fulcher quotes Urban:

'[The Muslims] have killed and captured many, and have destroyed the churches and devastated the empire. If you permit them to continue thus for awhile with impunity, the faithful of God will be much more widely attacked by them. On this account I, or rather the Lord, beseech you as Christ's heralds to publish this everywhere and to persuade all people of whatever rank, foot-soldiers and knights, poor and rich, to carry aid promptly to those Christians and to destroy that vile race from the lands of our friends. I say this to those who are present, it is meant also for those who are absent. Moreover, Christ commands it.'

Another chronicler of the First Crusade was Robert the Monk. Unlike Fulcher of Chartres, Robert did not go on crusade; however, it is generally agreed that he was in attendance when Urban spoke. Robert's account of the Pope's speech contains language intended to shock the reader:

'From the confines of Jerusalem and the city of Constantinople a horrible tale has gone forth and very frequently has been brought to our ears, namely, that a race from the kingdom of the Persians [the Seljuk Turks], an accursed race, a race utterly alienated from God, a generation forsooth which has not directed its heart and has not entrusted its spirit to God, has invaded the lands of those Christians and has depopulated them by the sword, pillage and fire; it has led away a part of the captives into its own country, and a part it has destroyed by cruel tortures; it has either entirely destroyed the churches of God or appropriated them for the rites of its own religion. They destroy the altars, after having defiled them with their uncleanness. They circumcise the Christians, and the blood of the circumcision they either spread upon the altars or pour into the vases of the baptismal font. When they wish to torture people by a base death, they perforate their navels, and dragging forth the extremity of the intestines, bind it to a stake; then with flogging they lead the victim around until the viscera having gushed forth the victim falls prostrate upon the ground. Others they bind to a post and pierce with arrows. Others they compel to extend their necks and then, attacking them with naked swords, attempt to cut through the neck with a single blow. What shall I say of the abominable rape of the women? To speak of it is worse than to be silent. The kingdom of the Greeks is now dismembered by them and deprived of territory so vast in extent that it can not be traversed in a march of two months. On whom therefore is the labour of avenging these wrongs and of recovering this territory incumbent, if not upon you? You, upon whom above other nations God has conferred remarkable glory in arms, great courage, bodily activity, and strength to humble the hairy scalp of those who resist you.'

Whatever Pope Urban's words truly were it is certain that they contained enough emotion to stir up hatred in the west, creating a strong desire in the hearts of the faithful to eradicate the infidels who were harassing fellow Christians in the east. If the words were not enough incentive, Urban offered a plenary indulgence (the remission of all sins) to all who would take up the cause, and further vowed that all property would be protected by the church as if it were its own. The offerings appealed even to those who had no property.

The idea that Urban's speech led to a mass exodus of commoners and kings to capture the Holy City of Jerusalem for Christendom is not an accurate one. From departure to conclusion, the campaign was far from a cohesive effort and this lack of Christian unity would continue throughout the era of the Crusader States during the twelfth and thirteenth centuries. In fact, the only thing that allowed the Christians to hold territory for as long as they did was an equal, and sometimes greater, lack of unity among their Muslim enemies. It was in this chaotic world of shifting allegiances and political intrigue that the Hospitallers, Templars and, during the final century, the Teutonic Knights would all have to operate.

The lack of unity first manifested itself in the days following Urban's speech, for it was not the kings and princes who were the first to leave, but rather the peasantry who would be the first to take up the cross: men and boys who had no real military skills outside the normal requirements of feudalism. Led by Peter the Hermit – a man whose depiction is often more romantic than factual – the Peasant or People's Crusade departed for Jerusalem with a force of probably 20,000, arriving at the gates of their eastern Christian brethren in Constantinople in May of 1096. Although Constantinople was a city that would plague the Hospitallers from the fifteenth century onwards, at the time of Peter's arrival at its gates it was under the control of the weakening Byzantine Christian Emperor, Alexius Comnenus. It had been the eastern Christians, defeated at the Battle of Manzikert in 1071 and pressured by the Turks ever since, that the western Christians had been sent to aid, but as far as the emperor was concerned the rabble gathered outside the gates of Constantinople were little better than the Turks and he quickly arranged for their transport across the Bosphorus. It was a body of water that many would not live to cross again. On 21 October, the Peasants' Crusade effectively came to an end when the Turks ambushed the army at Civetot near Nicaea, slaughtering the men and taking the women and children as slaves.

Others would follow the trail left by Peter the Hermit and his disastrous Peasants' Crusade, including Count Emrich of Leisingen, a minor lord from the Rhineland. Emrich was able to attract a good number of nobly born Germans to his cause. However, unlike the peasants who had rushed off to fight on foreign shores, Emrich saw Christ's enemies a little closer to home, slaughtering countless Jews at Worms and Mainz, and setting fire to the synagogue at Cologne. But his arrival in Hungary in June of 1096 would mark his farthest progress towards the east.

Emrich's army laid siege to the fortress of Wieselburg but when word arrived that the Hungarian king was returning with reinforcements, the army's discipline disintegrated and the garrison's defenders were able to destroy the Germans. Utterly routed by the Hungarians, Emrich and a few knights managed to escape and return to their homelands.

But where other efforts had failed, The Prince's Crusade would succeed. Again, this was not a singular united effort of the military might of the west; each of the several participants left in their own time and took their own route to the Holy Land. In total there were five armies that departed Europe between August and October 1096, arriving at Constantinople in the spring of 1097. The first to arrive was Hugh, the Count of Vermandois, who was the younger brother of the French king excommunicated by Urban at the Council of Clermont for adultery. He had set out in late August of 1096 and was joined by a number of knights who had survived Emrich's earlier debacle. The next army to arrive from the west was that of Godfrey de Bouillon, Duke of Lower Lorraine, a descendant of Charlemagne – a pedigree that certainly added to his status both before and after the crusade. Godfrey was accompanied by his two brothers, Eustace and Baldwin, and their cousin Baldwin of Le Bourg. Like Hugh's army, Godfrey's party had left in late August, but approached the east by way of Hungary, as the previous failed expeditions had done. Godfrey was followed by the armies of Bohemond of Taranto and his nephew Tancred, and Raymond IV, the Count of Toulouse, who had been accompanied on his journey by the papal legate Bishop Adhémar du Puy. The last of the crusader armies to depart for the east was that of Robert, the Duke of Normandy, the oldest son of William the Conqueror and the brother of King William II. Robert was accompanied by his brother-in-law, Stephen the Count of Blois, and Robert the Count of Flanders.

It is difficult to determine the size of the army assembled on Asia's western frontier. Medieval chroniclers had a tendency to record figures more for effect than accuracy. Certainly when chroniclers like Albert of Aix wrote that the crusaders numbered in the hundreds of thousands, their intent was to impress upon

Peter the Hermit is seen talking to his followers and Walter's soldiers in this nineteenth century illustration by Edouard Zier depicting the legendary but failed People's Crusade.

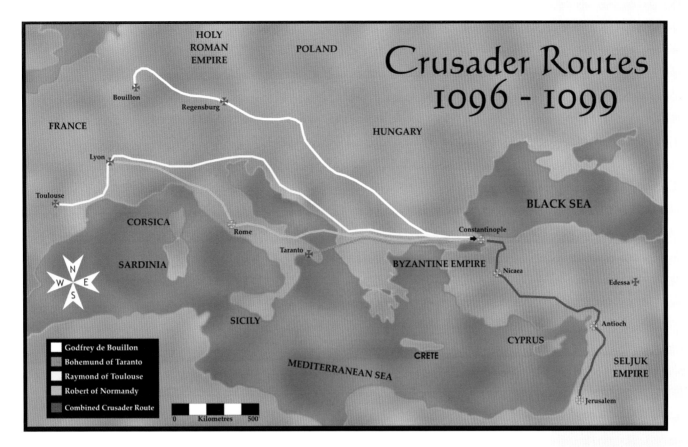

Crusader Routes
1096 - 1099

Legend:
- Godfrey de Bouillon
- Bohemund of Taranto
- Raymond of Toulouse
- Robert of Normandy
- Combined Crusader Route

0 Kilometres 500

their readers that the number was large. Sir Stephen Runciman, by examining the varying accounts of individual battles, arrived at a figure of approximately 4,500 cavalry and 30,000 infantry when the armies were combined. As mentioned before, this was not one cohesive force, but several individual armies, each with its own agenda and motives for being on crusade. The leaders of the armies were as suspicious of their co-religionists as they were of the enemies of their faith. Even the rival factions who had made up Peter's Peasants' Crusade had fought with one another over the spoils of war, and the campaign ultimately came to an end because of it. The leaders of the First Crusade proper, for all their existing wealth in Europe, were no less attracted by the glitter of gold than their pauper predecessors. However, despite their rivalries and infighting, they would succeed where the others had failed, scoring their first victory at the same place where the previous expedition met its demise, Nicaea.

After a subsequent victory at Dorylaeum at the beginning of July 1097, the crusader princes really began to pursue their own interests. Starting with Baldwin of Bolougne drifting off from the army to ultimately establish himself as ruler of Edessa, the crusader kings would begin to stay within captured territory, occasionally squabbling over who should keep it, as was the case with the capture of Antioch in 1098. Raymond of Toulouse and Bohemond of Taranto both wanted the city, but Bohemond succeeded, establishing himself as the second ruler of the Crusader States. These conflicts continued throughout the remainder of the long march to Jerusalem.

When the Franks had left their homes in the summer and autumn of 1096, there had been as many as 35,000 crusaders between the four armies. However, by June of 1099 when they crested the Judean hills and saw the Holy City for the first time, their number had been reduced to 14,000. For every kilometre as the crow flies the crusaders had lost six men, either through combat, starvation, sickness or the desire to settle down in the east. Less than half of those who had set out to seize

When the four main crusader armies left in the summer and autumn of 1096, they did not all take the same route to the rallying point of Constantinople.

Jerusalem from the Muslims were now left to complete the job.

This would be no easy task, for the city's defence had been left in the hands of its Fatimid governor, Iftikhar al-Dawla. While the Franks had been battling in Antioch in the summer of 1098, the Fatimids had been battling to regain control of Jerusalem. As Antioch's governor, Yaghi-Siyan had done during the siege of his city, Jerusalem's governor Iftikhar expelled the Christians from the city, lest they assist their co-religionists during the battle ahead. Additionally, he rounded up the flocks to deprive the crusaders

When the crusaders gained access to Jerusalem, Tancred pursued the Muslims to al-Aqsa Mosque where many had taken refuge. He offered to spare their lives if they would surrender and soon his banner was flying over the mosque; however, they were slaughtered by other crusaders the following day. In the years to follow, al-Aqsa would be home to the Knights Templar.
Bigstock/ Yan Vugenfirer

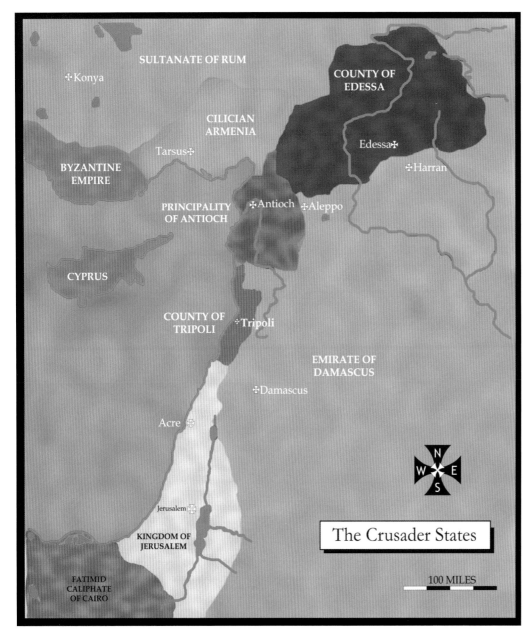

The boundaries of the so-called Crusader States were in constant flux throughout the period of Christian presence in the Levant. This map shows the County of Edessa, Principality of Antioch, County of Tripoli and Kingdom of Jerusalem as they would have appeared between the First and Second Crusades.

of food and burned anything that could be cut down and made into siege towers.

It is in this context that an interesting legend emerges about Brother Gerard. In the story, Gerard was not among the Christians expelled from Jerusalem before the crusaders arrived; rather, he was allowed to stay behind but ordered to help defend the city walls along with the other inhabitants. While the Muslim residents hurled rocks down upon the crusaders, Gerard is said to have cast loaves of bread shaped like rocks. When guards discovered that he was actually assisting his fellow Christians, Gerard was arrested and taken before the governor to answer to the charges. However, when the guards produced the evidence, Brother Gerard's loaves of bread had miraculously changed into rocks. Although the story is clearly a hagiographical account, it is possible that Gerard was allowed to stay behind in the city, and was subsequently arrested as the crusaders gained ground. As the rector of the hospital, it is quite possible that he and those who worked under him could have been an additional workforce to help deal with the wounded, no matter how rudimentary their abilities in medicine may have been. But the general harmony of accounts indicates that, for whatever reason, Gerard was left behind and was subsequently arrested, where he would remain until the Christians took the city.

The siege of Jerusalem lasted from 7 June 1099, when the crusaders first crossed the Judean hills, until 15 July when Godfrey de Bouillon's men finally crested the walls of the city sacred to three religions. Soon after Godfrey's men had gained access to the ramparts, the city's gates were opened wide, allowing the crusaders to flood through. Seeing that the city's defences had been shattered, the Muslims fled to the Temple Mount area where their predecessors had erected the Dome of the Rock and the al-Aqsa Mosque in the years that followed the first Muslim conquest of Jerusalem in AD638. Tancred pursued the Muslims and plundered the Dome of the Rock of its valuables before turning his attentions to the al-Aqsa Mosque, where many had taken refuge. He offered to spare their lives if they would surrender, and soon his banner was flying over the mosque.

Meanwhile, Raymond pursued the governor to the Tower of David, where Iftikhar surrendered not only the tower, but a considerable booty on the condition that he and his bodyguards would be spared and given the freedom to leave the city. The count accepted and honoured the governor's conditions, but others were not as lucky. Those in al-Aqsa who had surrendered in exchange for their lives were cut down the next day by a group of crusaders who ignored Tancred's banner flying overhead. Even the city's Jews, who had sought shelter in their synagogue, were killed when the Franks set the temple ablaze, as Emrich of Leisingen had done in Germany three years earlier. Every man, woman and child the crusaders came across was slaughtered, and had the Christians not been expelled from the city before the siege, it is possible that they too would have been among the dead. Perhaps the most gruesome of the contemporary accounts of the massacre is that of Raymond d'Aguiliers who described the carnage in gory detail:

'Piles of heads, hands, and feet were to be seen in the streets of the city. It was necessary to pick one's way over the bodies of men and horses. But these were small matters compared to what happened at the Temple of Solomon, [al-Aqsa] a place where religious services are ordinarily chanted. What happened there? If I tell the truth, it will exceed your powers of belief. So let it suffice to say this much, at least, that in the Temple and porch of Solomon, men rode in blood up to their knees and bridle reins.'

Although his sea of blood was most certainly a poetic exaggeration intended to shock his reader, d'Aguiliers nonetheless went on to endorse the slaughter: 'Indeed, it was a just and splendid judgment of God that this place should be filled with the blood of the unbelievers, since it had suffered so long from their blasphemies'.

Jerusalem had been captured, its Muslim and Jewish inhabitants slaughtered and its treasures divided between the princes who had come east to rescue the city. Two weeks after the capture, the Pope who had launched the campaign lay dead, before ever hearing the outcome of the crusade he had started with those now famous words, "Deus Lo Volt". But now that the mission's spiritual leader was dead, the victory called for a secular leader. Even in this the princes were divided, although a pretended humility was present throughout the discussions, which went on for several days. Raymond and Godfrey were the only serious contenders for the position. Raymond was initially offered the crown and title of King of Jerusalem, but feigned piety claiming that he would not wish to be king in a city where the King of kings had lived. The political manoeuvre, if that is what it was, backfired and Godfrey accepted the position on the condition that he would be referred to as *Advocatus Sancti Sepulchri*, or Defender of the Holy Sepulchre, rather than king. Of course, the difference in nomenclature did not change the fact that Godfrey was in every sense of the word elected as the first Christian King of Jerusalem.

Godfrey was, during his short reign, an enthusiastic supporter of Brother Gerard and his pilgrim hospital. It is said that Godfrey visited the hospital in the days that followed the conquest of Jerusalem and was impressed by what he saw. Not only were many of the wounded Christian soldiers being treated by Brother Gerard's men, but the Hospitallers were sacrificing their own food to ensure that those in their care were properly fed. Godfrey gave the fledgling Order his manor of Montboise in Brabant, their first donation of the crusader era. Several other leaders followed suit in patronising the hospital, and the thousands who returned to the west spread word of the good work Brother Gerard and his Hospitallers were doing in the recently captured city. Within a short period of time the hospital had obtained property in France, Spain and Italy, and began to establish daughter houses along the routes frequented by pilgrims travelling east.

It is interesting that by the time of Godfrey's deed to the Hospitallers, the St John being venerated was John the Baptist and no longer St John Eleemon. In his grant of Montboise, Godfrey refers to the hospital as "found in honour of God and his very holy mother and Saint John, precursor of the Saviour...". Regardless of whose honour Brother Gerard was doing his work in, over the next decade the hospital at Jerusalem continued to receive strong patronage from the west and new recruits from the east, largely men who, having settled in Jerusalem, had decided to lay down their swords for more noble pursuits. With the expansion in gifts and membership, Gerard proposed that the volunteers unite themselves into a religious body, taking the traditional monastic vows of poverty, obedience and chastity. This met with the general agreement of those involved in the hospital at Jerusalem, and the patriarch received their religious vows and clothed them in the black habit with white cross that would mark the Order's conventual dress.

In 1113, the Hospitallers received further official papal recognition from Pope Paschal II:

'Paschal, bishop, and servant of such as are the servants of God, to his venerable son Gerard, founder and Master of the Hospital at Jerusalem, and to his lawful successors forevermore. The requests of a devout desire ought to meet with a corresponding fulfilment. Inasmuch, as of thy affection thou hast requested, with regard to the Hospital

which thou hast founded in the city of Jerusalem, in proximity to the Church of the blessed John the Baptist, that it should be supported by the authority of the Apostolic See, and fostered by the patronage of the blessed Apostle Peter; We, therefore, much pleased with the pious earnestness of thy hospitality, do receive the petition with our paternal favour, and do ordain and establish, by the authority of this our present decree, that that house of God, your hospital, shall

Godfrey de Bouillon, shown in this nineteenth century painting, was unwilling to accept the title of king when crowned the ruler of the Kingdom of Jerusalem. Instead, he took the title Advocatus Sancti Sepulchri or Defender of the Holy Sepulchre.

now be placed, and shall ever remain, under the protection of the Apostolic See, and under that of the blessed Peter. All things whatsoever, therefore, which by the preserving care and solicitude have been collected for the benefit of the said Hospital, for the support and maintenance of pilgrims, or for relieving the necessities of the poor, whether in the churches of Jerusalem, or in those of parishes within the limits of other cities; and whatsoever things may have been offered already by the faithful, or for the future may through God's grace be so offered, or collected by other lawful means; and whatsoever things have been, or shall be granted to thee, or to thy successors, or to the brethren who are occupied in the care and support of pilgrims, by the venerable brethren the bishops of the diocese of Jerusalem; we hereby decree shall be retained by you and undiminished.

'Moreover, as to the tithes of your revenues, which ye collect everywhere at your own charge, and by your own toil, we do hereby fix and decree, that they shall be retained by your own Hospital, all opposition on the part of the bishops and their clergy notwithstanding. We also decree as valid all donations which have been made to your Hospital by pious princes, either of their tribute moneys or other imposts. We ordain furthermore, that at thy death no man shall be appointed in thy place, as chief and master, by any underhand subtlety, or by violence; but him only who shall by the inspiration of God, have been duly elected by the professed brethren of the Institution. Furthermore, all dignities or possessions which your hospital at present holds either on this side of the water, to wit in Asia, or in Europe, as also those which hereafter by God's bounty it may obtain; we confirm them to thee and to thy successors, who shall be devoting themselves with a pious zeal to the cares of hospitality, and through you to said Hospital in perpetuity. We further decree that it shall be unlawful for any man whatsoever rashly to disturb your Hospital, or to carry off any of its property, or if carried off to retain possession of it, or to diminish ought from its revenues, or to harass it with audacious annoyances. But let all its property remain intact, for the sole use and enjoyment of those for whose maintenance and support it has been granted.

As to the Hospitals or Poor Houses in the Western provinces, at Burgum of St Aegidius, Lisan, Barum, Hispalum, Tarentum, and Messina, which are distinguished by the title of Hospitals of Jerusalem, we decree that they shall for ever remain, as they are this day, under the subjection and disposal of thyself and thy successors. If, therefore, at a future time, any person, whether ecclesiastical or secular, knowing this paragraph of our constitution, shall attempt to oppose its provisions, and if, after having received a second or third warning, he shall not make a suitable satisfaction and restitution, let him be deprived of all his dignities and honours, and let him know that he stands exposed to the judgment of God, for the inequity he has perpetrated; and let him be deprived of the Sacraments of the Body and Blood of Christ, and of the benefits of the redemption of our Lord, and at the last great judgment let him meet with the severest vengeance. But to all who deal justly and rightly with the same, on them be the peace of our Lord Jesus Christ, so that not only here below they may receive the rewards of a good action, but also before the Judge of all mankind, they may enjoy the blessing of peace eternal.

I Paschal, bishop of the Catholic Church.
I Richard, bishop of Alboe, have signed.
I Calixtus, bishop of the Catholic Church.
I Landulphus, bishop of Beneventum, Have read and signed.

Given at Beneventum, by the hand of John, cardinal of the Roman Church, and librarian, on the 15th day of the calends of March, in the 6th indiction of the incarnation of our Lord, in the year 1113, and in the 13th year of the Pontificate of our Lord Pope Paschal II.'

Brother Gerard would continue to lead the Hospitallers for the next seven years, until his death in 1120. By that time, another group of men were beginning to offer their assistance to pilgrims, albeit with the sword and shield. Although the Knights Templar would be the first of the Military Orders of the crusader era, the Hospitallers would not be long behind. It would be Brother Gerard's successor who oversaw the Hospitallers' conversion from monastic carers to warrior monks.

CHAPTER 2
The Sword of Raymond Du Puy

Brother Gerard was succeeded by Raymond du Puy de Province, who was elected by the fraternity in accordance with the guidelines laid out in Pope Paschal's bull of seven years earlier. Du Puy was a 37-year-old French knight whose father had served as one of Godfrey de Bouillon's generals. He was also related to Adhémar du Puy, the late papal legate who had accompanied the crusaders east in 1099. It is not known if du Puy travelled east with his father during the First Crusade, although it seems unlikely, given that he would have been 13 at the time the crusaders left Europe. Like Brother Gerard, exactly how and when he arrived in Jerusalem is unknown, but like his predecessor, Raymond's primary focus and role, at least initially, was as administrator of the hospital. However, where Gerard is recognised as the Order's founder, Raymond is regarded as its first Grand Master, although this is a term du Puy seldom used himself except in a few letters written later in his career. Du Puy was also responsible for the Hospitaller Sisters of St John of Jerusalem which had been established in the hospital of St Mary Magdalene. Grand Master du Puy built on Brother Gerard's foundational work and the continued influx of men and materials from the Order's daughter houses in Europe expanded the hospital complex in Jerusalem throughout his term of office.

This illustration of Raymond du Puy, reprinted from Whitworth Porter's 1883 history of the Order, shows the type of garment the Hospitallers would wear until the thirteenth century. Du Puy is depicted with a cross and a sword, representing the two aspects of the Order during his Mastership.

This area, known as the Muristan (from the Persian word for *hospital*), was situated in the city's Christian quarter, and located just south of the Church of the Holy Sepulchre. Today there is little to mark the original Hospitallers' presence in the city other than a monument and garden erected in 1972 by the Order itself on the spot where its predecessor's first hospital once stood. The Church of Santa Maria ad Latinos, which was located in the northeast corner of the Muristan, and had been built by the original Amalfian merchants, was replaced with the Lutheran Church of the Redeemer, built over the ruins of the former

between 1869 and 1900. However, the Church of St John the Baptist, which was used by the Hospitallers throughout their time in Jerusalem, still stands, although it was taken over by the Greek Orthodox Church in the nineteenth century.

But in the twelfth century when Raymond du Puy was Grand Master of the Order and administrator of the hospital, the complex was actively involved in looking after the sick and poor travellers who passed through Jerusalem, impressing many visitors, including the German pilgrim and poet John of Würzburg who saw the hospital around 1160 and wrote of it:

The City of Jerusalem as it appeared during the early years of the Military Orders between the First and Second Crusades. At this stage in development the Hospitallers were evolving from a strictly hospital organisation towards a dual role as caregivers and protectors of pilgrims. Pilgrims visiting Jerusalem would enter the Holy City through David's Gate on the western edge of the city and make their way to the Church of the Holy Sepulchre in the northwest of the city. The Hospital of St John was located directly opposite the church. The Templars, who had originated as a militant order, were housed in the southeast of the city on Temple Mount next to the al-Aqsa Mosque, which then served as the Royal Palace. However, King Baldwin II granted the Templars the Royal Palace soon after their formation.

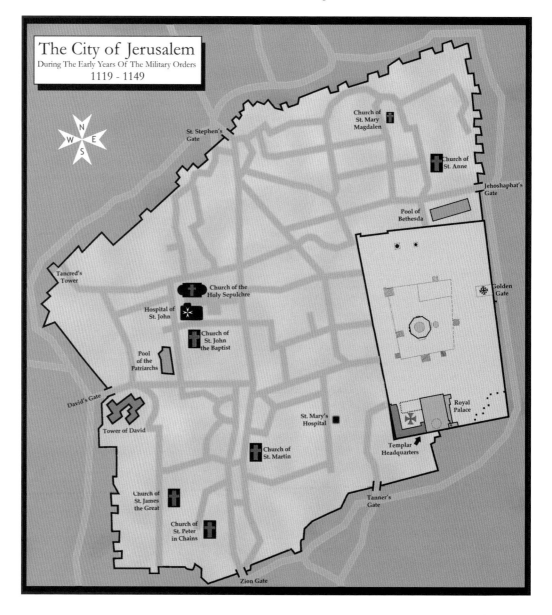

The City of Jerusalem
During The Early Years Of The Military Orders
1119 - 1149

'Over against the Church of the Holy Sepulchre, on the opposite side of the way towards the south, is a beautiful church built in honour of John the Baptist, annexed to which is a hospital, wherein in various rooms is collected together an enormous multitude of sick people. Both men and women. Who are tended and restored to health daily at very great expense. When I was there I learned that the whole number of these sick people amounted to two thousand, of whom sometimes in the course of one day and night more than fifty are carried out dead, while many other fresh ones keep continually arriving. What more can I say? The same house supplies as many people outside it with victuals as it does those inside, in addition to the boundless charity which it daily bestowed upon poor people who beg their bread from door to door and do not lodge in the house, so that the whole sum of its expenses can surely never be calculated even by the managers and stewards thereof. In addition to all these moneys expended upon the sick and upon other poor people, this same house also maintains in its various castles many persons trained to all kinds of military exercises for the defence of the land of the Christians against the invasion of the Saracens'.

When exactly the Hospitallers began to take on this militant role is hard to pin down. Certainly they were actively involved with the sword and shield by the time John of Würzburg visited Jerusalem in the mid-twelfth century, working apart from, but occasionally alongside, the Knights Templar, who themselves had slowly evolved since receiving their rule of order at the Council of Troyes in 1128, nine years after their formation in 1119. The French historian Réné-Aubert Vertot, in his history of the Order, makes the claim that the Hospitallers had taken up arms in the defence of Christendom well before the 1130s, citing a papal bull of that year in support of the idea. Writes Vertot:

'However, we learn from a bull of Pope Innocent II., bearing date A.D.1130, that the important services rendered the kings of Jerusalem by the hospitallers against the infidels, had been the admiration of Europe; which supposes, that they had been some time

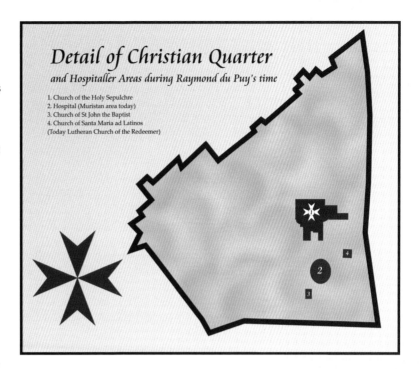

Detail of Christian Quarter
and Hospitaller Areas during Raymond du Puy's time

1. Church of the Holy Sepulchre
2. Hospital (Muristan area today)
3. Church of St John the Baptist
4. Church of Santa Maria ad Latinos
(Today Lutheran Church of the Redeemer)

Detail of the Christian Quarter in Jerusalem.

before in arms: and yet there is no carrying the epoch we are in search of higher than A.D. 1118, when Raimond Dupuy was dignified with the mastership of this new militia'.

Like many early writers, Vertot gives an earlier start to du Puy's term as Grand Master than was the case. Given that Brother Gerard died on 3 September 1120, it is from this date, or soon after, that du Puy began his leadership role in the Order, and not before. But regardless of which date is correct, it is well established that the Hospitallers began their military role well after the Templars, who did not take on the role until 1119. Other dates that have been suggested for the Hospitallers include the year 1126 because of a documentary reference to a Hospitaller constable; however, it is not conclusive that this office was of a military character at that time. Another reference to the Grand Master having travelled with King Baldwin II during a campaign against Ascalon two years later also does not prove that the Order was involved militarily.

The most probable date to indicate that the Hospitallers had established a military component to their Order is 1136, the year in which King Fulk of Jerusalem granted the Hospitallers his newly built castle at Beit

Jibrin, roughly 20 kilometres north of Hebron in the Kingdom of Jerusalem's southern reaches. This castle, which the crusaders called Bethgeblin, was used by the Hospitallers as a base to safeguard the kingdom's ports of Jaffa and Caesarea. Six years later the Hospitallers were given a number of land grants from Count Raymond II of Tripoli, including Krak des Chevaliers, which would become a key fortress for the Hospitallers for more than a century. Krak was a particularly important gift because it offered the only real protection to a large undefended trading area from potential attacks from the Muslims' fortified city of Homs. Over the next four decades the Hospitallers would continue to expand their fortresses in the Levant, and by 1187, when Saladin recaptured much of the territory the crusaders had gained since 1096, the Hospitallers owned twenty separate castles and fortifications in the east.

Regardless of when the Hospitallers embraced the model created by the Templars and their new knighthood, throughout the twelfth century fighting for Christ remained a secondary vocation for the Order, their primary concern still being to care for Christ's poor and sick. In fact, no mention is made of a militant role in the Order's rule until the closing years of the twelfth century. The original statutes created by Raymond du Puy in 1130 were simple when compared to the Templars original Latin rule, the latter document drafted largely by the Cistercian abbot and great promoter of the Templars, Bernard of Clairvaux, who based it on the Cistercian rule. The draft of Raymond's original Hospitaller rule was lost when the Christians lost Acre in 1291; however, in 1300 Pope Boniface VIII, at the request of the Order, issued a bull recapitulating the original rule as it was then remembered. From that document we see that a decade after taking control of the Order, Raymond du Puy was still very much focused on the hospitaller aspect of his Order.

In addition to the three monastic vows of poverty, chastity and obedience, the Hospitaller could expect nothing more than bread, water and clothing, the latter to be of a humble quality because, as du Puy felt, 'our masters, the poor, whose servants we profess to be, appear scantily and meanly clad, and it is not right that the servant should be proudly arrayed, whilst his master is humble'. But at all times those garments were to include 'crosses, to the honour of God and of His sacred cross'. Animal skins were forbidden from covering a Hospitaller's back and animal flesh was forbidden from filling his stomach from the third last Sunday before Lent until Easter.

Not only were the Hospitallers to clothe themselves according to their humble and pious duties, but their decorum in church and elsewhere was to be respectable at all times: brethren travelling in the cities and fortresses were to travel in groups of two or three, and were not to select their travelling companions, that decision being reserved for the Master; if women were present, the brethren were to safeguard one another's chastity, and they were not to permit a woman to wash their hands or feet, or even make their bed for them.

Should a Hospitaller commit a sin in secret, he was also to repent in secret, imposing a suitable penance upon himself. However, if his sin should become publicly discovered, he was to attend Mass on the Sabbath and after the congregation had left, he was to be stripped and beaten with rods by his superior or by brethren appointed by him. After the public flogging, he would be expelled from the Order. The expulsion seems to have been temporary if the brother were capable of redemption. In such cases he would return to the hospital, confess his previous sins and accept a suitable penance. Even then, his readmission was probationary for a period of one year, during which time he would be under the watchful eye of his brethren who would see that he sinned no more.

Should a brother sin in the presence of another, the witness was not to denounce the sin, either to the public or the prior of the convent. Instead, the witness to the sin was to chastise the offending brother directly, giving

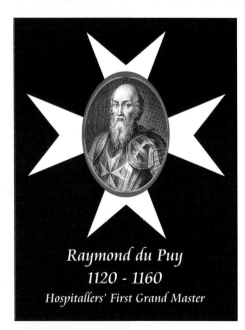

Raymond du Puy
1120 - 1160
Hospitallers' First Grand Master

him the opportunity to confess. If he did not, two or three other brethren were to be brought in to assist in the chastisement. If the offending brother remained obstinate in his confession, the details of his sin were to be outlined in a letter to the Master of the Order, to be dealt with in the chapter. No brother, however, was to accuse another without sufficient proof.

Internal disputes between brethren that created disturbances could be punishable offences if the superior caught sight of the uproar. In such cases, the offending brother would be made to fast for a period of seven days, receiving bread and water on the fourth and sixth days, which he would eat off the floor. If the disturbance resulted in physical violence between the brethren, the fast was for a period of forty days. Leaving the convent without permission could also result in a 40-day sentence of eating off the ground. In addition to the rules and regulations for the members themselves, Raymond's rule of 1130 also contained guidelines for admission of the sick. The applicant was to first confess his sins and take the holy sacrament. Afterwards he would be carried to his bed as though he were the Master himself. The Hospital's patients were to be fed every day before any of the brethren were given food. On the Sabbath the Epistle and Gospel were to be sung in the hospital, and holy water sprinkled around during the processional.

Although the Hospitallers put great distinction between themselves and those they cared for in their hospitals, the divisions within the Order were less apparent, at least during the twelfth century. Even after fully embracing a militant role there was not the class distinction between Hospitaller brother knights and brother sergeants that existed in the Templars – both knights and sergeants served as cavalry and were similarly armed, although a sergeant's armour may have been somewhat lighter to allow greater ease of movement when he was forced to fight on foot. Class distinction would take on a greater role in the thirteenth century with a further division in the brother knights to designate those who fought for the Order and those who served the Order in other capacities. But even then, the knights and sergeants remained in the same dress. It was not until 1259 that

the Hospitallers were instructed to adopt a distinct dress for the brother knights by the order of a papal bull from Pope Alexander IV:

'Since it has come to our knowledge that, amongst the brethren of your Order, both knights and others, there is no distinction or diversity of dress, contrary to the usual custom in most other similar institutions; on which account it comes to pass, that the love of many brethren of noble birth, who, casting aside the allurements of the world, under the garb of your Order, have chosen to devote themselves to the defence of the Holy Land, grows cold; we, therefore, being earnestly

The fountain in the foreground is in the Muristan area of old Jerusalem where the Order's hospital once stood. In the background is the Lutheran Church of the Redeemer built over the Church of Santa Maria ad Latinos in 1869. *Bigstock/ Vladimir Khirman* desirous that your Order may still continue by God's help, to be enriched with fresh donations, and may grow and increase in the votive offerings which it shall receive, do hereby grant to you, by the authority of these letters, permission to decree unanimously, and hereafter to maintain inviolate, the regulation, that the knights, brethren of your Order, shall wear black mantles, that they may be distinguished from the other brethren; but in campaigns, and in battles, they shall wear surcoats and other military decorations of a red colour, on which there shall be a cross of white colour, sewn on in accordance with that on your standard; in order that by the uniformity of signs, the unanimity of your spirits may be clearly apparent, and that thus, in consequence, the safety of your persons may be insured'.

The new rule of sartorial class distinction among the brethren was repealed within two decades, and both knights and sergeants-at-arms wore red garments with a white cross in battle from that point on. The evolution in dress had been slower than the Order's transition from scalpels to swords. For the first 135 years, the Hospitallers wore a tight-fitting, black monastic robe over their armour, which proved restrictive in battle. It was not until 1248 that the soldiers were permitted by Pope Innocent IV to wear wider surcoats, but even then it was restricted to dangerous areas. These garments carried the traditional eight-pointed Amalfian cross, which made its appearance on the garments in the early thirteenth century. Contrary to many depictions of early Hospitaller costume, the Amalfian or Maltese cross was not used in Brother Gerard's or Brother Raymond's time,

the white cross presumably being of a more traditional Greek or Latin design.

Although the hospitallers remained largely without the class distinction of the Templars in terms of arms, armour and outer garments, they were not without distinction among ranks in the field. In the earliest days the biggest distinction among brethren was between those who were priests and those who were not, although even those who were not priests were still monks by virtue of the fact they had taken monastic vows. This formed a part of the Hospitaller ceremony of reception, which was a solemn and simple affair. Like the Templar ceremony, the candidate for admission was first cautioned that appearances could be deceiving. While he might perceive the Hospitallers as a wealthy and well-dressed Order, membership among its ranks was not a life of luxury but one of service and duty, more often than not at a superior's orders. The new Hospitaller recruit could expect to fight when he wished to sleep and sleep when he wished to be awake; travel when he wished to stay in the convent and remain at home when he wished to travel abroad. For those who could endure such hardships, it was necessary, as part of the ceremony, to ask the Master or whoever was in charge for admission to the Order. The purpose of this requirement is not unlike modern-day fraternities that require assurance that candidates for admission are doing so of their own free will and accord. Once permission had been granted, the candidate was asked if he belonged to another Order, if he was married, and if he was in personal debt or servitude to any man. With the questions satisfactorily answered, the aspirant was asked to place his hands on a missal and take a vow of obedience to the Grand Master of the Order, promising to give his life for that loyalty if need be, and while alive always to be a serf and slave to the poor and sick. This oath was sworn to God, the Virgin and the Order's patron St John the Baptist. When the oath was completed, the man would take the missal to the altar, where it would be placed, and again taken up and given to the brother conducting the ceremony. The aspirant would then have the black mantle of the Order laid upon his shoulders, and his attention would be drawn to the white cross upon its breast, followed by an injunction to remember what it

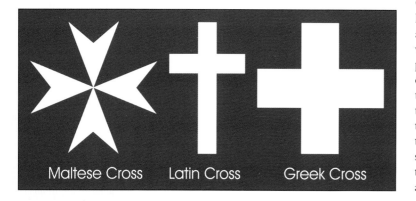

Maltese Cross   Latin Cross   Greek Cross

represented. The conductor of the ceremony would then give the new Hospitaller brother the kiss of peace, which he would then share with his new brethren. For the rest of his life, he would not return to secular life, and would follow the commands of his superiors.

The chief of the superior officers, as with the other Military Orders, was the Grand Master, who was elected by his brethren for life. The Master of the Order was in turn supported by a Grand Commander who fulfilled administrative duties similar to the Seneschal of the Templar Order. In both cases, the position was the second-in-command spot within the respective Orders. The Marshal of the Hospitallers was the third-ranked position, but was the superior officer with respect to the military side of the Order. His greatest responsibilities were on the field of battle where he was in charge of the military forces under the Master's direction. Under the Marshal was the Constable, which was largely an assistive position regarding organisational duties, and the Castellans who were commanders responsible for the Order's castles. During the twelfth century, the

Order's standard bearer, or Gonfalonier, was a position that was often rewarded for valour on the field of battle and open to any who fought for Hospitaller ideals. But this was not an uncommon thing among the Hospitallers and, as we have seen, set them apart from the more class conscious Templars. Until 1262, a Hospitaller Grand Master could as easily have been elected from among the brother sergeants as from the Order's knights. After 1262, a statute was passed prohibiting any but brother knights from becoming Master. Other offices existed within the Order and others would be added throughout the years as the need arose, such as the position of Admiral which was created in the fourteenth century after the Hospitallers took to the seas. However, in the years during which the sword of Raymond du Puy led the Order on the road to battle, the ranks among the brethren were minimal.

Formed before the victory of the First Crusade, the Hospitallers were slowly transformed by the new militant zeal brought east mostly by the French knights who had come to conquer Jerusalem. Nonetheless, as the

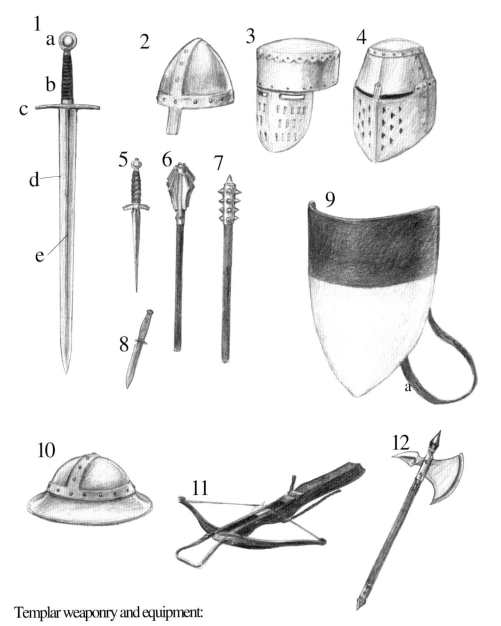

Templar weaponry and equipment:
1: Sword: (a) pommel, (b) grip, (c) cross guard, (d) blade, (e) fuller (groove). 2: Helmet, early12th Century, riveted iron plates with nose guard. 3: Helmet, late 12th Century with face guard. 4: Great helm, mid-late 13th Century, fully enclosed. 5. Knight's dagger, with slender blade for stabbing through gaps in armour eg. eye slits in helmets. 6 & 7: Maces. 8: General purpose knife. 9: Shield of reinforced wood, with leather strap or 'guige' (a) and cover painted black and white. 10: 'Kettle hat' or 'chapel de fer' helmet of riveted iron plates. 11: Crossbow. 12. War axe.

The Templar rule of order provides some precise details as to the types of weaponry the knights and sergeants carried. Within the Hospitaller Order, there was no great distinction in arms and armour, other than perhaps quality. The following diagram shows the standard tools of the trade during the crusading era.
Gordon Napier

Order's peaceful and beneficent Italian majority were replaced with the crusading French and their hatred of Muslims, the Hospitallers would, by the time of the Second Crusade, still continue their dual role as servants of the poor and soldiers of Christ. Although they never failed in fulfilling the former, they – like the Templars who fought along with them – were less successful in the latter.

On the morning of 19 March 1148, a number of Byzantine ships arrived on the shores of St Symeon in the Principality of Antioch. Aboard the vessels were the remnants of an army that included the Templar Master of France, Everard des Barres and 130 of his knights. However, for the locals enthusiastically waiting for the travellers to hit dry land, the presence of King Louis VII of France and his queen, Eleanor of Aquitaine, were of far greater importance. Eleanor's uncle, Raymond of Antioch, greeted them and took the royal couple and their entourage back to the capital, where they were shown several days of fine eastern hospitality. As was so often the case in the east, Raymond's generosity and graciousness were not so much a matter of

practising Christian charity as lobbying for political favour. No sooner had King Louis recovered from his journey than Raymond was bending his ear about a new campaign against his Muslim enemies. It would be unfair to place too much criticism on Raymond's motives or his desire to garner the king's support: Louis and Eleanor had not travelled east on a package holiday or for a family reunion; the king had journeyed east for a crusade and the prince was eager to get on with it.

In 1144, when the Hospitallers were guarding the Kingdom of Jerusalem's southern frontiers from Bethgeblin and the County of Tripoli's eastern frontiers from Krak des Chevaliers, the Crusader State's northernmost region lost its capital city of Edessa to Zengi, the Governor of Aleppo. The loss of Edessa in 1144 had prompted Pope Eugenius III to call for the new crusade; a cause which was enthusiastically promoted by Bernard of Clairvaux. In fact, it was through Bernard's influence that King Louis decided to take up the cross himself. But as Louis learned from Raymond, the Muslims had not rested in

the four years that had passed since the fall of Edessa; in fact, things had got progressively worse. Zengi's second son and his successor as Governor of Aleppo, Nūr al-Dīn, had established himself firmly along the Christian landscape from Edessa to Hama. What was worse, during the previous autumn, he had begun picking off Christian fortresses east of the Orontes River. With Nūr al-Dīn coming ever closer to his territory, Raymond was painfully aware that the Principality of Antioch could easily be the Muslim leader's next target and the prince hoped to set things right by hitting him on his own turf at Aleppo.

While Raymond could hardly be faulted for seeking help in dealing with the dangers presently facing the Principality of Antioch, those dangers may never have got a toehold in the region had he done something to address them in 1144. The political situation that existed in the Latin East at the time Zengi was planning to take Edessa had certainly worked in his favour. King Fulk of Jerusalem had died the previous autumn and his heir, Baldwin III, was still a child under the tutelage of his mother Melisende, the Queen of Jerusalem. Count Raymond of Tripoli was only marginally interested in Edessa's troubles due to the distance from his own county and the fact that the Hospitallers were occupying three fortifications within his territory. Raymond had been the closest and most able to offer Edessa assistance; however, there was ill will between Raymond and Count Joscelin of Edessa. As such, Raymond was not only unprepared to assist, he actually took pleasure in his co-religionist's plight.

However, Raymond was not the only Latin prince looking for the support of the French king and his army. Raymond of Tripoli had hoped to recover Montferrand, which had been lost to Zengi in 1137, the year before the Muslims captured the important city of Homs. It had been from this fortified city that Raymond of Tripoli had feared an attack and the principal reason he had given the Hospitallers Krak des Chevaliers. Now that Homs had been passed to Nūr al-Dīn along with the rest of his father's conquests, Raymond hoped to secure as much assistance as possible. Perhaps most eager for the king's assistance was Joscelin of Edessa himself, who was living in Turbessel, in what was once the

County of Edessa. The exiled count desperately wanted Louis to retake Edessa, for it was the fall of his former capital that had brought the crusaders east in the first place. Being tugged in several directions at once did not prompt the king to action, and he told Raymond of Antioch and the others who had bent his ear by messenger, that he was not prepared to take any course of action until he had fulfilled his crusader vows by visiting Jerusalem and seeing the sites sacred to his faith.

Despite his sudden departure for Jerusalem, Louis was actually the last of the westerners to arrive in the Holy City. Conrad III of Germany had landed at Acre in mid-April and set out for the Holy City, where he was warmly welcomed by King Baldwin III and his mother, Queen Melisende. Over Easter, the German king spent a few days with the Templars at their headquarters on the Temple Mount, where the Order no doubt filled him in on their thoughts on an appropriate campaign. Alfonso Jordan, the Count of Toulouse, had arrived in the east a few days after Conrad, where his arrival was also greatly celebrated, largely due to the fact that he was the son of the legendary Raymond of Toulouse, one of the leaders of the First Crusade. The count set out for Jerusalem to join his fellow crusaders, but during a brief stopover in Caesarea he suddenly took ill and died in the land in which he had been born forty-five years earlier.

Once Louis had finally arrived at Jerusalem and fulfilled his crusader vows, the westerners were invited to travel to Acre for a war council to plan their strategy. The assembly held on the Feast of St John – 24 June 1148 – was an impressive gathering. In attendance were King Baldwin III and Fulcher, the Patriarch of Jerusalem, as well as the Archbishops of Caesarea and Nazareth. Conrad III was accompanied by a number of his country's higher and lower nobility, as was King Louis. Also in attendance were the Hospitallers' Grand Master Raymond du Puy and the Templars' Grand Master Robert de Craon, the latter of whom had succeeded the founder of the Order, Hugues de Payens, in 1136. Conspicuous by their absence were the other leaders of the Latin East: Raymond was angry at Louis's sudden departure from Antioch and shunned any participation, while Joscelin of Edessa was in no position to travel anywhere for fear of losing further ground against his enemies. Raymond of Tripoli's absence was largely due to the death of Alfonso Jordan and the insistence of the deceased's bastard son, Bertrand, that Raymond was somehow involved in his father's death. Once again, as had been the case when Edessa fell four years earlier, the defence of Christendom would go on while the majority of the Crusader States turned their backs, hoping for the best.

History does not record the details of what was said during the great council of princes held at Acre in the summer of 1148 or who was in favour of taking what course of action. It is true that the crusade had been called in response to the fall of Edessa, but Nūr al-Dīn had murdered its remaining Christian inhabitants and destroyed its fortification in 1146 when Joscelin had tried to retake the city. Frankly there was little to recover and the crusaders must surely have ruled it out as an option. Another potential target was Ascalon to the south on the Mediterranean coast, near the Hospitallers' fortress of Bethgeblin. As the last port city in the region still under Muslim control, it would have been a welcome addition to the kingdom; however, there may have been some reluctance on the part of Baldwin III, who saw its capture as a possible future benefit to his younger brother Amalric. This left two options: Aleppo to the north and Damascus to the northeast. To the disappointment of the northern princes, the council voted to strike Damascus.

The city was of great religious importance to the Christians: it was on the road to Damascus that St Paul had converted to Christianity, and it was in Damascus that the tomb of St John the Baptist resided, among many other Holy Sites sacred to Christian faith in the region. However the decision to besiege Damascus had a more practical purpose than merely securing a few relics and additional sightseeing spots for travelling pilgrims to stop at. Damascus was an important centre of trade and communication and its capture would be as great a benefit to the Christians as its loss would be a setback to the Muslims. For an entire generation, the Kingdom of Jerusalem had coveted Damascus as a possession, repeatedly attempting to keep it under its

thumb through conquest or treaty. However, the most recent treaty between the Kingdom of Jerusalem and Damascus had been largely abandoned and the Damascenes were growing a little too friendly with Nūr al-Dīn. Ultimately the Damascus campaign was to be a pre-emptive strike in order to gain control of the city before their adversary from Aleppo did. It would prove to be a humiliating disaster.

The crusaders set out from Galilee in the middle of July with the largest army the Franks had ever put into the field. The Arab chronicler Ibn al-Qalānsī put the number of 50,000 between cavalry and infantrymen; however, as we have seen, chroniclers on both sides often exaggerated the numbers of combatants. Whatever the real number was, the bulk of the troops were made up of Louis VII's army and the Templars, although the Hospitallers contributed as many of their knights and sergeants as could be spared. Because the locals were more familiar with the territory, it was decided that King Baldwin and his men would lead the march, followed by King Louis and his men in the centre, with Conrad and his army guarding the rear against attack. On 24 July, the crusaders approached Damascus from the southwest, where they encountered the thick orchards that surrounded the city. The orchards were like a dense forest interlaced by mud walls which served to separate individual patches of land for farmers as well as act as a protective fortification for the city. The entire set-up created a labyrinth of narrow roads and pathways, which, while not a hindrance for the local farmers, proved to be difficult terrain for the crusaders to pass through. The decision to take this route was to fulfil the dual purpose of securing the fortified part of the city first and to provide the crusaders with a supply of food and water during the siege. However, there was more than lush fruit awaiting the crusaders behind the walls and amidst the trees, for the Damascenes had hidden themselves there and began attacking King Baldwin and his troops as they made their way through the narrow paths. As the army slowly marched on, the Muslims shot arrows down on the crusaders and stabbed at them with lances through slits in the mud walls. Although many men fell to the ambush, the crusaders persevered and slew or captured as many of the enemy as they could.

As the army pressed towards a nearby stream they were met by cavalrymen on the other side who began launching arrows to prevent the crusaders from reaching the stream. Parched from the journey and the battle, the army moved on towards the river, where they were met by an even larger force, which caused the line to halt. Unable to see the cause of the blockage, Conrad demanded to know what the hold-up was. When he heard that the enemy was blockading the river, he charged through the line with his lieutenants, dismounted from his horse and began to engage the enemy in hand-to-hand combat. With the river secured in front of them and the orchards cleared behind them the crusaders set up camp. Both the Franks and Damascenes began erecting barricades for the battle that lay ahead. The siege continued for several days after which events began to take a turn for the worse.

While the reasons suggested differ greatly between accounts, it is universally agreed that the crusaders left their supply of food and water on 27 July for the other side of the city, a position which afforded them far less than their previous base of operations. Sir Stephen Runciman suggested that the crusaders were driven from their position by the arrival of fresh reinforcements who had come to assist the city, but the early chroniclers were less generous. William of Tyre said that the Damascenes bribed some of the crusaders to lift the siege, while the Arab chronicler Ibn al-Athīr made the claim that the Emir of Damascus Mu'in al-Dīn appealed to the eastern Christians, questioning their loyalty to their western co-religionists. According to the Emir, if the western Christians captured Damascus they would keep it for themselves and should that happen the eastern Christians' possessions on the coast were sure to follow. In addition, he said that if it looked like he was going to lose Damascus, he would simply hand it over to his more powerful co-religionists and then the entire region would be in danger.

Regardless of the motivations for moving their position, the crusaders quickly went from the offensive to the defensive, and despite losing ground, began quarrelling amongst themselves as to what the final status of the city would be once captured. Jerusalem expected Damascus to be incorporated into its territory, while Thierry, Count of Flanders, who had travelled east with King Louis, wanted to hold it for himself. Baldwin, Louis and Conrad were in agreement, which angered the eastern barons and reduced their willingness to continue the fight. As rumours of bribery and treachery began to pass between the troops, the crusaders learned that Nūr al-Dīn and his men were on their way. The local barons began to persuade their western brothers that the time to retreat was now, and although Louis and Conrad were puzzled by the blatant disloyalty among their co-religionists, they nonetheless ordered the retreat. As the crusaders made their way back to Jerusalem with their tails between their legs, the Muslims harassed them with a greater zeal than they had during their approach to Damascus.

The failure to capture the Muslim city effectively brought the Second Crusade to a disastrous and unproductive end. The alliance between the western kings was over; Conrad returned at once to his homeland by way of Constantinople, and Louis, although he would spend another year in the east, made no attempts to engage in further military activities. From Attalia to Damascus, the east lay littered with the bloated and rotting corpses of dead crusaders left to bake under the sun. The decision to attack Damascus instead of Aleppo, as Raymond of Antioch had desired, ultimately allowed Nūr al-Dīn's base of power to grow and strengthened his alliance with Damascus. In 1149, the united efforts of Aleppo and Damascus led to Raymond's death at the Battle of Inab, and in 1150, Nūr al-Dīn captured and imprisoned Joscelin of Edessa, where he spent the last decade of his life. The inability of the eastern barons to set aside personal differences and work towards a common goal and a common enemy was beginning to push the Christians of the east closer and closer towards the Mediterranean Sea. It would only be a matter of time before they would be forced to cross it.

Some claimed that the failure to take Damascus was due to the Templars' greed for money, pride and even their jealousy of the western crusaders. Among those who took this point of view was Ralph of Coggeshall, an English Cistercian chronicler who wrote that the Templars had urged the crusaders to retreat after being offered a bribe from Nūr al-Dīn. Another contemporary chronicler, Gervase of Canterbury, held to the same belief, and added that when the Templars received their bribe, they found jars full of copper rather than the valuable coin they had expected. This was, according to Gervase, a miracle from God rather than treachery from the Muslims.

We may never truly know if the Templars forfeited the siege of Damascus in favour of financial remuneration, but Damascus would not be the last battle in which Templar greed would play a role, perceived or real. Five years after the failed siege of Damascus, the Hospitallers and Templars would both participate in the siege of Ascalon, a city situated on the Mediterranean coast, roughly 25 kilometres northeast of the Hospitaller stronghold of Bethgeblin and 10 kilometres from Gaza, which had been given to the Templars by King Baldwin III in 1150. Ascalon's fortifications were like a half circle, the radius on the shoreline and the semicircle on the landside facing eastward. William of Tyre described the city as being like a basin, that sloped seaward, girded round with artificial mounds, on which were built walls studded with towers. The stonework, according to William's account, was held together with cement, which made it very strong. There were also four gates in the circuit of the city's walls and one wall was flanked by two high towers.

The Hospitallers and Templars, together with King Baldwin's own men, began the siege in late January of 1153 and continued to besiege the city for months, their number added to at Easter with the arrival of pilgrims, among whom were many knights and sergeants. The Fatimid garrison at Ascalon was aided in June with the arrival of troops from Egypt who had come by ship to bring fresh supplies. With fresh forces on both sides, the siege continued on through the summer.

The largest of the siege towers rose a good distance above the city walls, allowing the Christians to rain down on the city with greater precision and accuracy. This they did until some members of the garrison sneaked outside one night in mid-August and set the massive tower ablaze. As clever as they thought they were, they did not factor in the direction of the wind and soon the flames were not only destroying the Christians' siege tower, but further weakening Ascalon's walls. By morning the walls had become so weakened from the previous night's flames and several months of Christian ballistics that they collapsed, creating a breach that gave the Franks their first opportunity in nearly seven months to capture the city. When the dust began to clear the Christians were greatly excited that a victory was at hand and immediately picked up their arms to enter the breach. The first to reach the breach was Bernard de Tremeley, the Grand Master of the Templars, along with a number of his men. In his account of the siege, William of Tyre said that de Tremeley would not let anyone into the breach except his own men so that they could have first pick in obtaining the spoils of war. Whenever a city was captured by force, whatever a man seized belonged to him and his heirs in perpetuity. De Tremeley entered the breach with about forty of his men, while some remained outside to keep others from getting in until the Templars had taken their share of the booty. Unfortunately for de Tremeley and his forty Templars, no matter how well trained, they were no match for the awaiting garrison who slew all but one man as soon as they realised that the odds were in their favour.

Realising that no further Christians were coming to attack, the Fatimids inside the garrison moved quickly to secure the breach, piling beams and other pieces of good-sized timber over the hole. As the fire of the previous night had now died out, they once again resumed their positions in the towers and renewed their defence immediately. Soon the Muslims were not the only ones looking down on the Christians from above; the executed Templars were tied to ropes and hung over the city's walls to taunt the Christians, who were already demoralised by the morning's events.

Tired from the long siege, and further enfeebled by the death of their Grand Master, the Templars had no trouble agreeing with Baldwin that perhaps the time had come to lift the siege. However not everyone was in agreement with the decision as both Raymond du Puy and Fulcher of Angoulême, the Latin Patriarch of Jerusalem, were opposed to lifting

uenir uprent:

the siege. The Hospitaller Grand Master argued that the loss of forty men that morning was but a setback; victory was near if they pressed the siege a little longer. Du Puy and the Patriarch's contrary opinion proved to be the correct one, and three days later on 19 August, the Fatimids surrendered Ascalon to King Baldwin.

Although William of Tyre's assertion that Bernard de Tremeley and his Templars acted in their own interests at Ascalon is commonly accepted, his is the only account of the battle which makes mention of the story. Given that William was not an eyewitness to the events and did not always see eye-to-eye with the Templars, it is possible that his account, derived from second-hand sources, was manipulated to deliver his own message.

This type of accusation rarely fell on the Hospitallers, although they were not without their critics, particularly after they had taken on the secondary role of fighting for Christ. After more than two decades of existence and constant warfare over chunks of land, there were still those who viewed monks who fight as an unacceptable combination. This attitude was more common among those who wore their monastic robes without sword belts than among the general easterner, but the offence may have had more to do with money and power than any real distaste for monks getting bloodied. Both the Hospitallers and the Templars were viewed by the local priests as a church operating within the church, and many resented the Military Orders' special privileges that freed them

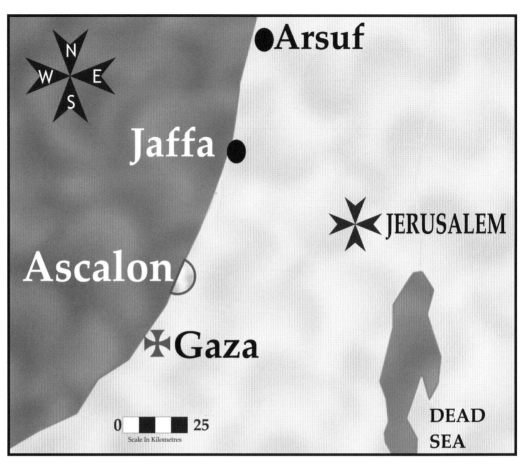

from paying church tithes. In fact, it was Fulcher of Angoulême, who had supported Raymond du Puy at Ascalon, who was the Orders' loudest critic. A year after the victory, Fulcher took issue with the Military Orders for refusing to pay tithes and for admitting excommunicated men into their ranks. The latter accusation was something the Templars had been actively involved in since their second Grand Master Robert de Craon revised the Order's rule in the 1130s. The Patriarch ordered both the Hospitallers and Templars to desist from the practice and start paying tithes. The Templars responded by firing arrows into his church door, the Hospitallers by firing arrows at his congregation, but only after shouting him down during his sermon. The following year Fulcher travelled to Rome to ask Pope Adrian IV to put the Templars and Hospitallers under his control, but Raymond du Puy's own trip to Rome added another facet to consider and when taken on balance, merely

prompted the Pope to reconfirm and expand the Hospitallers' privileges. The papal approval did not, however, settle the matter and the clergy began to look at both Orders with jealousy, splitting the focus of their often petty criticism where it had previously been launched at the Templars alone.

Although such criticisms would plague Raymond du Puy throughout his final years, neither he nor his Order had anything to hang their head about. Du Puy had honoured the memory of his predecessor Brother Gerard by maintaining and strengthening the Order's service to the poor and sick, while branching out to further serve travelling pilgrims with martial skills. His Order now rivalled that of the Templars, but little did he know in 1160, as he lay on his deathbed in the very hospital that he had helped maintain and grow, that his Hospitallers would continue long after the Holy Land they fought to protect had been lost, which would happen within a generation of his death.

CHAPTER 3
The Kingdom Falls

One morning, Nūr al-Dīn suddenly clutched his throat as he fell to the ground, dead. There at Damascus on 15 May 1174, Nūr al-Dīn, the man who had driven the crusaders back to the west, fell, struck down not by the dagger of his enemies, but by the complications of tonsillitis.

Before his death, Nūr al-Dīn had been planning to invade Egypt in order to take it away from an old associate of his named Saladin, whom Nūr al-Dīn, despite his previous esteem for the man, now viewed as a coward. He had sent Saladin to Egypt to work on his behalf, but his protégé had not made the progress against his Christian enemies to the north that Nūr al-Dīn had expected. Nūr al-Dīn saw this not so much as being afraid of the Christians as Saladin being afraid of removing them as a buffer between himself and Nūr al-Dīn. But Saladin was no coward, a fact that Nūr al-Dīn must have certainly known, for he, like his father and uncle before him, had long served the Zengid dynasty.

Salāh al-Dīn, or 'Saladin' as he is known in the west, was born Yūsuf ibn Ayyūb, the third son of Najm ad-Dīn Ayyūb, a Kurd who had served Nūr al-Dīn's father Zengi. When Zengi captured Baalbek from Damascus, it was Ayyūb who held the keys to the city for his master; however, when Zengi was murdered by a slave's dagger in 1146, Ayyūb quickly seized the opportunity to ally himself with Damascus by giving Baalbek back to them. Nūr al-Dīn

Salāh al-Dīn or Saladin, as he is known in the west, is shown in this modern interpretation of a contemporary twelfth-century depiction of the Muslim warrior.

was not amused by what he must have seen as disloyalty, but his displeasure was not sufficient to break his ties with Ayyūb's brother, Shūrkūh, who continued to serve the Turkish leader.

In 1154, Shūrkūh arrived before Damascus as Nūr al-Dīn's ambassador, but the governor of the city would neither let him in nor go outside the city to meet with him. Nūr al-Dīn, insulted at the treatment of his ambassador, descended on the city with a sizeable army, which was inside the city's gates within a week, having been granted entry by the citizens of Damascus. He instructed his men not to pillage the city, filled the markets with greatly needed produce and returned to Aleppo, leaving Ayyūb in charge as the conquered city's new governor, while Ayyūb's brother,

The Citadel of Aleppo was first constructed in the tenth century AD and was greatly expanded on during the thirteenth. Aleppo was the capital of the Zengid dynasty during Nūr al-Dīn's time and it is here that Saladin was educated.
Bigstock/ Shariff Che'Lah

replaced Shūrkūh as vizier of Egypt upon his uncle's death in March of 1169. However, this was not Saladin's first trip to Cairo. In 1163, he had been at his uncle's side when Nūr al-Dīn had sent the general to capture more territory for the Zengid Empire. The Egyptians invited King Amalric of Jerusalem to come to their aid and the king brought the Hospitallers and Templars with him, as both the Hospitaller Grand Master Arnaud de Comps and the Templar Grand Master Bertrand de Blanchefort were enthusiastic supporters of the campaign. After three months of besieging Shūrkūh's camp, both armies agreed to leave Cairo, but King Amalric received a handsome reward of gratitude for ridding Egypt of the threat of Nūr al-Dīn.

But the reward had not been sufficient to satiate Amalric's thirst for the gold of Cairo, a splendour he had seen first hand in 1163. The king, motivated by avarice and his own desire to topple the weak Fatimid rule, entered into an alliance with the Byzantine emperor for a second campaign in Egypt in 1168. The king was not alone in his avarice: Gilbert d'Aissailly, who had succeeded de Comps in 1163 was in favour of the campaign and had the support of the majority of his brethren in council. There were those opposed on the grounds that the Christians were operating under a peace treaty with the caliph of Egypt and they argued that the Hospitallers should honour that treaty, which was an opinion shared by the Templars and their Grand Master Bertrand de Blanchefort, who refused any participation in the campaign.

Although the Hospitallers succeeded in capturing the town of Belbeis, which d'Aissailly had made a condition of his Order's participation, the arrival of Nūr al-Dīn's army drove Amalric from his goal of Cairo and forced the evacuation of the small garrison of Hospitallers who had been left to guard Belbeis. Just as the Templars had been the scapegoats for the failed campaign at Damascus twenty years earlier, so too were the Hospitallers blamed for the disastrous campaign in Egypt. However, none took more blame than Gilbert d'Aissailly, who resigned from the Mastership of the Hospitaller Order and left the east, ultimately drowning between France and England. Regardless of who was at fault, Amalric would not invade Egypt again.

Shūrkūh, continued to serve the Turkish leader in a more offensive role. Less than a decade after the crusader's fiasco at Damascus, Nūr al-Dīn had succeeded in achieving what the Hospitallers and Templars had failed to accomplish with very few casualties.

It was in Damascus that the young Saladin received his early education, but once he reached the age of fourteen he entered military service at Aleppo under the tutelage of his uncle Shūrkūh, returning to Damascus four years later in an administrative capacity. Saladin continued to serve Nūr al-Dīn as part of his personal entourage and ultimately

Now that Saladin was stationed in Egypt, he was not prepared to take the chance of another Christian invasion. In November of 1170, he decided to strike at them on their own turf and marched on the Templar fortress at Daron. The Templars received assistance from King Amalric and a group of their brethren from the garrison at Gaza. Although the army was able to lift his siege of Daron, Saladin immediately marched on Gaza where he massacred the citizens of the lower town, but made no efforts to take the citadel. Soon after, Saladin returned to Egypt where he would continue to strengthen his position whilst trying to minimise that of Damascus.

By August of 1171, Nūr al-Dīn had sent word to Saladin that he wanted the country's Fatimid government and caliph gone and that if his representative in Egypt was not prepared to handle the job, he would have no problem making the journey in person. Despite Saladin's reluctance to comply with Nūr al-Dīn's orders, just a month later, two hundred years of Shia Fatimid rule came to

an end when the caliph al-Adid died. Within a week Saladin had what was left of the Fatimid royal family rounded up and imprisoned and set out on a campaign to attack the crusader castle at Montreal.

Saladin's siege of Montreal was going well. Amalric had received bad intelligence on the matter and left Jerusalem too late to be any help. As a result, the garrison at Montreal was all but ready to surrender the fortress when word arrived that Nūr al-Dīn was nearby at Kerak. Saladin immediately lifted the siege with the excuse that word had just arrived of problems in Upper Egypt, which required the army's immediate attention. The reality of the situation was that a confrontation with Nūr al-Dīn could have consequences for Saladin's position within Egypt, a position which he had worked hard to obtain and was unwilling to compromise.

For the next three years, Saladin followed his father's advice to lie low and sent frequent tributes to Aleppo to smooth things over with Nūr al-Dīn. But the treasure and riches sent

This bronze statue of Saladin on a rearing horse is located in front of the citadel in Damascus. The citadel in the rear of the photo was built in 1202 by Saladin's brother.
Bigstock/Styve Reineck

Belvoir Fortress,
located 20 miles south
of the Sea of Galilee,
was sold to the
Hospitallers in 1168 by
a French nobleman
named Velos. The
Hospitallers expanded
the existing fortress
into a large concentric
castle that served the
Hospitallers well until
it was besieged and
captured by Saladin in
1189. The Muslims
tore the fortifications
down in 1217, fearing
that the Crusaders
may one day recapture
the fortress.
Bigstock/George Kuna

from Cairo were not enough to appease Nūr al-Dīn and in 1173, he ordered Saladin to besiege the Christian fortress of Kerak. Once again, as he had two years previously at Montreal, Saladin lifted the siege the moment he heard Nūr al-Dīn was on his way to assist. However, this time he had a more legitimate reason for returning quickly to Egypt. His ageing father Ayyūb had been thrown from his horse and was seriously wounded. The old man died before Saladin reached Cairo. While Nūr al-Dīn was saddened by the death of his long-time servant Ayyūb, he was nonetheless angered by Saladin's disloyalty and vowed to move on Egypt the following spring. But as the seasons of 1174 passed, so too did Muslim power in Syria. By spring, Saladin's rival Nūr al-Dīn lay dead at Damascus; by summer word of his death had arrived in Cairo and Saladin was now sultan; and by the autumn the new sultan of Egypt was on the march to Damascus where he was received with open arms as

regent for Nūr al-Dīn's heir, Al-Sālih. In 1175, Saladin succeeded in adding Homs, Hama and Baalbek to his belt, and added Manbij and Azaz in 1176. Aleppo, however, would remain outside his grasp, despite his efforts to take the city. Upon his return to Damascus that year, he further taunted Nūr al-Dīn's memory by marrying one of his widows, Asimat ad-Dīn. By autumn he was back in Cairo, not only with the title Sultan of Egypt, but also King of Syria.

The Muslim world was not the only faction experiencing a shift in power; concurrent with Saladin's victories in the north, Christendom was experiencing difficulties of its own in the south. Amalric died of dysentery in July of 1174, leaving his thirteen-year-old son, Baldwin, as heir to the throne. Young Baldwin's age was not the biggest barrier to his kingship – he also suffered from leprosy. Despite his obvious shortcomings, four days after his father's death, he was crowned Baldwin IV in the Church of the Holy Sepulchre.

It was clear, however, that the Kingdom of Jerusalem would need a regent. The role, in all but name, was initially performed by Miles de Plancy, who was the deceased king's closest friend and Seneschal. However, de Plancy was not well liked and his unpopularity with the local barons paved the way for Raymond III, the Count of Tripoli, who was the king's closest male relative, to take over as regent. Raymond was the son of Raymond II of Tripoli, who had donated Krak des Chevaliers to the Hospitallers in 1142, and like his father before him, was a confrater or lay member of the Order. Three weeks after Baldwin was crowned king Miles de Plancy was assassinated at Acre and Raymond was a suspect in his death. Raymond may have been more popular with the local barons, but, like de Plancy, he was not without his opponents. In fact, his regency divided the kingdom into two factions with the Hospitallers and the Ibelin family being his main supporters. His opposition consisted of the Templars and westerners, both of whom sought a more militant approach to dealing with problems in the east. Among those to share this view with the Templars was a man named Reynald de Châtillon, who was released from prison in Aleppo in 1176 with a rabid hatred for Islam. However, Reynald's vendetta was as much personal as ideological. A few months after his release from prison, Reynald married de Plancy's widow Stephanie and through the marriage became Lord of Outrejordain. Since Reynald's bride was convinced that Count Raymond had played a hand in her husband's murder, it was clear which faction they would align themselves with. Likewise the Templars's problems with Count Raymond stemmed, at least in part, from personal motives. In 1173, a Flemish knight named Gerard de Ridefort came to Tripoli and entered into Raymond's employ. In exchange, the count had promised de Ridefort the hand of marriage of his first eligible heiress; however, when that opportunity arose a few months later, Raymond reneged on his promise. Instead of marrying her off to de Ridefort, Raymond gave her hand in marriage to a rich Pisan who offered the Count the princess's weight in gold. Soon after, de Ridefort joined the Templars, later to become Grand Master, but he would never forget Raymond's sleight.

The rift between the factions spread almost as rapidly as Baldwin's leprosy and with paralleled damage. The certainty of the new king's short life accelerated the need for succession planning if the kingdom of Jerusalem was to continue uninterrupted or uncontested. Baldwin had two stepsisters, Isabella and Sibylla, neither of whom had husbands. Sibylla, the elder, was the first to marry, uniting with William de Montferrat in October of 1176. However, just three months after the marriage, William died of malaria, leaving Sibylla pregnant with his child. It would be a few years before Sibylla would choose a husband, but in so doing she would marry a man who would give Saladin his greatest victory and the Hospitallers and Templars their greatest defeat.

Although Baldwin's reign would last but eleven years, the young king did not let his leprosy stand in the way of military action. Three years after having the crown placed on his head, the sixteen-year-old king personally delivered Saladin his first defeat at the Battle of Montgisard. Over the next eight years Baldwin would send his army to battles at Marj Ayyun (1179), Jacob's Ford (1179), Belvoir Castle (1182), Al-Fule (1183) and Kerak in Outrejordain (1183), and although defeated at Marj Ayyun and Jacob's Ford, the remainder of the battles were tactical draws.

Despite the king's ability to wage war, the fact remained that King Baldwin was slowly dying and his sister Sibylla had still not found a husband. Although she had fallen in love with Baldwin d'Ibelin and planned to marry him, he had been captured by Saladin along with the Templars' Grand Master Odo de St Amand at the Battle of Marj Ayyun in 1179. When Baldwin was finally released from prison, Sibylla told him that she could not marry him when he was in debt for the ransom that had bought his release; however, by the time d'Ibelin had secured the money to pay his ransom debt, Sibylla had found another man: a knight from Poitou named Guy of Lusignan. The couple were married at Easter 1180 and Guy was given Ascalon and Jaffa as his fief. It was a marriage that would create strife between Roger de Moulins and Gerard de Ridefort, the Grand Masters of the Hospitallers and Templars respectively.

Although de Moulins had been Grand Master since 1177, de Ridefort's administration began in 1185 as the political situation that had plagued King Baldwin's reign was coming to a close. The leper king finally succumbed to his illness in March of 1185, and was replaced by his nephew, Baldwin V, who died little more than a year later at the age of eight. Prior to his death, Baldwin IV had written in his will that should his nephew die before he reached the age of ten, Count Raymond was to resume his position as regent; however, there were those within the Kingdom of Jerusalem who did not wish to see the will fulfilled. With the assistance of de Ridefort and the Templars, Sibylla and Guy staged a coup in September of 1186 which ensured that they, and not Raymond of Tripoli, would rule the kingdom.

A nineteenth century romantic depiction of Gerard de Ridefort's impetuous charge against the Muslims at the Springs of Cresson on 1 May 1187, a battle in which Hospitaller Grand Master Roger de Moulins was killed.

Since the early days of the Military Orders, the Grand Masters held a special place in the Haute Cour of Jerusalem, holding the keys to the kingdom. There were three keys to the box that held the crown jewels. The Patriarch of Jerusalem and de Ridefort, both of whom supported Sibylla, each held one, while the third was held by de Moulins, who supported Raymond of Tripoli in his rightful duty. He refused to turn over the key, but ultimately threw it from his window in a fit of utter disgust over the matter. De Ridefort eagerly snatched the key from the dirt, seeing it not so much as the key to unlocking the crown jewels as the key to unlocking his revenge on Raymond of Tripoli for having refused him a bride all those years ago. As the Templars guarded the city gates to keep Raymond out, Sibylla was crowned Queen of Jerusalem by the Patriarch. Her first act as queen was to crown Guy as her king. According to some accounts, as de Ridefort left the Church of the Holy Sepulchre, he cried out that the crowning was payback for the marriage of the princess of Botron. It was not be de Ridefort's only move against Raymond of Tripoli, and throughout the winter of 1186, the Templar Master tried to persuade King Guy to march on Raymond and take Tiberius in order to bring him back into the fold. In a countermeasure, Raymond entered into a truce with Saladin to protect Tripoli and Galilee. King Guy, who tended to take whatever counsel was offered him at any given moment, may have made the move had he not been persuaded by Balian d'Ibelin to take wiser counsel. Instead of marching on Tiberius with arms, it was decided to march with diplomats and on 29 April 1187, the archbishop of Tyre together with de Moulins and de Ridefort set out for Tiberius. The plan was to pick up Balian at his castle at Nablus, but the younger Ibelin brother was tied up and sent the party north, promising to meet up with them at the Templars's castle at La Fève.

Concurrent with the embassy's move northward, Saladin's son Al-Afdal had requested Raymond to allow a scouting party from his army to move south. The request was little more than a polite formality because the truce Raymond had signed with Saladin allowed for it. However, it did not prohibit the count from sending word to the embassy to let them know what to expect. What should have been a friendly warning would soon turn to unnecessary bloodshed; upon receiving word that Muslims were afoot, de Ridefort moved immediately into action by summoning as many of his Templars as he could quickly gather.

On 1 May, the army – made up of about ninety knights from the two Orders, another forty local knights, 300 foot soldiers and the two Grand Masters – arrived at the Springs of Cresson, a little north of Nazareth. Below them was an army of approximately 700 Muslims, although contemporary accounts number them at 7,000. Being greatly outnumbered de Moulins and the Templar Marshal James de Mailly urged de Ridefort to retreat; however, de Ridefort would have no part of it. Instead of taking his Marshal's counsel, he taunted the man, telling him that he was too fond of his own blond head to risk losing it. The Marshal responded that he would die in battle a brave man, while his master would flee the field of battle like a traitor; it was a prophecy that would come true sooner than de Mailly thought. Gerard, insulted by the insubordinate comments of his Marshal, spurred his horse at once and led the charge down into the valley where the Muslims were waiting. When the battle was over, both the Marshal of the Templars and the Master of the Hospitallers, who had urged de Ridefort to retreat, lay dead in the field. Alongside their corpses lay the bodies of the knights and 300 sergeants who had entered the battle. Of those who had entered the field only four men survived, one of whom was de Ridefort.

The massacre at Cresson was undoubtedly a disaster brought on by de Ridefort's impetuous nature and, although he had sent ninety of his men to their deaths, they lived on in legend and lore for many years, as subsequent Templar leaders would use their martyrdom to maintain morale among troops before a battle or during a siege. The ancillary benefit of their martyrdom was the unification of the two political factions. It had been Raymond who allowed the Muslims to cross his land in the first place and, as such, part of the blame lay at his doorstep. Shortly after the massacre at Cresson, Raymond and King Guy patched things up, the truce with Saladin was ended, and the Muslim garrison stationed at Tiberius was expelled. For the first time in many years, it seemed like Christendom was once again prepared to turn its attentions towards a common enemy and Guy was able to assemble an army from Tripoli, Antioch and his own Kingdom of Jerusalem, the likes of which had never been seen. Unfortunately, it would prove to be too little too late.

A month after escaping the carnage at Cresson, Gerard de Ridefort was cracking into the coffers of King Henry II of England that were housed in the Templar treasury in Jerusalem. The money had been sent east as part of the atonement the English King had to make for his part in the murder of Thomas Becket in 1170. The money was to be banked to support the crusade east that Henry had planned to make, but never actually got around to. De Ridefort, however, was going to see to it that the money was put to use in hiring mercenary troops to avenge the shame the Muslims had brought on Christendom in general and himself in particular the previous month at Cresson.

De Ridefort was not alone in organising troops: the Hospitallers' newly elected leader Hermangard d'Asp was also preparing his men for the battle that lay ahead. While the two Orders made preparations to assist the Kingdom of Jerusalem, Saladin was bringing in troops from Aleppo, Mosul and Mardin that, when combined, would number 50,000 men. On 26 June, Saladin reviewed his troops at Ashtera and arranged them in marching formation. Taqī al-Dīn, Saladin's nephew, took the right wing; Kukburi, the Emir of Harran, the left wing; and Saladin himself, the centre column. The army marched north from Ashtera to Khisfin and then southward around the southern tip of the Sea of Galilee, where they stayed for five days, gathering intelligence on the Christians. Saladin crossed the River Jordan on 1 July, and sent half of his troops north to lay siege to Tiberius, while the other half moved west to Cafarsset where they set up camp.

Concurrent with Saladin crossing the Jordan, King Guy held a council meeting at the port city of Acre to lay plans for the Christian's plan of attack. Raymond of Tripoli knew that the summer heat would be a problem for both sides in the coming conflict, but realised that the army who attacked would

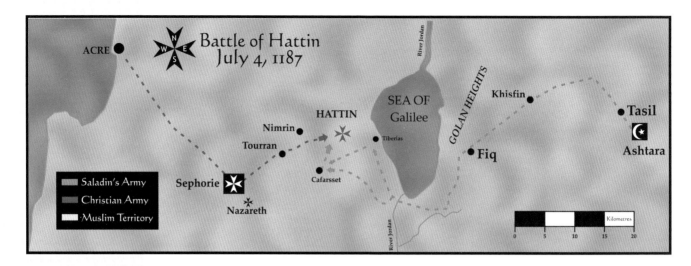

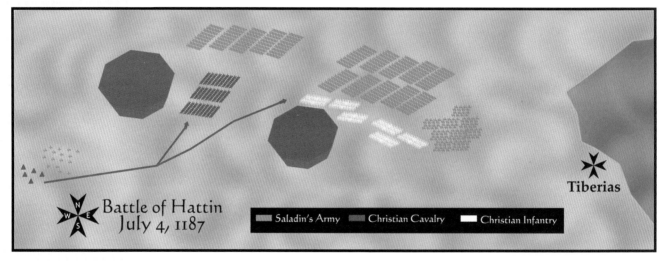

be at an immediate disadvantage. As such, it was his suggestion that the Christian army, which numbered some 38,000 men, including the mercenary troops hired with King Henry's money, should take a defensive stand. Raymond told the council that Saladin could not press the fight for long in the parched region and would be forced to retreat. Reynald and de Ridefort accused Raymond of cowardice and suggested a more militant approach. As was so often the case, Guy gave the Order to march towards Tiberius.

With the Hospitallers and Templars taking the rear positions, the Christian army arrived at Sephorie, northeast of Nazareth, on 2 July and set up camp. Like the orchards outside of Damascus forty years earlier, the spot was an excellent place to make a camp: there was plenty of water, pastures for the horses and the location would give them the advantage in the coming battle. But, like the fiasco of Damascus, the king would soon be persuaded to change locations. That evening a messenger arrived informing the Christians that Saladin had besieged Tiberius. Raymond again recommended the same defensive strategy he had offered earlier. Even though his wife was in the city's citadel, he was willing to lose her and let Tiberius fall for the greater good of saving the kingdom. This time King Guy took Raymond's advice and spread the word that the camp would hold their position. However, later that night Gerard de Ridefort returned to Guy's tent intent on bending his ear and making him abandon his plan. The Templar Master asked the king if he were prepared to trust a traitor, which is how de Ridefort regarded Raymond of Tripoli. It was a disgrace to sit idle while a Christian city so close by fell to the infidels. De Ridefort even threatened the king that should he remain inactive, the Templars would be forced to hang up their habits; the deaths of the brethren at Cresson must be avenged. Again, the malleable King Guy was persuaded and gave the order that the camp would march at dawn. Of course there was little he could say in opposition to Gerard's requests; had it not been for the Master of the Temple and his brethren, it would be Raymond of Tripoli and not he that was making the decisions.

When the sun rose the next morning, the Christians broke camp and left their favourable position at Sephorie for Tiberius, moving northeast towards Tourran. As the army was travelling through Raymond's fief, he, according to feudal custom, took the vanguard position. King Guy and his men made up the centre column, while Balian d'Ibelin, Reynald de Châtillon and the Hospitallers and Templars again formed the rearguard. Saladin, having received word of the Christians' movements, broke camp at Cafarsset and moved his troops in the same direction. As the Christians continued towards Tiberius, Muslim light cavalry began to skirmish the army, picking off horses and men one by one. As if this harassment was not enough to sap their morale, the Christians were now suffering from the heat, unable to quench the thirsts that had been building since they had left Sephorie that morning. By noon the army had all but come to a full stop. To solve the problem, Raymond suggested that the army change course and move towards the village of Hattin; it was but six kilometres away and the army could take water at the springs there, make camp and set out for Tiberius the following morning. Guy agreed and the army moved off in that direction. However, as the Christians were travelling downgrade towards the two hills known as the Horns of Hattin, Saladin had the advantage of being able to see what they were doing and ordered Taqī al-Dīn to move in to block their approach to Hattin.

With the vanguard blocked ahead, Saladin ordered his other wing to harass the Christian rearguard, which caused Raymond to order a second halt of the army. The Templars charged their Muslim tormentors in the hopes of driving them away, but the charge failed to deliver the desired result and the army, now exhausted from the abundance of heat and lack of water, decided to make camp where they were. Saladin had his men fire the brush in the area to torment the Christians with smoke and more heat.

Fighting broke out almost as soon as the army began to move forwards the next morning. Saladin sent his men in to attack the parched Christians, but the Templars repelled the aggressor with a counter-charge, which, although successful, cost them a number of their horses. As the fighting continued, the infantrymen who were to protect the knights lost morale and broke off from the main army in ever-increasing numbers heading towards the body of water glistening to their right, a body of water that was much further away than it appeared. It would be water they would never drink as many of the infantry were slaughtered; the rest were captured to be sold later as slaves.

With their protection destroyed there was little the remaining knights could do. Not even the disciplined Military Orders could gain much ground without the assistance of the infantry. The anonymous writer of *De Expugatione Terrae Sanctae per Saladinum* tells of the chaos and carnage that followed:

'The Templars, Hospitallers, and Turcopoles, meanwhile, were engaged in a fierce rear guard action. They could not win, however, because enemies sprang up on every side, shooting arrows and wounding Christians. When they had gone on for a little bit, they shouted to the King, asking for some help. The King and the others saw that the infantry were not going to return and that they themselves could not hold out against the Turkish arrows without the sergeants. Accordingly, by the grace of the Lord's cross, they ordered the tents to be put up, in order to block the Saracen charges and so that they could hold out more easily. The battle formations were, therefore, broken up. The units gathered around the Holy Cross, where they were confused and intermixed here and there. The men who were with the Count of Tripoli in the first group saw that the King, the Hospitallers, the Templars, and everyone else were jumbled together and mingled with the Turks. They also saw that there was a multitude of the barbarians between themselves and the King, so that they could not get through to return to the Lord's cross. They cried out: 'Those who can get through may go, since the battle is not going in our favour. We have now lost even the chance to flee.' Meanwhile, thousands and thousands of Syrians were charging at the Christians, shooting arrows and killing them.

Many knights now fought on foot; the weight of their chain mail hauberks and leggings putting them at a strong disadvantage; their only additional protection being the corpses of their fallen mounts and slain comrades. Raymond of Tripoli had fled the battle as did Balian d'Ibelin and Reynald of Sidon. However, there was little the count could do. When he led his men in a charge against the Muslims, Taqī al-Dīn had opened ranks, allowing the charge to pass through and then closed his formation just as suddenly. Raymond saw that charging uphill again would be as impossible as it would be futile and set off for Tyre.

'King Guy could also see that things were quickly going downhill and moved what was left of his troops uphill to the southern horn, where he set up the royal tent, perhaps hoping that its bright red colour would serve as a rallying point for the troops. But it was not long before the tent fell and those who guarded it along with it, the loss of the king's tent being as great a source of misery to the Christians as it was a source of joy to the Muslims. Soon after Guy's tent was pulled to the ground, the Christians lost another important symbol when the True Cross was wrested from Christian hands. The Arabic chronicler Imad al-Dīn wrote that "Its capture was for them [the Christians] more important than the loss of the King and was the gravest blow that they sustained in that battle. The cross was a prize without equal, for it was the supreme object of their faith. To venerate it was their duty, for it was their God, before whom they would bow their foreheads to the ground, and to which their mouths sang hymns."'

The earthly remnants of Christ's suffering and sacrifice were not all the Muslims had succeeded in capturing from the Christians. King Guy, Reynald de Châtillon, Gerard de Ridefort and William Borrell, the Marshal of the Hospitallers, as well as many other nobly born Franks were now Saladin's captives. Given

The fateful Battle of Hattin fought on 4 July 1187 is romantically depicted in this nineteenth century illustration. The massive defeat at Hattin would reduce the Christians' ability to fight off Saladin over the coming months and ultimately paved the way for the loss of Jerusalem.

the sheer magnitude of the slaughter, it is hard to imagine if they considered themselves lucky for having survived, or if they longed for the death their soldiers had embraced.

When the Franks had been brought to Saladin's tent, the sultan offered King Guy a glass of cool water; the first he had tasted since he had left Sephorie two days earlier. After Guy had his fill, he passed the cup to Reynald de Châtillon; however, the offering was not as welcomed by the sultan as it was by Reynald. "This godless man did not have my permission to drink and will not save his life this way," Saladin informed King Guy. Muslim custom dictated that if a man were offered food or drink, his protection was assured. This was a privilege which Reynald was not entitled to, especially since Saladin had vowed to kill him for his continued attacks on Muslim caravans and his plan to invade Islam's holiest cities. After being reminded of his many transgressions against the Muslims, Reynald was beheaded. In some accounts Saladin beheaded Reynald himself, while others indicate he ordered the job to be done, but regardless of who swung the scimitar, Saladin had taken his revenge on his enemy at long last. Seeing his friend beheaded before his eyes did little to quell King Guy's fears and he began to tremble anticipating a similar fate. Saladin reassured him that his life would not be taken; instead he was thrown in prison along with the Templars' Grand Master, Gerard de Ridefort.

However, other Hospitallers and Templars who had survived the ordeal did not share the same fate as their Master. The foot soldiers who survived Hattin had been rounded up like any other captured booty and treated as a marketable commodity, but the Hospitallers and Templars were highly prized by their captors, who anticipated a great ransom. Saladin was well aware of this and offered fifty Egyptian dinars for each of the captured members of the two Orders. The sum was sufficient to ensure that two hundred of Christendom's best fighting men were brought before him. Quite simply, Saladin was not interested in seeing the white- and red-crossed knights as slaves; he wanted them gone, although each was given the choice of conversion or death. As Ibn al-Athīr explained the matter, '[Saladin] had these particular men

killed because they were the fiercest of all the Frankish warriors, and in this way he rid the Muslim people of them.'

But Saladin was not content with ridding the east of the military Orders. As the remaining months of 1187 passed from one to another, so too did the various cities, towns and castles of the Levant pass from Christian to Muslim hands. Saladin's strategy was wise in that he struck at the Christians' coastal holdings first, effectively depriving any future Christian army arriving from the west the

This trebuchet outside Urquhart Castle in the Scottish Highlands is similar to what would have been used by Saladin to attack the cities he captured in the autumn of 1187.
Bigstock/Lance Bellers

opportunity of access by sea. Within a week of the Muslim victory at Hattin, the port city of Acre had surrendered to Saladin's army and within a month Toron, Sidon, Gibelet and Beirut had also capitulated. Ascalon, which had taken the crusaders several months to capture in 1153, had surrendered to Saladin on 5 September 1187 after being besieged for

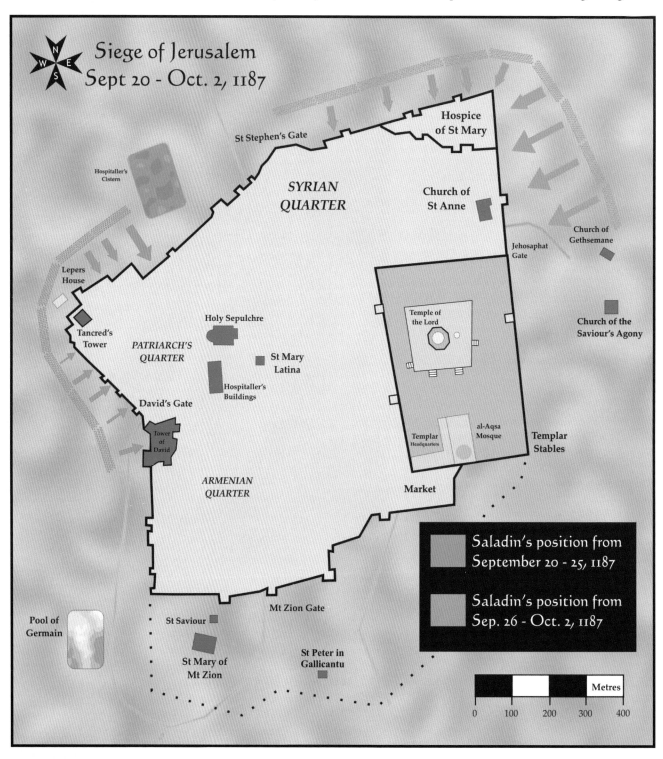

Siege of Jerusalem
Sept 20 - Oct. 2, 1187

St Stephen's Gate

Hospitaller's Cistern

Hospice of St Mary

SYRIAN QUARTER

Church of St Anne

Church of Gethsemane

Jehosaphat Gate

Lepers House

Church of the Saviour's Agony

Tancred's Tower

Holy Sepulchre

Temple of the Lord

PATRIARCH'S QUARTER

St Mary Latina

Hospitaller's Buildings

David's Gate

Tower of David

Templar Headquarters

al-Aqsa Mosque

Templar Stables

ARMENIAN QUARTER

Market

Saladin's position from September 20 - 25, 1187

Saladin's position from Sep. 26 - Oct. 2, 1187

Mt Zion Gate

Pool of Germain

St Saviour

St Peter in Gallicantu

St Mary of Mt Zion

Metres

0   100   200   300   400

less than two weeks. However, in the case of Ascalon, Saladin had some Christian help. The sultan brought King Guy and Gerard de Ridefort along to convince their co-religionists to surrender. Guy did as he was told, aided by the Templar Master, but their pleas were not well received by those behind the city walls who hurled insults at the men while Saladin's mangonels hurled projectiles at the walls. Nothing now remained of the kingdom's coastal holdings except Tyre, where many who had fled Saladin's onslaught were now huddled. Saladin could now turn his full attention on Jerusalem.

Prior to the siege of Jerusalem, Balian d'Ibelin, who was at Tyre, sent a request to the sultan asking to be given safe passage to retrieve his family from Jerusalem. Saladin agreed on the condition that Balian would stay in the city for no longer than one day, collect his family and leave again. However, when he arrived at Jerusalem, he found a city incapable of manning a defence against the coming siege and was persuaded to take the leadership role in the battle that lay ahead. He had given his word to Saladin, but now his duty to his people put him in the unfortunate position of having to betray his word. He wrote to the sultan explaining his position and Saladin not only accepted his apology but even sent his own men to escort Balian's family back to Tyre.

The situation in the Holy City, which had been home to both facets of the Hospitaller organisation, was grim. The Hospitallers, who once could be seen in their area around the Holy Sepulchre, and the Templars, who once filled the al-Aqsa, were now vastly outnumbered by the ghosts of their brethren who had fallen at the Battle of Hattin two months earlier. The reality was that neither Order had much more than three hundred knights in the east at any one time, although these would have been complemented and supported by much larger numbers of sergeants, turcopoles and mercenaries. Most of those had been killed or captured at the Battles of Cresson Springs, Hattin, and in defending the Christian outposts on Saladin's slow march down the Syrian and Palestinian coasts. In fact, in all of Jerusalem there were but two secular knights, and men of any sort were in short supply. Balian knighted every nobly born male over the age of sixteen and even knighted men of lower station. Those who were able to bear arms were given them.

On 20 September, Saladin's army arrived at Jerusalem and began their attack on the western side of the city the following day. For five days Saladin's mangonels hurled boulders and Greek fire at the walls, but the walls failed to give. Six days later he withdrew to the northern side of the city, which gave the inhabitants of Jerusalem hope that Saladin had broken the siege. However, their hopes, like the city's walls, were soon reduced to rubble, as the sultan's trebuchets resumed their volleys. As Jerusalem received its punishment, Saladin's miners worked on the walls, finally opening a breach on 29 September. The Patriarch and other nobles offered 5,000 bezants to any man who would move in to guard the breach, but there were no takers; it was realised that a continued fight would only cost more lives than had already been forfeited to save a city that could no longer hold off Saladin's army. The next day Balian left what little safety the crumbling walls of Jerusalem afforded him and sought an audience with Saladin in order to negotiate the terms of surrender. Saladin reminded Balian that the city was already lost and that the only option was unconditional surrender; however, Balian told the sultan that unless the Christians were assured of favourable terms they would destroy what was left of the city before his army could take it. The Dome of the Rock and the al-Aqsa Mosque would be razed to the ground and the Muslims inside the city would be slaughtered just as they had been when the city was captured nearly a century earlier.

With the prospect of entering a city in ruin, Saladin set the terms of surrender at 10 dinars for every man, five for every woman and one for every child. However, within the city were many of Christendom's poor who could not afford the ransom. Balian bought the freedom of 7,000 for the sum of 30,000 dinars, money taken from Jerusalem's treasury as well as those of the Templars and Hospitallers, the latter of whom, in keeping with their mission of looking after the poor, appear to have willingly contributed to the cause.

On 2 October, after besieging the city for less than two weeks, Saladin entered Jerusalem, bringing to an end the Christian's eighty-eight-year hold on the Holy City. However, unlike the Christian capture of Jerusalem in 1099, Saladin and his army entered the city with their swords sheathed. As the Muslims entered the gates, the Christians left in the opposite direction. Some had bought their freedom, others had their liberty bought for them and others faced the prospect of a life of slavery.

A decade had passed since the sultan had first marched on Jerusalem, only to be thwarted by King Baldwin IV and the Templars at Montgisard, but now the Templars had been removed from the Holy City and Saladin moved quickly to erase any memory of the Christian's presence on the Temple Mount. The great golden cross that once rose above the Dome of the Rock was torn down, the Holy sites were cleansed with rose water to remove the pollution caused by the Christians, and the al-Aqsa, which had been granted to the Templars by King Baldwin II in the 1120s, was restored to its pre-Templar purpose. With respect to the hospital

of St John, Saladin permitted ten Hospitallers to remain in the city to care for those who were too enfeebled to move. But when the grace period was over, the Hospitallers removed to their castle at Marqab, which they had purchased from a vassal of the Count of Tripoli a year before the Battle of Hattin. The sisters of the Order, however, would leave the Holy Land altogether for the various European hospitals operated by the Order.

Jerusalem was once again in Muslim hands and news from the east arrived in the west within a fortnight. Two weeks after the Christians conquered the city in 1099, Pope Urban II lay dead, having never learned of the good news; two weeks after the Christians lost the city in 1187, Pope Urban III also lay dead, having died soon after hearing the bad news. It would be his successor, Gregory VIII, who would launch the crusade that would give the Hospitallers and the Templars a common home for the next century. It would be the Christians' last century in the land across the sea which they called Outremer.

Ruins of the Hospital of Jerusalem are shown in this nineteenth century engraving originally published in Whitworth Porter's 1883 history of the Order.

AN ILLUSTRATED HISTORY OF THE KNIGHTS HOSPITALLER

CHAPTER 4
Acre

When King Richard I of England arrived at Acre in the spring of 1191, he found a city that had been under siege for nearly two years. He also found that his late father's enemy Philip Augustus, the King of France, had preceded his arrival by seven weeks. Both Philip and Richard had left the west around the same time and met up with each other in Italy, but the passage between there and Acre had been decidedly different for the two nobly born men. Richard's fleet had encountered bad weather and was forced to make stops at Crete and Rhodes, islands the Hospitallers would call home in the years to come. Two of Richard's ships had been wrecked on the coast of Cyprus, while another carrying the king's sister Joanna and his fiancée was forced to land at Limassol, a port on the island's southern coast. The island's self-appointed ruler, Isaac Ducas Comnenus, who was an ally of Saladin, had the shipwrecked passengers imprisoned; however, Joanna refused to leave the ship. When Richard arrived on 8 May he was not in a good mood from the journey, and the treatment his people had received did little to improve it. Four days later Richard conquered the island with the help of the English fleet, King Guy and the Templars.

On 5 June, the English fleet set sail from Famagusta on the eastern coast of Cyprus and landed the next day at Tyre, where they were refused entry to the city by orders of Conrad of Montferrat and Philip Augustus. King Guy and the Templars' Grand Master Gerard de Ridefort had been released by Saladin in 1188, but Guy found the gates of his former kingdom shut in his face. After hanging around the city gates for months, he moved on to Acre and began to lay siege to it. The Templars supported him and de Ridefort was killed in a skirmish early on. Despite the loss of the Grand Master, the Templars had remained loyal to King Guy.

When Richard arrived in 1191, the dispute over the Kingdom of Jerusalem was still going strong. Richard was a supporter of Guy's cause, while King Philip had sided with his cousin, Conrad. But Richard and his twenty-five galleys were better received at Acre and the arrival of the King of England brought both a fresh outlook and fresh troops to the battle, which had not been going well even after the arrival of the western Christians. By 3 July, the catapults finally managed to create a substantial breach in the wall, but all attempts to enter through it were repelled, as was a second attempt launched eight days later. However, by this time the garrison had already been prepared to offer their surrender as reinforcements promised by Saladin had yet to arrive. The terms of the surrender were set; 200,000 bezants were to be paid to the crusaders for the lives of the city's Muslim inhabitants and 1,500 Christians held captive by Saladin were to be returned along with the

King Richard of England and King Philip of France ride through the streets of Acre after its capture on 12 July 1191.
Jupiter Images

True Cross captured at the Battle of Hattin four years earlier. On 12 July, the Muslim inhabitants of Acre moved out of the city bound in shackles, while the Christians moved in bound with joy. With the city in Christian hands the nobles met to lay their claim to property and to resolve the dispute over the Kingdom of Jerusalem. It was decided that Guy would retain the crown until his death and thereafter it would pass to Conrad of Montferrat and his wife Isabella, the daughter of King Amalric of Jerusalem. Philip returned to France soon after complaining of illness; however, his departure was viewed as cowardice by the English.

The Hospitallers had remained reasonably unaffected by the aftermath of Hattin; Antioch, Tripoli and their own fortresses of Marqab and Krak des Chevaliers had remained in Christian hands. Now that the port city of Acre was once again added to the family, the Hospitallers would, in the coming months, move their convent and principal hospital from Marqab to Acre, where they would resume the work they had performed at Jerusalem for so long. In this they would be joined by a new Order dedicated to aiding the poor and sick, the Teutonic Knights of St Mary's Hospital in Jerusalem.

On 22 August, two days after massacring the 2,700 Muslim captives whose ransom had not been paid, Richard set off with his army for Jaffa. His goal was Jerusalem, but it would first be necessary to capture the port city as a base of operations. As the army marched down the coast they stayed close to the shoreline to benefit from the cool breeze and the support of the ships that followed the march down the coastline. The army was divided into three columns: the first column was composed of knights, and kept to the sea side, while the remaining two columns made up of infantrymen took the land side position. In the vanguard were the Templars, upon whom Richard relied throughout his crusade. It had been through his influence that Robert de Sablé, an Angevin who had travelled east with the king, had been elected to succeed de Ridefort as Master of the Order, despite the fact that he was not a Templar when he left England. In the rearguard were the Hospitallers, who were led by Garnier de Nablus, who was elected to the post in 1190.

As the Christian army marched down the coast their movement was shadowed by Saladin's light mounted archers who launched a series of attacks on the crusaders, riding in close enough to shoot and then retreating again as quickly as they had come. Despite the torments of Saladin's arrows, the army managed to maintain their discipline and the crusader infantry armed with crossbows took out a number of the Muslim archers.

Although the knights and their heavy charge often receive the bulk of attention in discussions of medieval conflicts, the discipline of the infantry is every bit as worthy of merit. As the knights were cooled by the sea breeze

and protected by two lines of human targets, the infantrymen in those lines sacrificed their lives to protect their nobly born counterparts and their horses. The medieval war horse was the tank of its day and the loss of one horse was a great cost to an army.

On 6 September, Richard's army passed through a wooded area about 16 kilometres north of Arsuf. Two weeks had passed since they left Acre and they had covered less than half the distance to Jaffa. Throughout the journey the Muslims had done little more than advance and retreat with their archers; however, that would change the next morning when the crusaders approached Arsuf. Saladin's men began a full assault around noon, but the crusaders resisted the attack. This was accomplished through the discipline of the common foot soldiers, who served as two rows of a flesh and bone wall between the Muslim archers and the Christian knights. The front line of infantrymen knelt with spear and shield, while the standing crossbowmen returned the attack. When the crossbowmen re-armed, the spearmen stood with their shields to provide them with cover.

Meanwhile, the knights were aligned in battle formation behind the front line: the Templars were at the southern end of the line forming the right flank along with the Bretons, Angevins and King Guy and his party; King Richard and his English and Normans troops made up the centre assisted by Flemish and French troops; in the rearguard were the Hospitallers. In total, the crusader army was made up of approximately 1,200 knights and 10,000 infantrymen. The Muslims numbered 20,000 men equally split between cavalry and infantry. As the day progressed it became increasingly difficult for the infantrymen to maintain a line of defence as the Muslims came closer and closer in their attacks, ultimately close enough to replace their bows and arrows for lances and swords. Soon the Christian infantry were falling in increasing numbers.

In the hopes of drawing the crusaders into an early charge, Saladin's troops focused their attacks on the Hospitallers'

The Teutonic Knights began in 1191 after the capture of Acre and, like the Templars and Hospitallers, made their headquarters in the port city.

division. The attacks began to take their toll on the Order and on several occasions Garnier de Nablus approached King Richard, begging him to give the signal to charge, but each time the king urged the Grand Master to instruct his men to exercise patience. Richard had a reputation for being adventurous, but he was a competent commander, and wanted to hold the charge until it could have the maximum possible effect. The Hospitaller Marshal did not see things the same way and when the Muslim assaults finally proved too much for him to endure, he and one of his knights broke rank and began the charge. Although the signal had not been given, all the Hospitallers assumed it had and charged after

King Richard is depicted in the melee that followed the Hospitallers' impetuous charge at the Battle of Arsuf in this illustration by Gustave Doré. Despite breaking ranks, the Christians emerged victorious.

their comrades. Within seconds horses were spurred down the Christian line as knight after knight joined the charge. Richard, seeing that there was no choice but to join the battle lest those who were already in it be slaughtered, ordered the Templars, Bretons and Angevins in their line to attack Saladin's left flank. Finally, the Templars were able to release the frustration that the Hospitallers had been unable to contain and their charge drove the Saracens from the field. Richard's column assaulted Saladin's right flank, while the Templars took care of the left. When all was said and done Saladin's army had been defeated, stunned by the Hospitallers' impetuousness and mopped up by the Templars' discipline, a reversal of how things had gone at Ascalon nearly thirty-eight years earlier when it had been the Templars who had felt they could go it alone. Although the losses had been relatively light on both sides, the Muslims had been repelled. Following so soon after the capture of Acre, the battle was a great morale-boosting victory for the Christians in general and the Military Orders in particular. It had been the first open battle since the Battle of Hattin four years earlier and neither the Hospitallers nor the Templars had forgotten the role their Order had played there or the great price their fallen brethren had paid during the battle.

Although the victory at Arsuf undoubtedly boosted morale for the Hospitallers and Templars, the Muslims resumed their taunting Parthian shots the next morning, following the crusaders as they made their way towards Jaffa. However, they did not engage in a full assault as they had at Arsuf as Saladin understood that attacking the boxed formation of infantrymen the crusaders used to protect their cavalry was like besieging a fortress; the efforts to draw out the knights were too great and the result too damaging. Richard pressed on to Jaffa relatively unopposed and took the city on 29 September, after which he fortified it with ditches and a wall in anticipation of having to defend it from Saladin. But Saladin was busy at Ascalon, levelling it to the ground to prevent it from being of any strategic value to the crusaders.

Richard entered into negotiations with both the Templars and Saladin soon after taking control of Jaffa: the purchase of Cyprus with the former, the surrender of Jerusalem with the latter. However, Richard soon found his allies to be more agreeable to his terms than his enemies. Saladin had sent his brother Al-'Ādil to handle the negotiations and returned to the sultan with Richard's first offer, which was really a demand. The king wanted Jerusalem, all of its land west of the Jordan and the return of the True Cross. The offer was refused, but Richard's second offer must have seemed just as unreasonable: Al-'Ādil should receive all of Palestine currently controlled by Saladin, while Richard's sister, Joanna, should receive all the area captured by the king thus far. To balance things, Al-'Ādil would get Joanna as a bride and the couple would live in Jerusalem, with access to the Holy City open to Muslims and Christians alike. Additionally, the True Cross was to be returned to Christendom and the Hospitallers and Templars were to be restored with all of their properties captured after Hattin. Joanna was less inclined to accept the offer than Saladin was. As things stood, if Richard wanted Jerusalem, he would have to take it.

Shortly after Christmas Richard's army was within 19 kilometres of Jerusalem and although those who had come on crusade wanted to lay siege to the Holy City, both Garnier de Nablus and Robert de Sablé urged caution. The consensus of the two Grand Masters was that even if they succeeded in taking the city by force, it would be virtually impossible to hold once the crusaders returned west. Richard took the counsel, perhaps hoping that a peaceful solution was still possible, and spent the next four months at Ascalon rebuilding the city Saladin had razed to the ground following his defeat at Arsuf. From March until August, Richard and Saladin alternated between fighting and negotiating with each other, the common stumbling block being Ascalon, which Saladin wanted destroyed for good.

While Saladin and Richard were trying to come to terms over Jerusalem, others were trying to decide who should wear the crown belonging to the entire kingdom bearing its name. Although the matter had been decided uponsome time previously, it remained largely unaccepted, and to this end Richard called a council of the barons to decide the matter. When presented with the choice between Conrad and Guy, the council unanimously chose the former, which shocked Guy. Three days after receiving the favourable news, Conrad was murdered in the streets of Tyre by two assassins. The marquis's murder did not, however, mean that Guy took the crown. Although Conrad was dead, his widow Isabella was the rightful heir to the throne and soon after chose Henry, Count of Champagne, as her new husband. Although Guy had lost one kingdom he would soon gain another, for the following month, Richard bought Cyprus back from the Templars and sold it to the deposed king. It would be one of Guy's descendants who would offer the Hospitallers and the Templars refuge on Cyprus 100 years later.

On 28 August 1192, three years to the day that Guy had begun his siege of Acre, Saladin's final offer was presented to Richard: The Christians were to keep the coastal cities they had captured as far south as Jaffa; Jerusalem as well as other sites sacred to the faith would once again be open to Christians, and both sides were free to travel through each other's lands. There was one condition: Ascalon was to be destroyed. Richard was agreeable to the terms but unwilling to swear an oath because he was a king. On 2 September, the Masters of the Hospitallers and the Templars, together with Henry of Champagne and Balian d'Ibelin, took Richard's hand and swore on his behalf, adding their names to the document. The next day the Third Crusade came to a close when Saladin added his own signature, completing the truce.

For the first time in nearly five years Jerusalem was once again open to Christians and many of the crusaders who had come east to rescue the city took advantage of visiting it;

Richard was not among them. On 9 October 1192, the King of England set sail for home, having never seen the city he had come to rescue. He died seven years later after being shot while besieging a castle in his own lands. Saladin had died in 1193, and the territory he had captured throughout his career was divided among his relatives, who fought amongst one another over land and titles. The Muslim unity that Saladin had created dissolved after his death.

Richard's life had ended, but the city he had helped to capture during the Third Crusade remained very much alive and was now the capital of a much smaller Kingdom of Jerusalem. The Hospitallers who had looked after the poor and sick a stone's throw from the holiest site in Christendom for more than a century, now occupied extensive property in Acre, as did the Templars, who occupied the peninsula of the port city as their main headquarters in the east. However, whereas many of the eastern Christians had been dependent on revenues from their eastern land holdings, the Hospitallers, like the Templars, had not lost their important network of farms and manors in the west, all of which continued to send men, money and arms to their eastern brethren. While the link between east and west would help the Military Orders survive, the link between the eastern and western churches would grow further strained, which would only push Christendom closer to the shores of the Mediterranean.

In 1202, Pope Innocent III called for another crusade with the purpose of regaining Jerusalem for Christendom by striking the Muslims in Egypt. But the crusaders, seeing the glitter of gold at Constantinople and led astray by the promises of pretenders to the Byzantine throne, attacked and looted the city in 1204, destroying it and the already fraying bond between the eastern and western churches.

However, relationships were not the only thing crumbling in the east in 1202. A major earthquake shook the Hospitallers' castle at Krak des Chevaliers and did to the fortress what Nūr al-Dīn and Saladin had failed to do the century before. But the Hospitallers repaired the damage caused by the earthquake and took the opportunity to undergo a substantial expansion. When completed the fortress could support 2,000 soldiers, although

Crusaders are shown loading a boat with the spoils of war after sacking Constantinople in 1204 in this medieval illustration. The misguided crusade would further strain relationships between the eastern and western churches.
Jupiter Images

The angled interior walls of Krak des Chevaliers, surrounded by a moat, added to the impossibility of getting inside the fortress. Located on the fortress's more vulnerable southern side, the base of the angled wall is 80 feet thick.
Bigstock/Styve Reineck

it is doubtful that the Hospitallers ever had more than 60 of their own men stationed there at any one time.

The Hospitallers' other major fortress at Marqab was the site of a conflict between the Order and their rivals the Templars. According to Whitworth Porter the Templars had designs on a castle owned by the Count of Tripoli's vassal who had sold Marqab to the Templars in 1186. When the Templars seized the castle, the vassal appealed to the Hospitallers for protection, which they were only too happy to provide with full military force. The situation, says Porter, alarmed the eastern ecclesiastics to the point where they appealed to the Pope to intercede. The Pope decided neither of the Orders was in the right and ordered the Hospitallers to return the castle to the Templars, and for the Templars to return it to de Marqab after a month had passed. Such conflicts between the Hospitallers and the Templars were not uncommon, but they did not always involve castles and armed brethren.

Another dispute took place at Acre in 1235, where the Templars and Hospitallers both operated a mill on the River Belus. The Hospitallers' mill was upstream from the one operated by the Temple and whenever the Templars would back the water up to power their mill, it would flood the Hospitallers' fields. This caused the Hospitallers to hold back the flow of water altogether, which left little more than a trickle downstream making the Templars' mill useless. The dispute went on for some time, ending up in the papal court, after which Pope Gregory IX ordered Guerin de Montacute, the Grand Master of the Hospitallers, and Armand de Périgord, the Grand Master of the Templars, to reach an agreement.

Gregory's criticism of the Hospitallers and Templars was not confined to disputes between the two Orders. In 1236, he threatened the Military Orders with excommunication to prevent them from co-operating with the Muslim Assassins sect against Bohemond V of Antioch. The source of the complaint was Bohemond himself, who wrote to the Pope complaining that the Grand Master of the Hospitallers was in an alliance with the enemy.

Pope Gregory instructed the local ecclesiastics to order the Hospitallers to stop any connections with the Assassins, and for good measure he sent a similar letter regarding alleged connections between the assassins to the Templars. Although the Templars are often accused of acting in their own best financial interests, the censure of the Pope in 1236 shows clearly that the Hospitallers could be every bit as swayed by money as the Templars, who also received an annual tribute from the Assassins. He would also send other letters critical of the two Orders and their mission. In 1238, he wrote to Armand de Périgord criticising him and his Templars for failing to protect pilgrims travelling from the Holy Sepulchre back to Jaffa. Jerusalem had been opened to Christians once again because of the truce the Holy Roman Emperor Frederick II had negotiated at the end of the Sixth Crusade, a campaign the two Orders had been reluctant to join. In the same month that Gregory chastised the Templars for failing in their original mission, he wrote to Bertrand de Comps, the new Grand Master of the Hospitallers, accusing the Order of things that would not be heard again until the Templars were arrested in France in 1307. In short, they had disregarded their three monastic vows of chastity, poverty and obedience: the first by allowing prostitutes into their houses; the second by holding personal property, changing the wills of the dead for their own profit, and spending money that was intended for the sick and poor; the third by admitting thieves, murderers and heretics into their Order.

Ultimately, nothing would come of the papal letters. Although the Orders were subservient to the Pope and his church, the reality was that both the Hospitallers and Templars were wealthy and powerful. However, while they could escape the wrath of papal power with apologetic wording, they were often unable to escape military power, particularly when it overwhelmed their own.

The Khwarezmian Tartars were driven south by the Mongols and became allies of the Sultan of Egypt. In 1244, they captured Jerusalem.
Jupiter Images

In 1244, the Christians suffered their greatest defeat since Hattin, in a battle during which the Military Orders were particularly devastated. In August of that year the Holy Sepulchre was again cut off to Christians when the Khwarezmian Tartars, allies of the sultan of Egypt who had moved south to escape the Mongols two decades earlier, captured Jerusalem – it would be the last time Christians would have control of the Holy City until 1917. Two months later the Hospitallers formed part of a Christian army composed of the Templars, the Knights of St Lazarus, the Teutonic Knights and the Kingdom of Jerusalem, who joined forces with Muslim allies from Homs, Outrejordain and Damascus, to take on the Egyptian–Khwarezmian alliance. The Christians fielded an army of about 11,000 men, roughly equally split between infantry and cavalry.

Guillaume de Chateauneuf, who had become Master of the Hospitallers two years previously, brought 351 men, and the Templars' Grand Master Armand de Périgord brought 347 of his troops. The sultan of Egypt had sent roughly an equal number of men, made up of Mamluk and Bedouin cavalry.

The two armies met at La Forbie, northeast of Gaza, on 17 October and after some back and forth skirmishes, the Christian army left a well-defended position to attack the Egyptians and soon found themselves surrounded by their enemies and their Khwarezmian allies. In the end the Christians lost roughly half of their soldiers and would never again field as large an army in the east. The Military Orders suffered heavy casualties. Although the Knights of St Lazarus fielded a small number of combatants, none lived to fight again, and the Teutonic Knights lost all but three of their men. The Templars lost 314 men, including the Grand Master. The Hospitallers lost all but twenty-seven of their men, and although Grand Master de Chateauneuf survived, he did so as a prisoner bound for Egypt. He would spend the next six years of his life in prison, during which time Jean de Ronay, the Grand Prior of Jerusalem, would fill the role in all but title.

In the disastrous Battle of La Forbie, the Hospitallers were defeated by an army that included a young Mamluk emir named Baibars. Within a decade of the Battle of Al Mansurah in 1250, (another Christian defeat in which the Hospitallers took heavy casualties) Baibars had secured, by conquest, the position of sultan of the Mamluk Empire. In 1263, when Hugues de Revel was Master of the Order, the sultan agreed to a truce with the Christians on the condition that a number of Muslims held in captivity be released; however, the Hospitallers and Templars, who were using the prisoners as skilled craftsmen, refused to release them. This brought the negotiations to an abrupt close and the sultan marched into Christian territory where he sacked Nazareth, destroyed the Church of the Virgin and launched an attack on Acre. Although Baibars managed to sack the suburbs, he never actually laid siege to the city itself. However, three decades later the Mamluks would succeed in taking the city from the Christians forever.

CHAPTER 5

Prisoners of Overwhelming Sorrow

The final two decades of Christian presence in the Holy Land were particularly costly for the Military Orders in terms of fortifications. In 1271, Baibars took Montfort Castle from the Teutonic Knights, Safita from the Templars, and most devastating for the Hospitallers, the formerly impenetrable Krak des Chevaliers, which was under-garrisoned at the time of Baibars' attack in April. The loss of so great a fortress drove the Hospitallers towards the Mediterranean, back to Acre and to their basalt castle of Marqab, which was now their largest. Even this fell in 1285 when Baibars' successor, Qalāwūn, captured it after a month-long siege, an attack that was launched while he was operating under a peace treaty with the Christians. The Hospitallers were permitted to leave with their possessions and retreat to Tripoli.

In January of 1289, a Mamluk informant working for the Templars named Badr al-Din approached their Grand Master William de Beaujeu with the news that Qalāwūn was preparing to attack Tripoli. De Beaujeu wasted no time and immediately informed the city of the dangers that awaited them; however, instead of receiving the news with appreciation and making the necessary preparations, de Beaujeu's warning was disregarded. The city fell to the Mamluks three months later on 26 April, but where the sultan had allowed the Hospitallers to leave their castle at Marqab, he put the residents of Tripoli to the sword.

Pathways through Krak des Chevaliers were designed in a zigzag pattern, creating a maze-like passage that would slow potential invaders to a near crawl. Openings were built into the design high above the pathway, allowing defenders to attack invaders with arrows, rocks or hot oil.
Bigstock/Steve Estvanik

The Mamluks had succeeded in pushing the Christians to the water's edge. All that remained was to besiege the port city of Acre, capture it, and the Christians who were lucky enough to survive the carnage would retreat to their homelands.

Two years after the fall of Tripoli, Qalāwūn's son Al-Ashraf Khalīl attacked Acre. He arrived at Acre on 5 April 1291 and began his siege of the city the following morning. For the first week the battle consisted largely of skirmishes outside the city walls; however, by 11 April, the massive Muslim mangonels, which had taken two days to build, began their assault on

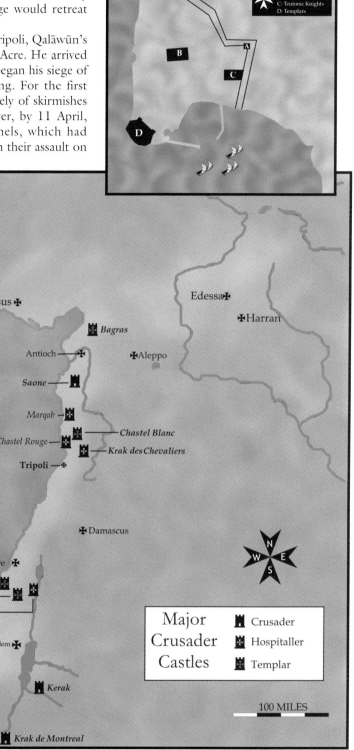

Acre 1291

A: Accursed Tower
B: Hospitallers
C: Teutonic Knights
D: Templars

✠Konya

Tarsus ✠

Edessa✠

✠Harran

✠ Bagras

Antioch — ✠

✠Aleppo

Saone

Famagusta —
Kolossi —

Marqab

Chastel Blanc

Chastel Rouge

Krak des Chevaliers

Tripoli — ✠

✠Damascus

Acre ✠

Castle Pilgrim —
Castle of La Feve —
Belvoir —

Jerusalem ✠

Kerak

Major
Crusader
Castles

Crusader

Hospitaller

Templar

100 MILES

FATIMID
CALIPHATE
OF CAIRO

Krak de Montreal

the city walls. One of these had been brought from the Hospitallers' former castle of Krak des Chevaliers. Because Acre was a coastal city, the Christians had the advantage of receiving assistance by sea and to this end, a number of ships, one of which was armed with a mangonel, began an assault on the Mamluk forces. As their own weapons were concentrating on the city's walls, they were unable to use them to assault the ships, but a violent storm soon had the ships rocking to the point that the mangonel was destroyed.

On the night of 15-16 April, de Beaujeu and his Templars joined Othon de Grandson and the knights of the minor Military Orders of St Thomas and St Lazarus in a sortie from the Gate of St Lazarus against a Muslim army from Hama. The intention had been to set fire to one of the massive siege engines; however, the incendiary fell short of its mark and lay burning on the ground. In the process many were either killed or captured. Three days later, a second sortie was launched from the Gate of St Anthony under the lead of Jean de Villiers and his Hospitallers who were backed by a few Templars. This sortie also failed because the Muslims, having gained advance warning of the attack, lit torches so that the Hospitallers may as well have been fighting in daylight. This brought the sorties to an end due to the number of lives already lost.

In total the Christian forces at Acre amounted to about 800 knights and 14,000 foot soldiers between the Orders and the secular population. This was added to two weeks later when King Henry II of Cyprus arrived on 4 May with a fleet of 40 ships containing another 100 knights and an

The Hospitaller Marshal Matthew de Clermont is shown defending the walls of Acre in this nineteenth century oil painting by Dominique Louis Papety depicting the fall of the city in 1291.

additional 2,000 foot soldiers. The arrival of fresh troops restored the faith of the besieged.

Despite bringing military reinforcements, the Cypriot king felt the best solution to the problem was a diplomatic one. To this end a ceasefire was called and two knights, William de Villiers and William de Cafron (a Templar) were sent to propose a truce with the sultan. When the diplomats arrived at the sultan's tent the first words out of his mouth were to ask if the knights had brought him the keys to the city. Khalil went on to tell them that it was the city and not the citizens he was interested in and that if the city would surrender, the citizens would be spared. No sooner had he spoken than a crusader mangonel from inside the city flung a rock near to the tent. Khalil was outraged and threatened to kill the knights, but was stopped by one of his men. De Cafron and de Villiers returned to the city and Khalil returned to his siege. Soon after, 3,000 of Acre's nobility fled the city to take refuge on Cyprus.

Over the next few weeks the sultan's miners continued to work on the city's towers and walls, and by mid-May, the Hospitallers, Templars and other defenders were preparing to defend the city from inside its inner walls. Mining operations had proven effective and parts of the King's Tower, the Tower of St Nicholas and the Gate of St Anthony, where the Hospitallers had launched their failed attack a month earlier, were crumbling. On 16 May, the Hospitallers returned to the gate along with the Templars and together they succeeded in repelling an attack, but the assault may have been little more than a diversion. Regardless of the sincerity of the assault, within hours the Accursed Tower in the city's northeast corner would be the key defensive position. Two days later the battle would be brought to the streets of Acre through a breach in the tower, which was then being defended by the Hospitallers, Templars and Henry's troops from Acre and Cyprus. Despite their efforts, the tower soon fell to the Mamluks, who pressed their way into Acre on the morning of 18 May.

The counterattack fell to the Military Orders led by the Hospitallers' Marshal Matthew de Clermont, Grand Master Jean de Villiers and the Templar's Master William de Beaujeu.

The citadel at Acre was built by the Ottomans over the original Hospitaller fortress. Much of the original fortress has been restored below ground.
Bigstock/L David

Both the Marshal and the Grand Master hollered out to those who were in retreat, urging them back to battle for Christ's sake, but few answered the call. In the fighting that followed de Villiers took a spear to the shoulder, an injury that nearly cost him his life; however, his fate was better than that of his Templar counterpart, William de Beaujeu. According to the account of the anonymous Templar of Tyre, de Beaujeu was fighting without a shield, and as he raised his arm he was struck by a javelin, which lodged itself a hand's width under his exposed armpit. The Templar Grand Master, now mortally wounded, was carried by his bodyguards and led throughout the city by de Clermont seeking refuge, ultimately arriving at the Templar castle on the peninsula. De Beaujeu's bodyguards did not wish to take their dying Grand Master through the gate for fear of opening it to a Mamluk attack, so they took him through a courtyard where the Order piled their horse manure. It was here that the Hospitallers' Marshal remained, holding the Templar Grand Master until the latter died amid the dirt and excrement that surrounded them, a fitting visual epitaph to the two Orders' history in the Holy Land.

Returning to the fight, de Clermont lost his own life the same day while defending a part of the Genoese quarter with a small number of his knights. It was a somewhat fitting if not ironic place to die. Thirty-five years earlier the Hospitallers had sided with the Genoese in their conflicts with the Venetians, the latter of whom were supported by the Templars. The conflict had arisen over land owned by the monastery of St Sabas, but claimed by both the Venetians and Genoese. The conflicts which lasted more than a decade had damaged or destroyed some of Acre's fortifications, and ultimately, although indirectly, aided in diminishing the port city's ability to withstand a prolonged attack. But the conflicts between the Genoese and Venetian merchants were at an end and many of their number had already left for the island of Cyprus as the attempts to hold Acre grew more futile with each passing moment.

Those who remained in the city received no greater mercy from the Muslims than the Muslims had received 192 years earlier when the crusaders stormed Jerusalem at the end of the First Crusade. Those who managed to escape the slaughter gathered at the headquarters of the three Military Orders, although most had gathered at the Templars' headquarters where the era of the Crusader States would come to a close.

On 20 May, the Hospitallers and Teutonic Knights, besieged in their headquarters and realising the futility of defending the city any further, surrendered their fortified towers and departed Acre forever. Soon after, a Mamluk negotiator was sent to the Templars' fortress to ensure that they followed suit. The Templars accepted the terms and let the Mamluks into the compound; however, once they entered, the Muslims began to abuse the inhabitants, an event echoed by both the Christian and Arab sources. The Mamluk chronicler Abu al-Mahasin, who wrote one of the most detailed and interesting of the Muslim accounts of the siege of Acre, provides the details of what happened after the Templars surrendered their fortress:

'[The sultan] sent them a standard, which they accepted and raised over the tower. The door was opened and a horde of regulars and others swarmed in. When they came face to face with the defenders some of the soldiers began to pillage and to lay hands on the women and children who were with them, whereupon the Franks shut the door and attacked them, killing a number of Muslims. They hauled down the standard and stiffened their resistance. The siege continued'.

During the next week, as the Templars continued to defend their compound, the Order's Marshal Peter de Sevrey sent some civilians and the Templars' treasury to Cyprus, where a large number of refugees had already gathered. On 28 May, the sultan once again offered terms of surrender, but when the Marshal and some of his brethren emerged to discuss the matter, they were executed for having killed the Muslim prisoners the previous week. No sooner had the Marshal's body hit the ground, than it was followed by those of five Muslim prisoners thrown from the Templars' tower in retaliation for their leader's execution. It was not long after that the sultan's miners succeeded in bringing the fortress's walls crashing to the ground, and with them the Christians' hold on the city.

Much of what remains of the Templars' headquarters at Acre today has been flooded by a rise in sea level, but in the days that followed its capture in 1291, it was Mamluks and not water that flooded the streets, the end result of the rising tide of Islam that the crusaders had come eastward two centuries earlier to fight. Unlike the men who had swarmed the Mediterranean coast in 1099, many who had fled Acre in 1291 were not invaders, but rather people who had been born in the very city they were now forced to leave. To them, the loss of Acre was not so much a political or religious defeat as it was a personal one: they had lost their homes, their possessions, and most tragic of all, their loved ones. The Templars had also experienced great loss at Acre, for not only had they lost their Master and many of their companions, they had lost their headquarters, which they had occupied for the last century.

However, while the Templars would soon be removed from the ongoing war with Islam, the Hospitallers would take on a new role in that fight. Although the next two and a half centuries would see the Hospitallers pushed closer and closer to the European continent, they would never cease in their attempts to shield to the west from the spread of Islam. As he recovered from the spear wound to his shoulder, Jean de Villiers wrote a letter to Guillaume de Villaret, who was then Prior of St Gilles, telling him of the great battle the brotherhood had just passed through and the tragic fall of Acre. He ended his letter with his feelings on that loss and his new place of refuge:

'And thus I and some of our brothers escaped, as it pleased God, most of whom were wounded and battered without hope of cure, and we were taken to the island of Cyprus. On the day that this letter was written we were still there, in great sadness of heart, prisoners of overwhelming sorrow.'

PART 2: KNIGHTS OF RHODES

CHAPTER 6
From Acre to Rhodes

The two decades that followed the Christian exile from Acre were decidedly different for the Hospitallers and Templars. While the former, adapting to their present situation, rose in prominence and success, the latter, less able or willing to adapt to new challenges, easily fell prey to their enemies on both sides of the religious divide. For the Hospitallers, the exile to Cyprus marked the launching point for their long-term survival; for the Templars, the debarkation on Cypriot shores marked the beginning of a period that would see their once burning flame extinguished, not by the swift cuts of the sword of Islam, but by the gentle movements of a pontiff's quill.

Although it is commonly thought that the loss of Acre in 1291 marked the end of the crusading era, the notion is a false one. While it is certainly true that the Military Orders were seen as the natural scapegoats for the loss of Christendom's (by then) tenuous grip on the Holy Land, there was still a desire on the part of Rome to recapture that which was lost. Although he had shown little interest in the port city when it was under Christian occupation, other than threatening to excommunicate anyone who traded with the Mamluk sultan, the sudden loss of Acre ignited a crusader's zeal in Pope Nicholas IV, so much so that he did everything he could to arouse the same feelings among those who might answer the call of his crusading

sermons, but his call went largely unanswered. The long, drawn-out and mostly fruitless wars with the Muslims had dulled western enthusiasm for yet another campaign on eastern shores. Likewise, the Pope's attempts to gain support in the east among the Greeks and Armenians proved futile, as did his sending twenty galleys to attempt to gain ground along the Armenian coast.

Nicholas called for a number of councils to be held in February of 1292, when the clergy would discuss the challenges of undertaking a new crusade, including the possibility of uniting the Military Orders, a notion that had been tossed around at the Council of Lyons in 1274, but was rejected, largely because the Spanish kings were concerned that a united Military Order would be too powerful. Although the councils convened on schedule, Nicholas died in April before ever hearing their reports.

Outside the Military Orders, whose entire *raison d'être* had been fighting for Christ and occupying the lands he once travelled, there were few willing to aid them in their cause. This was largely due to the fact that Christendom shared the same problems of disunity that Islam was going through in 1099; a lack of religious cohesion that allowed an unorganised and uncooperative band of crusader armies to capture Jerusalem and hold it for nearly a century. Civil disputes in Armenia, naval battles between the Venetians

A Hospitaller knight circa 1350-1400 is shown in this original image by David Naughton Shires after a depiction of knights of the era found in the Grand Master's Palace at Rhodes. The Hospitallers conquered Rhodes in 1309 and would call the island home until 1522 when they were evicted by Suleiman the Great. Plate armour would evolve considerably during this time.
David Naughton Shires

Right: The priory of St John of Jerusalem at Clerkenwell in London is shown in this mid-seventeenth century etching by Wenceslaus Hollar. St John's Gate was constructed in 1504 by Prior Thomas Docwra. Although much larger in scope than the Hospitallers' English holdings at the time of the loss of Acre, they and other Langues were fearful of losing their properties to monarchs who felt they had been given to the Order to support their war against the Muslims and not for their present idle conditions.

and Genoese over trade and further strife between the Genoese and the Ibelin family on Cyprus all reduced the probability and possibility for creating a united front against the Muslims. If help was to come from the west, it would have to be from the Orders' own reserves or from what they could secure on their names and reputations.

Support for the Templars' cause seems to have been minimal, and their Grand Master Jacques de Molay spent the three years following his election in 1293 travelling England, France, Aragon and Italy in search of arms, horses and other supplies to replace those lost in recent years. Such was not the case for the Hospitallers, who saw an influx of members from the west coming to Limassol in response to Grand Master Jean de Villiers' request for reinforcements. In concert with the arrival of fresh members of the Order to Cyprus, the coffers of every western priory were emptied and sent to support the Order, as they often had been when the eastern brethren were based on the mainland. A large part of the difference in support may have been due to the disparity in the two Orders' western holdings. Writing in 1250, Matthew de Paris suggested that the Hospitallers were then in possession of 19,000 manors, while the Templars possessed 9,000.

Support and wealth were not the only differences between the two Orders during the closing years of the thirteenth century. Both had been put to sea and, although both would use the sea in their plans, the Templars focused their maritime interests on the island of Arwad (Ruad) with the idea of retaking the mainland for Christendom, while the Hospitallers turned their attentions to protecting pilgrims travelling by sea. As many of those ships were also carrying merchandise to and from Europe, the Hospitallers' efforts in protecting European ships from Muslim attacks were seen, not so much a crusading effort, as an effort to provide an armed guard for European commerce. Throughout two centuries in the Levant, the Hospitallers' and Templars' efforts on behalf of Christendom had been of little real value to the majority of Europeans. But now, when all they had fought for had been lost and there was little hope of taking it back, the by-product of the Hospitallers' newfound maritime zeal created a sense of gratitude

among a greater number of westerners, particularly those who benefited directly or indirectly from commerce in the east. In this sense, the Hospitallers' ability to adapt saved the Order from the fate that would ultimately befall the Templars. It is interesting that an Order started by Italian merchants, would, two centuries later, again come under the figurative protection of merchants, while literally protecting the same.

But where the Templars would feel the heat of a monarch's torch some years later, both Military Orders were feeling pressures from monarchs in both the east and the west, pressures that were abated only after the election of Pope Boniface VIII in 1294. Prior to this time, there was a desire on the part of the kings of England and Portugal to take back the properties of the Military Orders on their lands on the grounds that they were never intended to support them in idleness. On his election as Pope, Boniface interceded and put pressure of his own on the kings, causing them to back off. Similarly, he intervened in a situation brewing on Cyprus where Henry II, who had accepted the crusaders as his guests, was rapidly becoming uncomfortable with their presence. Henry, fearing that the Hospitallers and Templars would soon be as powerful on his island as they had been in Palestine, refused to allow them to purchase any new lands and levied the same poll tax on both Orders that he required his own subjects to pay. Despite Pope Boniface's demands to abolish the 'horrible and detestable' tax, Henry ignored his edict, persisted in his taxation demands and ramped up his means to annoy the Orders as much as he could, purely out of spite for the Pope meddling in Cypriot matters.

Those matters came to a head in 1306 when the Templars assisted Henry's brother Amaury and a number of the Cypriot nobility in

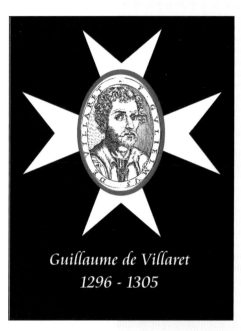

Below: Guillaume de Villaret was the Order's twenty-fourth Grand Master and was the Prior of St Gilles at the time of the fall of Acre. It was to Guillaume that Grand Master Jean de Villiers wrote from Cyprus telling him that the Hospitallers and exiled Christians were prisoners of overwhelming.

Guillaume de Villaret
1296 - 1305

Far left: Kolossi Castle, located outside Limassol, Cyprus, was built in 1210 by the crusaders and given to the Hospitallers by King Hugh III. One of the purposes of the castle was to protect a sugar production facility that adjoined the castle. The present castle was built in 1454. Bigstock/Vlasis Vlasidis

The temple of Virgin Mary in the hill of Filerimos was built in the fourteenth century by the Hospitallers. This location was one of the first areas captured by de Villaret and his men in the autumn of 1306.
Bigstock/Panagiotis Karapanagiotis

ridding the island of its king. There are several claims as to the Templars' level of involvement: in one account, the Templars' Grand Master Jacques de Molay and the Bishop of Limassol drew up the papers to depose Henry and install Amaury in his stead, while another indicates that the Templars lent the usurper 50,000 bezants, suggesting that the Templars financed the coup. Although de Molay did not personally orchestrate the move against King Henry, he and the Templars were nonetheless involved, and their involvement would have consequences in the years to follow, when Amaury was murdered and Henry reinstalled on the throne. By contrast, the Hospitallers had, despite more than a decade of receiving no special favours from the king, supported Henry in the dispute.

Although the Orders had been rivals for more than two centuries, the new Pope, Clement V, wished this disagreement to be their last, and was intent on joining them under one banner. On 6 June, the Pope sent a letter to Cyprus summoning to France both Jacques de Molay and the Hospitallers' new Grand Master, Foulques de Villaret, who had succeeded his uncle Guillaume in 1305, to discuss the prospect of uniting the Military Orders. The concept of a united Order was doomed from the start. The Franco-Mongol alliance which had proven successful for the Military Orders in helping Mahmud Ghazan capture land in Syria at the turn of the century had failed to maintain or gain new ground in the following years, and by 1302, the Mamluks had driven the Templars from the island of Arwad back to the security of Cyprus, taking those Templars captured in the conflict to Cairo where they were killed. With Ghazan dead and lacking a similar strong ally in the east to support a combined Order, there was little point in discussing a concept that neither the Hospitallers nor Templars were enthusiastic about. Although de Molay heeded the Pope's summons and departed for France in the autumn of 1306, de Villaret did not answer the Pope's call until August of the following year, having been engaged elsewhere, namely in his quest to capture the island of Rhodes as a home base for the Hospitallers, from which they could more effectively do battle with the pirates disrupting Christian trade and commerce in the Aegean.

Rhodes had originally been a dependency of Constantinople; however, the crusader occupation of the capital city during the Fourth Crusade in 1204 had left the little island of Rhodes vulnerable to attack, something the Genoese succeeded in doing in 1249 with the assistance of Guillaume de Villehardouin, prince of Achaea. The Genoese held the island until it was captured a short time later by the Nicaean Emperor John II, thus bringing it back into the Byzantine fold. However, over the years, the further weakening of the Byzantine Empire led to Rhodes opening its ports to merchants and Mediterranean pirates of all faiths, who were given a free rein and shelter within Rhodian harbours, and made the island their home.

Our Lady of Philerimos is a Byzantine icon owned by the Hospitallers and believed to have been been found after the capture of the hill of Filerimos in 1306. The tempera painting on wood, shown here in a mid-nineteenth century Russian copy, was encased in a jewelled frame. The icon was among the Hospitallers' most revered items and would follow them from Rhodes to Malta in 1530 and from Malta to Europe in 1798.

Unlike the subsequent sieges of Rhodes in 1480 and 1522, the Hospitaller conquest of the island in the years between 1306 and 1310 is a confusing matter to digest because there are no primary sources to draw from, and even the most respected of medieval scholars tend to gloss over this pivotal point in Hospitaller history, offering few details as to exactly how they captured the island. Other historians, particularly those writing up to the nineteenth century, tend to romanticise the chain of events, as was the common practice at that time. Even where historians are in harmony with respect to that chain of events, they are at odds as to when events took place. For example, Vertot, writing in the eighteenth century, tells us that the Hospitallers 'planted the grand master's standard on the top of the breach, August 15, 1310, and carried the place'. Writing in the nineteenth century, Porter tells us that Foulques de Villaret 'determined again to deliver an assault. This he did on the 5th day of August, 1310, and with complete success. Before nightfall on that day the white cross banner of the Hospital was waving over the ramparts of Rhodes'. However, modern historians, including David Nicolle and Christopher Tyerman, suggest that the Hospitallers moved their headquarters to Rhodes in 1309, which would indicate an earlier conquest than the date of 1310 offered by some historians, but apart from agreeing that the Order began its conquest of the island in 1306, they offer little in the way of specifics as to how the victory was obtained – a necessary caution when no primary sources are to be found.

Without primary sources, sifting through the various accounts of the siege can be problematic in determining precisely when and how the Hospitallers came to conquer Rhodes. Also problematic is the question surrounding their real motivation. This is particularly so when dealing with those accounts that attempt to analyse the Hospitallers' decision to move to Rhodes in light of the Templars' fate in 1307. It has been posited that the Hospitallers sought out Rhodes as a home base to escape a similar fate to that awaiting the Templars in France, but this is an untenable argument. De Villaret declined the Pope's request to travel to Rome because he was already involved with his plans

for Rhodes. It is highly unlikely that he could have known what would happen to the Templars in 1306, given that the Pope, despite suggestions by later writers to the contrary, did not know what the King of France had in store for the doomed Order at that time. Even if rumours of criticism had arrived on Cypriot shores prior to Jacques de Molay's departure, it is unlikely that de Villaret would have given them any greater weight than the criticisms that had been levelled against the Orders following the fall of Acre, nearly a decade earlier, or that had been levelled against his predecessors in the mid-thirteenth century. It seems most likely that the Hospitallers' wish to secure Rhodes as a base was a combination of their desire to get away from the pressures of Cyprus and their desire to increase their naval operations, something Nicholas IV had ordered them to do following the loss of Acre in 1291. If there was a decision on the part of de Villaret to isolate the Order from a papal or monarchical attack, it was done after the Templars' fate had been sealed, rather than before. Quite simply, Rhodes would serve the Order well. No longer would they be taxed or limited in their dispositions, the island was close enough to the Syrian coast to enable them to be effective when need be and it was closer to the Aegean to better enable them to thwart or engage in piracy as the situation required.

Regardless of their motivations in capturing Rhodes, the Order still needed to actually do so before they could enjoy the fruits of their labours. Rhodes was nominally under the control of the Byzantine Empire, which had recaptured the island during the First Crusade. However, in the ensuing years it had opened its ports to Muslim pirates who had taken up residency along with the Rhodian natives. De Villaret's early surveillance of the island, probably in the spring of 1306 as is commonly agreed, showed him that Rhodes would not be an easy or quick conquest. Having assessed the island's most vulnerable points of defence, the location and size of its towns, and the overall scope of the undertaking, de Villaret had the necessary information to make an assault on the island, but not without help.

On 27 May, the Hospitallers signed an alliance with a Genoese freebooter named Vignole de Vignoli to combine their naval and land forces to capture the island. In June, de Villaret set sail with his fleet of two galleys and two other boats, carrying five hundred infantry, six turcopoliers and thirty-five knights. The Hospitaller ships met up with de Vignoli's own pair of galleys and the six vessels set sail towards Kastelorizo, a small island on the coast of Asia Minor, 110 kilometres from Rhodes. In several accounts of the story, we are told that de Villaret kept the mission secret from his infantry of mercenaries, telling those outside his Order and his Genoese supporters that they were going on crusade. However, as the story goes, de Villaret's reason for putting into port had nothing to do with his alleged crusade: the stoppage was to send a group of spies to Rhodes, while an embassy travelled north to Constantinople to meet with Andronicus II (Andronicus Paleologus) to ensure that the Order would be given sovereignty over the island once it had been captured. In exchange for the emperor's agreement, de Villaret would supply an annual allowance of men and money to the empire. Although Andronicus had the most tenuous grasp on the island, he declined de Villaret's request, perhaps thinking it would be easier one day to take the port city from the Muslims and pirates than from the Hospitallers. The Grand Master's spies, however, returned from Rhodes with better news: the island was a diamond in the Aegean and well worthy of being captured for the Hospitallers' new home.

Whether an embassy was dispatched to Constantinople or not, it is probable that Vignoli's men were the spies sent ahead to the island. Despite their growing successes as seamen, the Hospitallers were far less experienced than the Genoese. Regardless of the path to Rhodes, the initial assault in June of 1306 against the main port proved unsuccessful, but by autumn the Fortress of Faraklos on the island's eastern coast had fallen to the alliance. By November, the hill of Filerimos at Trianda on the western coast, eight kilometres southwest of Rhodes, had also fallen to the Order and their Genoese supporters, a point of debarkation that the Turks would use 174 years later in their attempt to wrest the island from the Hospitallers. Just how the Hospitallers captured Filerimos, which would become

home to one of the Order's most sacred relics, is one area of the Rhodes conquest story that was certainly embellished by the early historians. According to traditional accounts, it was not through martial prowess that the fortress was captured, but through cunning and the assistance of a resident Greek. Taking a cue from Ulysses' deception of Polyphemus in Homer's *Odyssey*, the Hospitallers were said to have sneaked into the fortress under sheep skins along with the returning flock. What is more likely to have happened is that the Hospitallers gained access to the fortress, either with the assistance of a traitor or through their own cunning, when postern gates were opened to allow the grazing sheep to return to the fortress for the night.

Accounts of the capture of the city vary greatly. The story as told by Porter is that, after the spies and embassy sent to Constantinople returned to the port, the fleet weighed anchor and set off westward towards their island prize, at which time the infantry, consisting of recruits de Villaret had procured from Europe, possibly when he went to visit the Pope in 1307, were finally apprised of their real mission. Arriving at Rhodes, the sudden debarkation of troops onto the shoreline caught the locals by surprise, and, having no time to prepare, they put up little resistance. Although de Villaret and his men succeeded in making small work of gaining control of the open country, the fortified city over which the standard of the Muslim crescent flew would be another matter altogether. Not only did the Hospitallers have to contend with the Saracens themselves, but Emperor Andronicus, on hearing that the Hospitallers had landed at Rhodes, sent his own auxiliary force to help expel the Christian invaders.

However, de Vallaret's deception had begun to demoralise and diminish the men long before Andronicus would attempt to do so with the sword. The European recruits, who were enthusiastic when they believed the mission had been a crusade against the Muslims to take back Palestine for Christendom, were far less enthused about capturing a little island purely for the personal gain of the Hospitallers, an Order which, despite its popularity among the merchant class, was viewed with suspicion and envy by many. Within short order, the only men de

St Ubaldesca shown in this Italian painting was born near Pisa in 1136 and joined the Hospitaller sisters at the age of fifteen. From that time until her death at the age of 70, Ubaldesca worked in the infirmary at the Pisan monastery. She died on 28 May 1206 and her body was enshrined at Calcinaia, the place of her birth.

Saracens and orthodox Christians were not the only ones put out to sea by the battle: numerous Hospitallers had fallen victim to the Saracens' swords, others to those of their eastern co-religionists. De Villaret simply had too few men left after repelling the ground forces to press on with an assault on the city. Putting out to sea with his fleet, he determined to starve the city by blockade while he waited for fresh recruits to arrive from Europe. Manpower was not the only support the Grand Master sought from Europe. Offering the future revenues of the Hospitaller Order as security, he obtained a substantial loan from Florentine bankers, funds he used to hire additional mercenary forces who had no problem fighting on de Villaret's behalf, regardless of whether his crusade was religious or personal. The assault was renewed on 5 August 1310 and succeeded where previous attempts had failed; the banner of the Hospitaller Order now waved proudly over the ramparts from which the Muslims and their standard had been torn. Other accounts of the siege, while agreeing that Emperor Andronicus had in fact sent reinforcements to combat the Hospitallers, assign them an entirely different role in the series of events that led to the downfall of the city. Rather than disembarking at Rhodes to draw their swords on the Latin Christian aggressors, the troops first dropped anchor at Cyprus, after being carried off course in bad weather. The ship was seized by a Cypriot knight, who convinced the captain, a Rhodian sailor, into changing his mission from warrior to negotiator, with the plan of talking his fellow islanders into surrendering to the Hospitallers.

Villaret was left with were those who wore the habit of the Hospitaller Order. One by one, the European recruits lost all desire to fight an unrighteous battle and abandoned the Grand Master and his personal crusade.

With only his own men to continue the assault on the city, de Villaret found his troops outnumbered and the besiegers quickly became the besieged, as the Hospitaller camp was encircled by a combination of Saracens and Byzantine Greeks. Despite the odds, the Hospitallers pressed on with the same militant zeal that had served them well for two centuries. In the end, a small and tired band of soldiers succeeded in driving the battalions to their galleys, and then out to sea. However, the

Whether the city gates were opened voluntarily or by force, it is generally agreed that Foulques de Villaret and his Hospitallers walked through the city gates at some point in 1309, marking the beginning of the Order's 213-year reign on the island. Although it would take more than two centuries for the Hospitallers to be expelled from Rhodes, it would only take a decade for the Grand Master, who had secured their new home, to be expelled from the Order. During that time, de Villaret would witness how the Templars' losses were to become the Hospitallers' gains.

CHAPTER 7
A Templar Interlude

The story of the Templars' meteoric rise to wealth and power and their subsequent legendary fall from grace into Christian oblivion has been told many times over the past seven centuries. Yet with each retelling the story has been slowly twisted and moulded to fit the personal agendas of the storytellers, leaving a legacy for the Templars that either paints the Order as innocent martyrs ensnared by a greedy king and a corrupt pope, or as the dregs of Christendom well worthy of far harsher penalties even than they received. Somewhere down the middle road lies the truth, and before examining the Hospitallers' role in picking up the pieces after the Templars' dissolution, it is important to understand the Templars' demise, devoid of the mythical and apocryphal embellishments.

Although the fingers of condemnation for the loss of the Holy Land had been pointed at the Holy See, the European monarchs and even the citizens of Acre itself, the natural scapegoats for the debacle were the Hospitallers and the Templars, as well as the minor Military Orders. Criticism of the Orders was certainly nothing new and can be traced back to the twelfth century and the founding of the Templars under Hugues de Payens when morale among the Order was low due to complaints over the very concept of the warrior monks. By the mid-thirteenth century we find Matthew de Paris writing critically of both the Templars and Hospitallers in his account of events preceding the battle of Al Mansurah in 1250:

'When the count of Artois [Robert I] heard this he was highly indignant and, excited and flushed with anger and pride, replied, "See the time-honoured treachery of the Temple!

Jacques de Molay, the last Master of the Knights Templar, is shown in this popular nineteenth-century interpretation. He was born in 1244 and joined the Order in France in 1265. De Molay was elected Grand Master in 1293, the same year Hospitaller Grand Master Jean de Villiers, who fought at Acre, died.

The ancient sedition of the Hospitallers! What deceit hidden for a long time, now appears openly in our midst! This is what we predicted long ago in a prophecy which has now come true. The whole country of the East would have been conquered long ago had it not been for the Templars and Hospitallers and others who call themselves religious, who have hindered us, the laymen, with their deceit. Look how the capture of the sultan and the complete confusion of paganism lies open to us, as well as the permanent exaltation of the law of our Christians, all of which this Templar here is doing his best to prevent with his fictitious and fallacious arguments. For the Templars and Hospitallers and their associates, who are fattened by ample revenues, are afraid that, if the country is subjected to Christian laws, their supremacy will come to an end.'"

The count's accusations, although clearly issued out of anger, must have reflected to some degree his true feelings. He was certainly not alone in them, and similar accusations continued to be levelled at both orders, as well as the Teutonic Knights, throughout Christendom's remaining years in the east. Although the accusations, criticism and condemnations had no real effect on the Orders, the fall of Acre changed the playing field. One of the reasons for the desire to unite the Military Orders was that Pope Nicholas IV had suggested that the rivalry and quarrels between the Hospitallers and Templars over commercial interests had played a substantial role in the disaster. However, the Pope's public criticism of the Orders' avarice seems to have had little effect on either group in the years that followed, least of all the Templars. A well-known example of their greed occurred at Balantrodoch under Preceptor Brian de Jay in the late thirteenth century and is known as the 'Eperstone affair'. Eperstone farm, located near Balantrodoch, was owned by Christiane of Eperstone, who had received it from her father. Christiane married an idle man named William of Haukeston who, upon marriage, became legally entitled to do with his wife's property as he wished and decided to grant it to the Templars in exchange for a corrody. The corrody was common in the Middle Ages and was usually offered by an abbey, monastery or other religious houses such as those operated by the Military Orders, who provided the corrodian with accommodation within the area operated by the house, food and drink, heat and light, and in some cases an annual allowance of clothing. All of this was given in exchange for service, money or property. On William's death, the Templars moved in to

Balantrodoch, in Temple, Midlothian, had been owned by the Templars since their early years. In the late thirteenth century, Preceptor Brian de Jay was involved in the Eperstone affair, which became a well-known example of Templar greed.
Douglas Bewick

AN ILLUSTRATED HISTORY OF THE KNIGHTS HOSPITALLER

seize his wife's home as payment for the favours her dead husband had already made. In the process of physically removing Christiane from the house, she clung to the door post and was immediately relieved of her fingers by a Templar's sword. Although King Edward I intervened and restored the widow with her rightful property, she was evicted again at the start of the Anglo-Scottish wars in 1296. Two years later, Brian de Jay was leading a band of Welsh mercenaries en route to Kirk Liston to meet Edward I. When he stopped at Balantrodoch, he was approached by the widow's son, Richard Cook, who pleaded with de Jay to return the home to his mother. Instead, the Templar preceptor convinced Cook to act as a guide for the troops and had the man murdered along the South Esk River by one of the Welsh mercenaries where the body was left to rot. Brian de Jay was killed a few days later at the Battle of Falkirk and the Templars maintained possession of the property until they, like Christiane, were ejected under bloody means.

Although the corrodian, William of Haukeston, was not a member of the Order, the treatment of his family after his death in the Eperstone affair was in stark contrast to the way the Order's *fratres conjugate*, or married brothers, were dealt with in the early years when the Templars were still operating under the original Latin rule of the Order. Similar to the corrodian, the *fratres conjugate* accepted their situation with the Templars by offering the Order a return on their death. However, if the married brother died prior to his wife, as was clearly the case in William's situation, a portion of his estate was to be given to the Templars; the rest went to the widow for her future support.

The Eperstone story is a documented event and a fitting example of Templar greed in the years immediately preceding their downfall. It shows how the Order was viewed as corrupt, particularly in Scotland where they had sided with Edward I against William Wallace at the Battle of Falkirk, an interference in civil matters that was a departure from the Order's prohibition against fighting fellow Christians.

However, the Templars' meddling was not exclusive to the strife between England and Scotland, nor was it exclusive to merely civil matters. The Order had supported the French King Philip IV in his grievances against Pope Boniface VIII in 1303 and even offered him refuge for three days in 1306 when the king found himself on the wrong end of an angry mob and had to seek shelter in the Paris Temple. It would prove to be a favour the Templars would not be able to bank on.

King Philip IV of France is shown returning to Paris in battledress after his victory at Flanders in this sixteenth-century woodcut based on a statue that once existed in Notre Dame Cathedral.

anything but fair. Inheriting a debt from his father's reign as king and always on a quest to finance his own military operations, Philip fiddled with the currency, persecuted the Jews and Lombards, and even levied a tax on the clergy in his lands. This last action had prompted Pope Boniface VIII to issue the bull *Clericis laicos* in 1296, which prohibited secular rulers from taxing the churches without his approval. Philip's response was to forbid the clergy on his lands from sending any money to Rome at all. Pope Boniface was not amused and began the process of excommunicating the French king in 1303. However, William de Nogaret, one of Philip's ministers, and Sciarra Colonna, one of the Pope's Italian enemies, descended on the pontiff and had him arrested. Although he was freed from prison, Boniface VIII died soon after the humiliating ordeal. Philip had turned on the very man who had made his crusading grandfather Louis IX a saint. As such, it should come as no surprise that he would turn on the men who had helped free his grandfather when he was in an Egyptian prison, long before he was canonised.

However, Philip faced a problem in that the Templars answered only to Pope Clement V. Prior to his coronation in 1305, Clement was known as Bertrand de Got and had served as Bishop of Bordeaux, which made him a subject of the King of England rather than the King of France. Although Philip and Bertrand had been childhood friends, Bertrand had remained a strong supporter of Philip's enemy Pope Boniface VIII during their conflict; however, the unique combination allowed Bertrand to be well poised for an elevation to Pope when Boniface's successor, Benedict XI, died. The election was a long drawn-out affair, due to political controversies hanging in the air from Pope Boniface's reign, but Bertrand was not related to the Colonna or Orsini families which had caused the Pope's problems; his status as Bishop of Bordeaux made him acceptable to the anti-French factions, and the fact that he was a Frenchman by birth made him acceptable to the King of France. Long-term political strife prompted Bertrand to be coroneted at Lyons rather than Rome. In fact, as Pope Clement V, he would serve his entire reign in France, ultimately choosing Avignon as his base of operation in

Philip IV ascended the throne in 1285 and perhaps more than any of his ancestors – a pedigree that could be traced back three centuries to Hugh Capet, the founder of the Capetian dynasty – Philip regarded his throne as having been given to him in trust by God. Of course, having his grandfather proclaimed a saint during his reign certainly did nothing to diminish Philip's belief that his monarchy met with divine approval.

Throughout his reign Philip was known as 'le Bel' or 'the fair', a term of reference connected with his good looks rather than an accommodating personality. In fact, his actions as king, even before his attack on the Templars, clearly show that he was often

1309, a base that would be used by his successors until 1378.

Although this resistance to reigning in Rome has been offered as evidence of Pope Clement's subservience to King Philip, the fact remains that, like Pope Urban II who launched the First Crusade, the political situation in Rome was such that the new Pope did not feel safe in Italy. In fact, the entire notion that Pope Clement was in league with King Philip in orchestrating the Templars' demise is an apocryphal reimagining of the chain of events, crafted in hindsight and hatred. Although weak in will and credulous in his acceptance of information, Clement was not a dishonest man: his desire to launch a new crusade was sincere, and uniting the two Orders was to be the method of ensuring that the mission was successful.

Talk of a united Order was not the only rumour being circulated about the Templars. While Grand Master de Molay was discussing his ideas with the Pope, rumours were circulating that the Templars were not the devoted Christians they wished everyone to believe. The rumours were started by Esquin de Floryan, a former preceptor of Montfaucon, who had been expelled from the Order. De Floryan had begun his accusations against the Templars when he offered to sell them to the King of Aragon; however, a lack of interest on the part of the monarch soon put de Floryan in the hands of Philip's chancellor, William de Nogaret, who saw promise in his story. When Esquin finally had an audience with the king, he told Philip that when the Templars were received, they were instructed to deny Christ and spit on His Holy

The Palais des Papes in Avignon became home to numerous popes after Pope Clement V established his papacy there in 1309. Construction of the palace commenced in 1334 by Pope Benedict XII. The papacy would remain at Avignon until 1378.
Bigstock/Rusty Elliott

Cross. During their reception they were forced to kiss the receptor on the mouth, navel and buttocks and, because the Templar rule prohibited them from having sex with women, the new brethren were told that it was permissible to engage in sexual activity with each other. And perhaps most horrifying of all, the Templars did not worship God, but rather an idol.

After hearing the renegade Templar's account, Philip informed the Pope of what he had learned and turned the matter back over to his right-hand man, de Nogaret, who began an immediate investigation of the Templars, interviewing a number of brethren who had been expelled from the Order, and conducting a survey to ascertain the scope and scale of Templar properties in France. To avoid suspicions, the assessment was broadened to include all religious Orders who held land in the kingdom, including the Cistercians and Hospitallers.

Pope Clement wrote to Philip in late August 1307, informing him that he was planning his own investigation in response to the accusations levelled against the Templars, but that he would not begin until October. Philip had no intention of waiting that long and issued a letter to his bailiffs throughout the kingdom in mid-September, outlining the Templars' crimes and ordering their arrest at a later date, which was to be kept secret until the time had arrived. In the early morning hours of Friday 13 October 1307, Philip's men acted upon the orders they had received a month earlier, and in a series of simultaneous raids on Templar properties throughout France, they rounded up 15,000 people, the majority of whom were not even full members of the Order.

Three days after imprisoning the Templars, Philip wrote to

Although the Templars were accused of worshipping a severed bearded head, neither of the two heads the Order owned was male. Among the Templars' actual relics was a head believed to belong to St Euphemia of Chalcedon, an early Christian martyr.
Jupiter Images

the other western rulers explaining the actions he had taken against the Order, as well as the reasons why, and urged them to do the same as he had. None complied, and although Philip was undoubtedly surprised by their reaction, Pope Clement was appalled; not by their failure to comply, but rather by Philip's failure to seek his permission before arresting the Templars, but there was little he could do. The Templars were already being interrogated and Philip was not about to let them loose.

Within a week of their arrests, Philip put the Templars through a series of interrogations to extract confessions to confirm the accusations levelled against the Order. The 138 Templars arrested in Paris began to give their depositions on 19 October, and to ensure that only the right information was received, the jailers were instructed to keep the brethren in isolation, to inform them that both the king and Pope were aware of the scandalous nature of their reception ceremonies and that they would be pardoned if they confessed to the accusations against them, while a refusal to do so would result in death. To help persuade the Templars to comply, the jailers were instructed to use threats and torture before sending the brethren to meet with the inquisitors. The tactic worked and Philip got the confessions he desired.

When Esquin de Floryan bent Philip's ear with accusations against his former Order, he listed but four faults. By August of 1308, when the charges against the Order had been formally drawn up, they had been greatly embellished and expanded into a clever stew of the standard charges of heresy, similar to those issued against the Cathars and Waldensians of France, as well as misinterpretations about actual Templar practices. In addition to de Floryan's claims that the Templars denied Christ and defiled the Cross, engaged in sodomy, kissed their receptor on the buttocks and worshipped idols, there were now accusations that the Templars did not believe in the Mass and other holy sacraments of the Church, that they believed the Grand Master and other high-ranking officers could absolve them of their sins, and that they were even permitted to confess their sins to a brother of the Order.

The idol that de Floryan claimed the Templars worshipped slowly evolved into the

AN ILLUSTRATED HISTORY OF THE KNIGHTS HOSPITALLER

claim that the Order venerated a bearded head, which they touched with the cords they wore around their waists. The reality of the matter is that the bearded head simply did not exist, at least not among the Templars, although it was common for the Hospitallers to venerate a representation of the severed head of St John the Baptist. However, this did not mean that the Templars did not own a head or two. Among the many holy relics acquired by the Order was a head believed to have belonged to one of St Ursula's 11,000 virgins, as well as the head of St Euphemia. The former was kept in Paris, while the latter was housed in the east.

However, the Templars did confess to these and other charges, prompting Clement to issue the bull *Pastoralis praeminentiae* in late November, ordering the arrest of the Templars throughout Christendom, an order that was not met with immediate or unanimous compliance. In England, the Templars were reluctantly rounded up, but they did not receive the same treatment as in France; even after Clement ordered that they be tortured, none were willing to use the means to extract confessions. In Cyprus, King Amaury was reluctant to arrest the Templars because they had supported him in his coup against his brother, and even when he did, the Templars were simply confined to their own estates; in Venice, the investigations into the Order were conducted by the state, while the Templars remained free; in Naples, torture was used; however, King Charles II of Naples was a relative of Philip. In Germany, the Templars arrived at the council in Mainz armed and accompanied by the local barons who swore to their innocence, and as a result they were set free. In Aragon, the Templars proclaimed their innocence while entrenched in their castles and although James II besieged them and arrested the Order, they were freed in 1312 and granted pensions. However, in France the Templars did not receive any such justice from Philip the Fair.

Displeased with Philip's handling of the Templars, Pope Clement demanded that the matter in France be turned over to the Church's authority and in February of 1308, he suspended the trial, but Philip continued to garner public support for his actions against the Templars and lobbied the Pope to resume the trials. The Pope finally capitulated in July, but insisted that the trials continue under the direction of the clergy. In August of 1308, he issued the bull *Regnans in coelis* that called for a general council to be held on 1 October 1310 at Vienne in order to deal with the matter of the Templars. However, the commission he appointed to investigate the Order was having so much difficulty in obtaining corroborating testimonies that the council was postponed a year, finally convening on 16 October 1311. After three years of investigations the papal commission determined that the Templars were innocent of the charges, but it would be necessary to ensure that the Order was reformed and its rule brought in line with orthodoxy. The commissioners believed that the rule, as written, was fine, but that unwritten and unorthodox practices had been allowed to creep in.

The Church fathers, who had gathered at the Council of Vienne, were, for the most part, doubtful of the Order's guilt and seemed genuinely interested in hearing what its members had to say. However, Philip had no intention of allowing this to occur and continued to apply pressure on the Pope, bringing matters to an abrupt end on 20 March 1312 when he personally arrived at Vienne accompanied by a sizeable army. Two days later Pope Clement held a meeting with a number of cardinals and his special commissioners, who voted by a four-fifths majority to dissolve the Order. The result of the meeting was the bull *Vox in excelso*, which was read publicly on 3 April, and dissolved the Order for all time. In the end it was the Templars' defamed reputation and not their alleged guilt that dissolved the Order. After fighting for Christendom for nearly two centuries the Templars were destroyed, not by their enemy's sword, but by their benefactor's quill:

'Therefore, with a sad heart, not by definitive sentence, but by apostolic provision or ordinance, we suppress, with the approval of the sacred council, the order of Templars, and its rule, habit and name, by an inviolable and perpetual decree, and we entirely forbid that anyone from now on enter the order, or receive or wear its habit, or presume to behave as a Templar.'

Chinon Castle is located on the banks of the Vienne in Chinon, France. It was here in the castle's tower that Templars were imprisoned and later investigated by Clement's papal commission of August 1308. From those investigations came the famed Chinon Parchment which gained media attention in 2007.
Bigstock/ Edyta Pawlowska

In recent years much has been made about the Chinon Parchment, a document that during the height of the Da Vinci Code craze and attention surrounding the 700th anniversary of the Templars' arrest, was transformed into something it was not. Contrary to media headlines which asked 'Were the Templars pardoned by the Pope who killed them?', the Chinon Parchment does not disclose some secret absolution of the Templars by Pope Clement V. Additionally, the document was not a new discovery hidden deep in the bowels of the Vatican's Secret Archives. *Archivum secretum* properly translated is 'private archives' and simply refers to the private archives of the Vatican, where important documents, including the Chinon Parchment, are kept. Although an important rediscovery, if one can consider a well-protected document as lost, the Chinon Parchment was hardly new ground; obscure, certainly, but hardly unknown. Published in Étienne Baluze's 1693 work *Vitae Paparum Avenionensis* (Lives of the Popes of Avignon), the Chinon Parchment documents the 1308 papal inquiry into the Templars' guilt. The recommendation of the papal commission following the inquiry was to reform the Order and its rule, merging it with the Hospitallers,

as had been proposed several times over the years. However, this was not acknowledged at Vienne because Philip strong-armed Clement into dissolving the Order, as we have seen.

The eradication of the Templars left the Pope with the problem of what to do with their properties throughout Christendom. Three suggestions had been put forth during the Council of Vienne: the property would either be turned over to the Church with revenues used to pay for crusading efforts, used to fund a new Military Order to replace the Templars, or turned over to the Hospitallers. Although the majority of those gathered at Vienne were in favour of creating a new military and religious Order, Clement overruled the decision, granting the property to the Hospitallers. The decision was ratified in the bull *Ad providam*, which Clement issued on 2 May 1312:

'The property should become forever that of the order of the Hospital of Saint John of Jerusalem, of the Hospital itself and of our beloved sons the master and brothers of the Hospital, in the name of the Hospital and order of these same men, who as athletes of the Lord expose themselves to the danger of death for the defence of the faith, bearing heavy and perilous losses in lands overseas. We have observed with the fullness of sincere charity that this order of the Hospital and the Hospital itself is one of the bodies in which religious observance flourishes. Factual evidence tells us that divine worship is fervent, works of piety and mercy are practised with great earnestness, the brothers of the Hospital despise the attractions of the world and are devoted servants of the most High. As fearless warriors of Christ they are ardent in their efforts to recover the Holy Land, despising all human perils. We bear in mind also that the more plentifully they are supplied with means, the more will the energy of the master and brothers of the order and Hospital grow, their ardour increase and their bravery be strengthened to repel the insults offered to our Redeemer and to crush the enemies of the faith. They will be able to carry more lightly and easily the burdens demanded in the execution of such an enterprise. They will therefore, not unworthily, be made more watchful and apply themselves with greater zeal.

'In order that we may grant them increased support, we bestow on them, with the approval of the sacred council, the house itself of the Knights Templar and the other houses, churches, chapels, oratories, cities, castles, towns, lands, granges, places, possessions, jurisdictions, revenues, rights, all the other property, whether immovable, movable or self-moving, and all the members together with their rights and belongings, both beyond and on this side of the sea, in each and every part of the world, at the time when the master himself and some brothers of the order were arrested as a body in the kingdom of France, namely in October 1307. The gift is to include everything which the Templars had, held or possessed of themselves or through others, or which belonged to the said house and order of Knights Templar, or to the master and brothers of the order as also the titles, actions and rights which at the time of their arrest belonged in any way to the house, order or persons of the order of Knights Templar, or could belong to them, against whomsoever of whatever dignity, state or condition, with all the privileges, indults, immunities and liberties with which the said master and brothers of the house and order of Knights Templar, and the house and order itself, had been legitimately endowed by the Apostolic See or by Catholic emperors, kings and princes, or by other members of the faithful, or in any other way. All this we present, grant, unite, incorporate, apply and annex in perpetuity, by the fullness of our apostolic power, to the said order of the Hospital of Saint John of Jerusalem and to the Hospital itself'.

Although the Hospitallers must certainly have been troubled by the fate of their long-time rivals and allies, it is also certain that the idea of obtaining Templar properties would have been an exciting opportunity. Given that the Order had to borrow money to assist in conquering Rhodes only a few years earlier, the additional estates in the west would ensure that it could continue to thrive. Although properties in the Kingdoms of Castile, Aragon, Portugal and Majorca were exempt from the bull's terms at the insistence of the Spanish kings, the Hospitallers' access to properties they had been granted was neither immediate nor easy. In France, where the Templars' troubles had begun, the Hospitallers paid a total of 250,000 livres to King Philip and his successor between 1313 and 1318 to access the properties they had been bequeathed, on top of cancelling Philip's debt to the now defunct Order. In England, the transition was even more problematic, largely owing to King Edward II having taken a considerable share for his own needs. Some estates were given away; others had their revenues expropriated for the king's own purposes. Between selling off grain, livestock and other resources, Edward fattened his own revenues by approximately £1,500 per year. Under threat of excommunication, Edward finally turned the matter over to parliament and the former Templar properties were finally taken from the hands of English lords who had claimed them as escheats; even then the Hospitallers had to make concessions and compromises in many cases to take them from those who held them hostage. By 1338, there were still approximately fifteen Templar properties that were under the control of English lords. Those that had been turned over were often of a greater burden than they were of any real value to the Order: mills were either in a state of disrepair or not working at all; buildings were dilapidated; and the Hospitallers were responsible to provide for the corrodians who had made arrangements with the Templars. Additionally, revenues from the lands had to be used, in part, to pay for the maintenance of former Templars now living in monasteries. This requirement had been included in the bull *Considerantes dudum*, issued four days after *Ad providam*. Having the leaders of the Templar Order in custody, Clement decreed that those Templar brethren imprisoned elsewhere were to be disposed of by the judgement of provincial councils. The Pope's order called for those who had already been acquitted or would be acquitted in the future to be provided for out of the Templar estates that were to be handed over to the Hospitallers. Evelyn Lord in her book on the Knights Templar in Britain has estimated that by 1338, less than a decade before the Order would be forced to defend its new home for the first time, Hospitaller revenues from former Templar properties in England were £1,442, just slightly less than King Edward II had been receiving while holding the lands hostage.

Elsewhere, the Hospitallers did not fare as well. It has been estimated that half of the Templars' property in Europe fell into the hands of lay people rather than the Hospitallers. However, the transfer of Templar assets allowed the German Hospitallers to expand into Brunswick and Halberstadt, whereas, prior to the dissolution, the Order had been largely confined to Austria, Breisgau, Silesia and Switzerland. As was the case prior to the loss of Acre, the purpose of the farms and vineyards of the west was to provide resources for those who battled for the cause in the east. By the time Jacques de Molay, the last Grand Master of the Templars, was burned at the stake on 18 March 1314, an act that marked the end of the Templars' story, de Villaret and his Hospitallers were reaching the peak of their own.

The last grand Master of the Templars, Jacques de Molay, is shown being burned at the stake on 18 March 1314, in this nineteenth-century depiction of the event that effectively brought the Templars' story to a close.

CHAPTER 8
Resignations and Dragons

Under de Villaret's leadership the Hospitallers of Rhodes continued to expand their land holdings in the Aegean and Mediterranean, holdings that now ran from Lerro in the north to Castelrosso in the south, along the coast of Asia Minor. As such, the Order dominated a large stretch of the Turkish coastline and either forced the Muslims to move their naval operations further north or denied them access to the seas altogether, as was the case with the Turkish Beylik of Mentese, directly opposite Rhodes on the mainland.

The acquisition of new lands to support Rhodes did not merely benefit the Hospitallers martially; each of the islands under Hospitaller rule offered its own specialities. Lerro and Calamo provided the Order with valuable marble, while Nisyros had an abundant supply of porphyry and Simie was known for its fine wines and sponges, and was home to some of the best ship carpenters in the Dodecanese. The small island also acted as an observation post for the Order where news of oncoming danger could be communicated either by signal fires or swift boats.

Under the Hospitallers' protection, Rhodes quickly became a port of call for European traders who brought valuable commodities from the west and returned with exotic merchandise from the east. No longer would the Hospitallers merely offer European ships protection at sea; they could also offer safe harbour for travelling merchants. As commerce increased, so too did the Hospitallers' fleet, until it was able to cover the Levant, protecting against or engaging in piracy as required, guarding Christian vessels and their cargo, and attacking Muslim ships and procuring their stores.

This naval dominance was made all the easier by the situation in Asia Minor after the disintegration of the Seljuk Sultanate of Rum into a number of Ghazi emirates, independent small Turkish beyliks ruled by tribal leaders. Although the Germaniyans and Karamans were the largest of the competing clans,

The courtyard of the hospital built by the Hospitallers on Rhodes is similar to the image of the ruins of the hospital at Jerusalem. Despite a drastic change in the Hospitallers' role as crusaders following their move to Rhodes in 1309, the Order remained strongly dedicated to its hospital work.
Bigstock/Magomed Magomedagaev

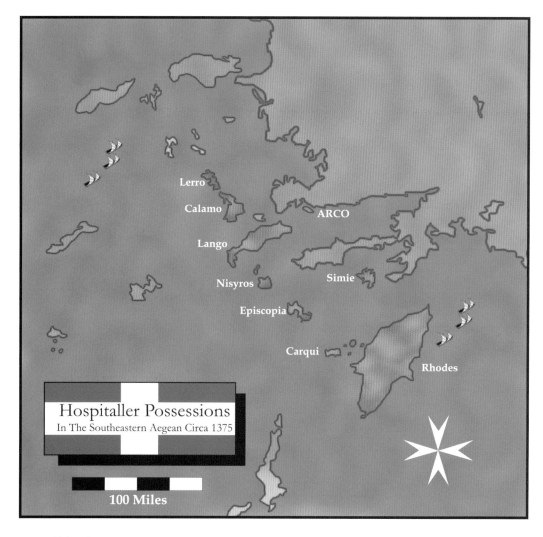

Lerro

Calamo

ARCO

Lango

Nisyros

Simie

Episcopia

Carqui

Rhodes

Hospitaller Possessions
In The Southeastern Aegean Circa 1375

100 Miles

it would be the Ottomans under Osman I and his successors who made the most gains, slowly nipping away at Byzantine borders until eventually the Ottoman Empire took its place. However, during de Villaret's time in office, Osman's battles were confined primarily to land, although the Turks did capture the island of Lango in 1319. The Order's real maritime threat was the Mamluk Empire and they were less intrusive than they might have been; the weakening of crusader and Mongol forces allowed Al-Nāsir Muhammad to concentrate on his empire's own internal struggles.

With its increased wealth and prominence, the Order began to attract a number of new recruits, and although Hospitaller recruiting practices had remained unchanged for centuries, the world in which the Order sought recruits had. In the early days of the

Military Orders many of the young men who sought association with the Hospitallers and Templars were nobly born second and third sons who, in a feudal society, would be left without an inheritance. Joining one of the Military Orders allowed them to carve out a place in the world befitting their earthly rank, although they would be giving up the luxuries they once knew. Even the ignobly born men who would take a lesser role in the Orders did so to escape what would be a grim life of servitude to the aristocracy. By the fourteenth century, the elite position of that aristocracy was being challenged by the growing prominence of an emerging middle class, leading to a trend among the aristocracy to once again embrace chivalry. Unlike joining the Teutonic Knights in the Baltic states, there was little likelihood of ever having to draw a sword after joining the Hospitallers unless one were posted to Rhodes, and even then it was less likely than it had been in the past. As such, new recruits were not drawn to the Order for the thrill of adventure and a chance to fight against the enemies of Christendom; the vast majority of Hospitallers would hold nothing more than administrative positions within the Order. Likewise, religious contemplation was less a driving force in attracting recruits than it had been in the twelfth and thirteenth centuries, largely due to changing attitudes about religion. Whereas the recruits of the previous two centuries had been brought in largely on the strength of crusading as a concept and an ideal, the notion of crusading was beginning to wane: the Holy Land had been lost and people seemed resigned to the fact; the Hungarians were doing a decent job of preventing the landward expansion of the fledgling Ottoman Empire and the Venetians were more interested in maintaining peace with the Muslims than starting a potential war.

In a world that regarded crusading and crusaders as of little necessity beyond protecting western merchants from Muslim pirates, chivalry as a garment to be worn to create class distinction and was increasingly less controlled by religious thought, it is not surprising to find that fourteenth-century Hospitallers were not content to leave behind a life of luxury for one of austere poverty. While they were quite prepared to fight and die (as unlikely as that may have been) for the cause, they were not willing to endure the monkish practices of their historical predecessors, as dictated in the rule of order. This is not to say that the Hospitallers gave up their religious duties: important feasts were honoured, religious observances kept and all of the island's knights worked in the great hospital that looked after the sick and poor, as the Hospitallers had done at Jerusalem before the First Crusade. As the sun set each evening the Order's chaplains would say a prayer for the sick, the poor, the pilgrim, the benefactor, the commoner and the king.

A tendency towards excesses observed in a number of young impetuous recruits did not meet with the approval of the veterans of the Order, who, having lived through the Templars' troubles, were always a little concerned that they may be the next group to be targeted by Pope or king, but it was difficult to rein in the intemperate behaviour of the younger members of the Order when their leader was, with each passing day, spiralling farther out of control with respect to his own observance of the Order's rules and regulations.

Rather than acting like the leader of a Military Order, de Villaret began to take on more and more the airs of a monarch, as if Rhodes were his personal kingdom, rather than the headquarters of an Order of which he was chief administrator. De Villaret's growing arrogance, although unacceptable to his men in principle, was nonetheless accepted in fact, as none were willing to think too poorly of a man under whose leadership the Order had been able to occupy Rhodes and subsequently Leros (1314) and Kos (1315). However, past glories could only carry the man so far, and by 1317, de Villaret's arrogance led to the grumbles previously spoken only in undertones being loudly voiced in open complaint. As a result, de Villaret was summoned before the council to give an account of himself and his handling of the Order's accounts. Allegations had been levied against the Grand Master that Hospitaller revenues had been misappropriated and used for his own lavish excesses, including copious gifts to his growing retinue of sycophants. Even in this, de Villaret acted as if he were a monarch above condemnation and answerable to no man, rather than an elected leader who was answerable to his Order and its rules.

Fed up with their Grand Master's lack of accountability, a number of Hospitallers staged a coup, bribing one of the Grand Master's servants to allow them in at night when they could assassinate de Villaret in his sleep. However, on their arrival they soon discovered that the servant had either betrayed them from the start or had a change of heart and had made de Villaret aware of the plot

Foulques de Villaret was elected in 1305 and resigned as Grand Master in 1319.

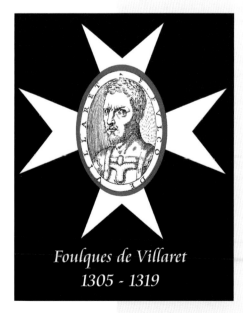

Foulques de Villaret
1305 - 1319

meeting of council, Maurice Pagnac, the leader of the insurrectionists, was elected to succeed the now well-fortified Grand Master. But Pagnac's unanimous election was not the end of the matter. Although the Order had sent an account of what happened to Pope John XXII, de Villaret, from the security of his Lindos castle, had done the same. The two letters prompted the Pope to respond to both claimants for the leadership of the Order, but if de Villaret had hoped for the full sympathetic ear of the Pope, he was to be disappointed:

'We are sorry to learn that you have been assaulted and compelled by your own Knights to fly from the city of Rhodes into a fortress in another part of that island; and although their conduct appears to have been highly incorrect, still you are accused of having excited it; we therefore cite both them and you to our presence, in order that we may investigate the affair, and base our decision on correct information.'

against him. Regardless of the servant's timing in telling him, the Grand Master and his entourage took the news at face value and went to the Hospitaller castle at Lindos and fortified themselves against their enemies. If de Villaret hoped his removal to Lindos would gain him sympathy among those neutral to the conflict, he was wrong. The situation swayed more to the opposition camp and after another

Pagnac was likewise summoned to appear before the Pope at Avignon in order to offer his testimony in settling the dispute. Until then, Pope John appointed Gerard de Pins, a well-respected knight of the Order who had remained neutral during the conflict, to assume the role of acting Grand Master or *locum tenens*. Unfortunately for Pagnac, the closer the ships came to France, the farther the possibility of his chances at the Hospitaller

helm seemed to drift. Far removed from the island de Villaret ruled like a dictator. All that was known of the man was that he was a hero of Christendom in an era when all the heroes of Christendom had either died or been burned at the stake as heretics; a lone crusader in the Aegean, fighting for a dying cause. The situation was no better at Avignon, where, despite any upset the Pope may have had at de Villaret's conduct, there was no movement towards favouring Pagnac, a man who many in Europe saw merely as a usurper to de Villaret's rightful claim to the Grand Mastership.

In the end, neither man succeeded in his claim for the honour. Maurice Pagnac, elderly when he made his move, died having never achieved his desire. Foulques de Villaret, although reinstated as Grand Master in 1319, was reinstated solely on the understanding that he would immediately resign. In consolation for doing so, de Villaret was given the priorship of Capua, in southern Italy, a position he was to hold for life; however, continued administrative problems led to him being reassigned to the Priory of Rome, before ultimately being removed from all authority, given a pension, and allowed to live out the rest of his life in southern France as a common brother of the Order. Upon his resignation, de Villaret's successor was chosen from amongst the knights who were within travelling distance of Avignon. On 18 June 1319, Hélion de Villeneuve was selected as de Villaret's successor, but the new Grand Master did not take his residency at Rhodes until 1332, preferring to rule his Order from France for his first 13 years.

Although the Hospitallers' system of 'Langues', or 'Tongues', based on the geographical divisions of the Order had been in place prior to moving to Rhodes, it was under de Villeneuve that they received further

Hélion de Villeneuve
1319 - 1346

refinement. Beginning in 1320, the *pilier*, who headed each Langue, also took on one of the Order's great offices: Provence provided the Grand Commander, Auvergne the Marshal, France the Hospitaller, England the turcopolier (commander of light cavalry), Italy the admiral, and Spain provided the Order's drapier; Germany played no special role at this stage of the organisational evolution. De Villeneuve had a number of impressive accomplishments during his career, including assisting in the destruction of one hundred Turkish vessels in 1334 and joining forces with the Papal League

Left: **Hélion de Villeneuve was elected Grand Master on 18 June 1319, but did not travel to Rhodes until 1332, ruling his Order from France for his first 13 years.**

Above: **Street of the Knights in Rhodes. It was here that each of the Order's Langues had a separate inn. In 1320, de Villeneuve assigned special offices for each of the Langues' leaders.** *Bigstock/Panagiotis Karapanagiotis*

in capturing Smyrna (Izmir) in 1344. Despite the successes of his administration, he is often mentioned in association with his successor Dieudonné de Gozon.

De Gozon was elected in 1346, and although Vertot claimed that he nominated himself for the position, Porter cites a letter of Pope Clement VI that references the man's reluctance to accept the post. This, combined with his subsequent two offers to tender his resignation, is offered by Porter as evidence that the man was not the arrogant leader Vertot made him out to be. But the myth is not the only dragon to be slain. In fact, it is an incident involving a real dragon that connects de Gozon with his predecessor.

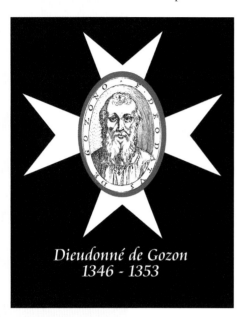

Dieudonné de Gozon 1346 - 1353

Dieudonné de Gozon was elected Grand Master in 1346 and is perhaps best known for a legend that has him slaying a dragon on Rhodes in 1332.

The fanciful story took place in 1332, the year that de Villeneuve finally arrived on Rhodes, a period of time when the island was fearful not of the attack of its Muslim enemies but of further attacks from an enormous creature, said to be a dragon that lived in a marsh at the foot of Mount St Stephen, about two miles from the city of Rhodes. Whatever it was, the creature continued unopposed in its insatiable hunger for sheep, cattle and even the occasional shepherd boy who got too close to the water's edge. The tradition says that several knights had ventured to slay the creature, but after none returned, de Villeneuve forbade his knights from any further incursions against the great beast that had been reported, by those who had seen it and lived to tell the tale, as being a large creature covered in thick scales impervious to sword or arrow.

Neither the beast nor the Grand Master's decree deterred a young de Gozon who asked for a leave of absence and travelled to his father's castle in the Languedoc where he built a model of the great beast to be studied as he would any other opponent of war. De Gozon, realising that the underbelly of the beast was unprotected, trained his dogs to attack the model at that point in preparation for an assault on the real thing when he returned to Rhodes. Anticipating that the Grand Master would forbid him to destroy the beast, de Gozon landed along the coast rather than in the great harbour, made his way to the Chapel of St Stephen, and left his two squires to come for him if he were successful in slaying the dragon or carry the news if he failed in his mission.

When the inevitable fight with the great beast began, de Gozon soon learned that his lance and sword were of little use, but the beast's tail was effective for throwing him from his mount. Picking himself up from the ground, de Gozon could see the underbelly of the beast had been exposed by the attack of his dogs. Wasting no time for the creature to regain its footing, de Gozon thrust his sword into the exposed softness, ending the reign of terror the beast had held over the islanders.

As the tradition goes, de Villeneuve did not congratulate the knight on having slain the dragon or lavish him with thankful praise, but rather chastised him for his disobedience, and, depending on the account, either expelled him from the Order or put him on probation. However, the public outcry at the mistreatment of the heroic knight resulted in de Gozon's reinstatement. Although the story of de Gozon's dragon is clearly a romantic fable, what is probable is that the man killed some form of marshland nuisance, either a large snake or crocodile, that other knights had failed to hunt down, and the story of his success continued to be inflated long after his death to the epic proportions it eventually obtained.

Whatever de Gozon's dragon may have been, if it were anything at all, the real dragon to rise from the sea and threaten the Hospitallers' island was the Ottoman Empire, an emerging empire that began to rise around the same time that the Hospitallers were setting their eyes on Rhodes. Although the Ottoman Turks would make great inroads over the next century, it would not be until 1480 that they would launch a massive assault on the tiny island. By that time it would be the cannon's fire and not the dragon's that Christendom would be worried about.

CHAPTER 9
Siege of Rhodes 1480

When the Sultan Mehmed II captured Constantinople on 29 May 1453, it effectively put an end to more than a millennium of existence for the Byzantine Empire. Although already fragmented into a number of Greek monarchies, Constantinople was the capital of the empire, whatever might remain of it. It had been threatened many times in the past. In fact, it had been the sound of Turkish horses' hooves growing ever nearer to her gates after the Battle of Manzikert in 1071 that had prompted the eastern Christians to plead to Rome for assistance in driving off the Muslim invaders, a call to action that had prompted Pope Urban II to preach the First Crusade in 1095. And although their western co-religionists had driven back the rising tide of Islam and established permanent settlements in the east, it was only a century later that another generation of western Christians would once again cross the Bosphorus. However, this time it was with the desire of conquering, rather than assisting, their eastern cousins at Constantinople, an act of aggression that left a lasting legacy of bitterness over the betrayal of the western crusaders even after the reconquest of the city in 1261.

The Ottoman forces that laid siege to Constantinople in the spring of 1453 were not the soldiers who had attacked the city with the simple swords and siege engines of years gone by. This new aggressor had come with a

Mehmed II, shown in this fifteenth-century oil painting by Gentile Bellini, was the Sultan of the Ottoman Empire from 1444 until 1446 and again from 1451 until his death in 1481. In 1453, he conquered Constantinople and subsequently attacked Rhodes in 1480.

number of bombards or cannon. Although cannon had been known in the Muslim world as early as the late thirteenth century, the weapons Mehmed II brought with him to the walls of Constantinople had evolved considerably in both size and destructive power. One of the most formidable was a

19-tonne bronze unit that required sixty oxen and two hundred men to move and was capable of firing a 600lb ball. Although these primitive cannon were powerful, they lacked the ability to fire in rapid succession, requiring several hours to cool between discharges. This allowed the Byzantines to repair damage as it occurred and reduced the overall effectiveness of the new siege weapon. Despite its limitations, the cannon and the man who put it to use against the walls of Constantinople caught the attention of the Hospitallers stationed at Rhodes.

Mehmed II saw himself as the Alexander the Great of a new era, and was a man equally gifted in matters of war or letters. He was well versed in both Arabic and Greek literature, science and philosophy, and was able to speak Turkish, Arabic, Greek, Latin, Hebrew and Persian. The fourth son of the Sultan Murad II and a slave girl, Mehmed had ascended the Ottoman throne in 1444 at the age of twelve when his father abdicated in his favour. However, after an unsuccessful first reign which lasted only two years, Mehmed would have to wait until his father's death in 1451 to once again resume control of the Ottoman Empire. Mehmed was just nineteen when he resumed the throne and within two years the more mature ruler had managed to capture Constantinople, a victory that increased his image not only among his countrymen but in his own mind as well.

His first act upon entering Constantinople as conqueror was to go to the Hagia Sophia and convert it to a mosque, but the symbolic and physical retrofit of the nine-century-old Byzantine Christian cathedral was not his only design upon the city. In an effort to restore Constantinople to its former glory and to expand it as the new capital of the Ottoman

Empire, Mehmed invited the Greeks and Genoese to return to the city, offering them their former homes and his personal guarantees for their safety within Constantinople's newly rebuilt walls. Additionally, in an effort to further repopulate the city, the sultan deported both Muslims and Christians from Anatolia and the Balkans, forcing them to settle in the city, now called Istanbul (a corruption of a Greek name meaning 'the city', by which it had been known colloquially since the tenth century.)

Like his father before him, the young sultan expanded the Janissary infantry to help act as a standing army. Although the first Janissaries were composed of war prisoners and slaves, by the late fourteenth century Janissaries were drawn entirely from the devsirme system, a process by which young Christian boys were taken from their families, converted to Islam and enrolled in one of four Ottoman institutions: palace, scribes, religious and military. Regardless of the selected vocation, by the time of Mehmed's second ascendancy to the Ottoman throne the best and brightest from the devsirme system replaced the Ottoman ruling class at all levels of society and effectively replaced the power base of the Turkish nobility.

Nowhere was this more effective than in the Janissary soldiers who had been developed as elite military forces loyal to the sultan alone, rather than to any individual Ottoman nobleman. In this sense the Janissaries were similar to the Mamluks, a group of soldier converts to Islam who ultimately seized power in Egypt in 1250 and went on to expel the Christians from Acre in 1291. However, unlike the Mamluks, the Janissaries remained loyal to their overseer, the sultan, whom they regarded as their father, the corps itself serving as their family.

Together with his armies, the foremost of which were the Janissary soldiers, Mehmed went on to conquer Serbia in 1459 and the Peloponnese peninsula the following year. By 1461, he had gained ground into Anatolia as far as the Euphrates, but resistance from the Mamluks in Syria halted his eastern progress. During the next decade, Mehmed would substantially increase his efforts in the Dodecanese, forcing Tilos and Chalki to evacuate to Rhodes in 1470 and 1475 respectively. It would be another five years before the sultan would besiege the largest and most heavily fortified of the islands.

It is doubtful that Mehmed's desire to conquer Rhodes was entirely for the purpose of exterminating the Knights Hospitaller stationed there, although it would certainly serve his purposes better if they were removed from the Aegean entirely. Having described himself as 'the lord of two lands and two seas', a reference to his land dominance of Anatolia and the Balkans and his naval prowess in the Aegean and Black seas, Mehmed was desired to increase his Ottoman Empire even further by invading Italy. As such, Rhodes would offer him a perfect base to launch a naval campaign. Before he could set his sights on southern Italy, he would first need to wrest Rhodes from the Hospitallers, something Grand Master Pierre d'Aubusson was not prepared to let happen.

Like Mehmed, d'Aubusson was born into nobility and had experienced war early in life. He had fought both the Turks and the Swiss by the time he was twenty-one, and on his return to France he obtained permission from King Charles VII to join the Hospitaller Order. In the same year that Mehmed ascended the throne for the first time, d'Aubusson was stationed at Rhodes. The young Hospitaller novice from the Langue of Auvergne quickly rose in prominence within his newfound Order. In 1454, a decade after his admission into the Hospitallers, he was sent by Grand Master Jean de Lastic to Europe to secure arms and alms to prepare for a Turkish attack that de Lastic felt could come at any time.

By 1460, he was appointed Castellan of Rhodes and soon after was elevated to the post of Captain General of the City. It was in this capacity that d'Aubusson personally oversaw the upgrade to Rhodes' defences which included the erection of a seaward curtain wall and several new towers, the expansion of all landward ditches and the installation of a boom chain across the island's commercial harbour. Central to d'Aubusson's shoring up of fortifications was the construction, in 1465, of the Fort of St Nicholas, built at the point of the harbour mole over an earlier Arabic structure. Philippe le Bon, the Duke of Normandy, donated 12,000 crowns in gold towards the erection of the new tower in honour of the Burgundian soldiers who had held the previous fort against an earlier Mamluk attempt to

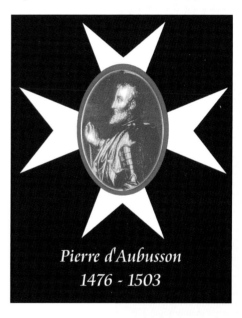

Pierre d'Aubusson was Grand Master from 1476 until 1503 and led the Hospitallers in the defence of Rhodes against an Ottoman attack in 1480.

Left: The Fort of St Nicholas at Rhodes was built in 1465 when Pierre d'Aubusson was Castellan of the city. It went on to play a major role in the siege of 1480. The two bronze deer in the harbour are located where the famous Colossus of Rhodes is believed to have stood. *Bigstock/Ivo Velinov*

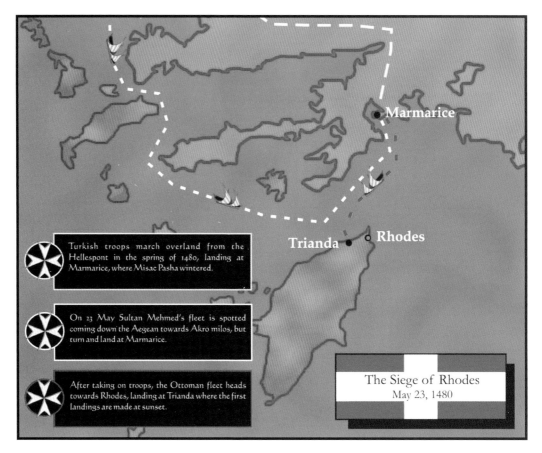

Turkish troops march overland from the Hellespont in the spring of 1480, landing at Marmarice, where Misac Pasha wintered.

On 23 May Sultan Mehmed's fleet is spotted coming down the Aegean towards Akro milos, but turn and land at Marmarice.

After taking on troops, the Ottoman fleet heads towards Rhodes, landing at Trianda where the first landings are made at sunset.

The Siege of Rhodes
May 23, 1480

gain control of the island in 1444. As a token of their gratitude for the duke's contribution, the Hospitallers had Philippe's shield carved into the tower and above the door. With the city's walls refortified against an imminent Ottoman attack, the Hospitallers charged each of the Order's eight Langues with the responsibility of guarding individual sections of the city's walls. It would be another fifteen years before the attack finally came, by which time d'Aubusson was in full control of the Order and its men, who continued to safeguard the city's walls.

Early in 1476, d'Aubusson had been elected Grand Prior of the Langue of Auvergne, but due to the age and infirmities of Grand Master Giovanni Battista Orsini, and the fact that the two men were close friends, d'Aubusson was Master of the Order in all but name, a situation that was rectified on Orsini's death in June of that year. Anticipating Mehmed's intentions towards Rhodes, one of d'Aubusson's first acts as Grand Master was to seek assistance, both financial and material,

from the various western houses of the Hospitaller Order, as well as from Pope Sixtus IV and King Louis XI. Despite his best efforts in apprising them of the necessity of sending assistance, d'Aubusson's defensive forces at the time of the siege consisted of no more than six hundred members of the Order and approximately 2,000 auxiliary troops, hardly a match for the fifty ships laden with Turkish soldiers that Mehmed would send to Rhodes with the hopes of conquering the island.

Mehmed's herald, who set sail in the winter of 1479, was a member of the Imperial house of Paleologus who had converted to Islam after the fall of Constantinople. In his quarter-century service to Mehmed, Paleologus had risen in the Ottoman ranks to the title of pasha and was appointed Mehmed's commander-in-chief. Sailing down the Dodecanese with a number of Turkish galleys to survey Rhodes, Paleologus Pasha performed a number of raids, torching a few small villages along the way. However, his attempt to gain ground on Rhodes, to wear down the garrison ahead of the full attack, proved disastrous. Although his landing went unopposed by the Hospitaller garrison, the pasha found the surrounding land deserted. With his troops spread out in their quest for plunder, they were taken by surprise by the Hospitallers who slaughtered a number of Turks, driving the rest back to the beaches where they had landed. Realising that his small fleet was not sufficient to take on Rhodes, Paleologus sailed for Marmarice on the Turkish mainland and spent the winter waiting for the sultan's fleet and army to arrive the following spring.

At dawn on 23 May 1480, Turkish ships were spotted coming down the Aegean towards Akra Milos (the island's northwestern tip) and it appeared that the battle the Order had been anticipating for many years was about to ensue. However, rather than heading towards shore, the fleet abruptly turned away from the island and headed towards Marmarice. It was here, where Paleologus had settled in for the winter, that Turkish troops travelling over land had rallied awaiting the sultan's fleet. After the embarkation had concluded, the fleet again weighed anchor and turned back towards Rhodes, landing around sunset at the Bay of Trianda on the island's western coast. The attack on the city began the following morning.

The closest extant account of the siege of Rhodes in 1480 was written by d'Aubusson himself, and while it is true that history is always written by the victor, the Grand Master's account, a letter sent to the Holy Roman Emperor Frederick III, is both concise and modest in its retelling of the nearly three-month-long ordeal. As such, it is probable that it is as accurate an account of the events as we are likely to read and far more reliable than the more romantic accounts by authors like Vertot, who wrote extensively of the Order in the eighteenth century. It is here presented in its entirety as translated in Major General Whitworth Porter's 1883 revised edition of *A History of the Knights of Malta or the Order of St. John of Jerusalem*:

'Most invincible and serene prince; it appears to us in no way incongruous that we should describe to your Imperial Majesty the incidents which have occurred in the siege of the town of Rhodes; by the Turks in its attack, and by

ourselves in its defence; now that the day of battle has had a prosperous ending, to the honour of the Christian name; and we do not doubt but that your Imperial Majesty will derive no little pleasure from our victory. The Turks having encamped around the city sought diligently for points of attack; they then endeavoured to shake and destroy the ramparts on all sides with their cannon, and soon showed plainly what their intentions were, and for that purpose surrounded the city with guns and mortars, and with them overthrew nine of its towers and a bastion, and struck and destroyed the magisterial palace. It seemed, however, most convenient to them to assault and press the city upon three sides principally: the attack of the tower on the mole of St. Nicholas appearing the most advantageous for concluding the affair; by means of which they deemed that the city would the most readily fall into their power. This tower is a stronghold, at the extremity of the mole, which juts out into the sea in a northerly direction as far as the harbour extends, and is visible to approaching mariners, who may either keep close to it or easily avoid it. On the westward is situated the chapel of St. Anthony, at a distance of barely 200 paces, with the sea between. The advantages of the place having been therefore perceived, the Turkish army strove by every means in their power to get it into their possession. They brought three huge brass bombards to batter down the tower, whose size and power were incredibly great, and which threw balls of stone of nine palms, and they placed them in the chapel of St. Anthony. Wonderful to relate, and most calamitous to behold, this renowned fort, which appeared of such surpassing strength, after having been battered by 300 stone balls, had the greater part of its extent destroyed, overthrown and ruined. The enemy, who beheld the ruins with exultation, filled the air with their shouts, which vain rejoicing was, however, speedily converted into sorrow. For we, being anxious for the safety of the tower, beholding its great and fearful ruin, strove to prop up the remainder of the wall; and since such a course appeared the most judicious, after so complete a downfall, we decided upon protecting, not the tower only, but also the mole of St. Nicholas itself. With the most vigilant care and numberless inventions, 1000 labourers worked day and night without intermission, who dug a deep ditch, and constructed a bulwark with timber on the top of the mole, around the tower, and in the midst of its foundations, and completed an impregnable redoubt at a great cost. There we placed a guard of our bravest warriors within the ruins of the mole, and supplied them with stores and ammunition. At the end also, and foot of the same; we placed other garrisons, both at the eastern and western extremities: because at those points the ramparts ended, and the sea is fordable, so that it was necessary to watch and defend them, lest the Turks should pass there, and attack us in the rear. And on the walls of the tower we placed bombards, which should sweep the spot during an attack. Fireworks were also prepared to attack the fleet. Twice did the Turks storm the tower, and the new work on its ruins; the first time, when they thought it easy to capture with only moderate force, before daylight at early dawn; when they attacked the place in triremes [oared warships] prepared for the purpose, and fought vigorously. But our men, who were intent upon the defence of the post, were constantly on the watch. So the enemy was driven back discomfited. And in that battle nearly 700 Turks were killed, as we learned from the deserters. After the lapse of a few days, however, enraged at their former repulse, they again attacked the tower with a powerful marine, and with ingenious skill; shaking and destroying our repairs and new bulwarks with their heavy artillery, and some were completely destroyed. We, however, promptly repaired whatever they overthrew. To carry out the attack, they then got ready triremes well supplied with munitions, and ingeniously prepared for the fight, and certain other heavy vessels (called commonly 'parendarias'), in which were heavy guns and stones; that they might establish themselves upon the mole and tower, which they thought they were secure of, and from that point annoy and breach and capture the city itself. They also prepared certain flat-bottomed boats, from which some of the boldest among them reached the mole, and constructed a bridge with the most wonderful skill; which was to cross from the church of St. Anthony to the mole at the foot of the tower. But we, suspecting what would

occur after the first attack, had laboured with all our strength and ingenuity, added to our munitions, increased our fortifications, and did not spare the most serious expense; for we judged that the safety of the city depended on the spot. In the middle, therefore, of the night, the Turks, on the thirteenth of the kalends of July, burning with a fiercer ardour than ever, approached the tower with the utmost silence, and attacked it on all sides with the greatest impetuosity; but our ears were pricked up, and we were not asleep. For when we discovered that the foe was arrived, our machines commenced to hurl their stones, our soldiers girded on their swords, and missiles of every description being hurled from the tower and mole, overthrew and repulsed the enemy; the battle was carried on with the utmost vehemence from midnight until ten o'clock. Numberless Turks, who had reached the mole from the boats and triremes, were killed. The floating bridge, laden with Turks, was broken by the missiles from our machines, and those who were on it were thrown into the sea. Four of the triremes, and those boats which were laden with guns and stores, were destroyed by the stones hurled upon them, and were sunk. The fleet was also set on fire, and forced to retire; and thus the Turks departed, beaten and defeated. Many of their leading commanders fell in this battle, whose loss was deeply mourned for by the army. Deserters, who joined us after the battle, told us that the Turks had received a severe check, and that nearly 2,500 had been slain. But when the Turks lost all hopes of capturing the tower, they turned all their energies, their ingenuity, and their strength, on an attack of the town itself, and although the whole city was so shaken and breached by their artillery that scarcely the original form of it remained, still their principal attack was directed against the part of the walls which encloses the Jews' quarter, [southeast part of the city] and looks towards the east; and against that part which leads to the post of Italy. For the purpose therefore, of destroying and breaching those walls, they brought eight gigantic and most enormous bombards, hurling stones of nine palms in circumference, which played upon the walls without ceasing night and day. Nor did the bombards and mortars placed around the city cease from hurling similar stones, the fall of which added greatly to the general terror and destruction. We therefore placed the aged, the infirm, and the women in caves and other underground spots to dwell, which caused but few casualties to occur from that infliction. They also prepared another description of annoyance, by using fire-balls and lighted arrows, which they hurled from their ballistae and catapults, which set fire to our buildings. We, however, careful for the safety of our city, selected men, skilled in the art, who, ever on the watch, put out the fires wherever the flaming missiles fell. By these precautions the Rhodians were preserved from many mishaps. The infidels also attempted to approach the city underground, and excavated winding ditches, which they partly covered with timber and earth, that they might reach the ditches of the city undercover; and they built up batteries in many places from which they kept up an unceasing fire, with colubrine and serpentine guns, and harassed and wearied our men, and also thought it would be an advantage to fill up that portion of the ditch which is adjacent to the wall of the spur. They continue without ceasing, therefore to collect stones, and secretly to throw them into the ditch, so that part being filled up by their labours to the level of the opposing wall, they could form a pathway in the shape of a back, from which they could conveniently enter upon the walls of the town. We, however, perceiving the attempt of the foe, watched over the safety of the city, and throughout the town, and castles, and ditches, inspected carefully where repairs and munitions were required; which the Turks perceiving, turned again in despair to the Jews' rampart, and other spots; whilst we, with repairs and supports, restored such places as they had ruined, with stakes of the thickest timber, firmly planted into the ground, and covered with earth, and roots and branches interlaced, which clinging together most tenaciously and firmly, sustained the shock of their missiles, and protected the breach, lest the rampart falling into the city should afford them an easy descent. We also made similar bulwarks, with stakes interlaced with brushwood and earth, as cover for our men, and as an obstacle to the Turks when climbing up. We also prepared artificial fire, and other contrivances, which might prove useful in repelling the attack of the Turks. We also

thought it advisable to empty that part of the ditch which the Turks had filled with stones; but as that could not otherwise be done secretly, from the situation of the ditch, we made for ourselves an exit beneath the stones, and secretly brought them into the town. The Turks who were nearest to the ditch, however, remarked that the heap of stones diminished, and that the facilities for an ascent would be reduced, unless they rapidly carried out the attack they contemplated. Thirty-eight days had passed in these labours; and during that time 3,500 huge stones, or thereabouts, were hurled at the ramparts and into the town. The Turks, perceiving that the opportunity of storming the town was being gradually taken away from them, hastened on their preparatory works, and on the day before the assault, and that night, and even on the early morning itself, they battered at the walls without intermission with eight huge bombards, hurling enormous rocks; they destroyed and overthrew the barriers that had been erected behind the breach; the sentries, look-outs, and guards of the ramparts were mostly killed, and it was hardly possible to mount the wall, except by taking the utmost precautions, and by descending a little at the sound of a bell, and afterwards continuing the ascent. Nor was time given us to repair the ruined fortification; since the vigour of the bombardment never relaxed, and in a little time 300 stones, or thereabouts, had been discharged. The bombardment having concluded, the Turks, at the signal of a mortar, which had been placed there the day previous, mounted the breach, on the seventh day of the kalends of August, in a vigorous and rapid attack; and the ascent was, as we have already said, easy for them, easier than it was for our men, who had to use ladders. Annihilating the guard who had been placed on the summit of the rampart, who were unable to resist that first onset, before our reinforcements could ascend the ladders, they had occupied the spot, and planted their standards there. The same thing occurred at the bastion of Italy, whose summit they gained. The alarm was given on all sides and a hand-to-hand encounter commenced, and was carried on with the utmost vehemence. Suddenly, our men opposing themselves to the foe, on the right and left of the rampart, drove them from the higher places, and prevented them from moving about on the walls. Of the four ladders, too, which had been provided for the descent into the Jews' quarter, one had been broken by our order; but having ascended by the others, we opposed ourselves to the enemy, and defended the place. There were, in truth, 2,000 most magnificently armed Turks upon the walls, in dense array, opposing themselves to our men, and striving, by force of arms, to drive them away, and expel them from the place. But the valour of our soldiers prevented us from giving way. To the first body, however, the Turks, who had gained the walls, there followed an immense multitude of others, who covered the whole country, the adjacent breach, the valley and ditch, so that it was hardly possible to see the ground. The deserters state that 4,000 Turks were engaged in the assault. Our men drove about 300 of the enemy, who were upon the rampart, back into the Jews' quarter, where they were killed to a man. At that conflict we raised the standard bearing the effigy of our most sacred Lord Jesus Christ, and that of our Order, in the presence of the enemy; and the battle raged for about two hours around the spot.

The siege of Rhodes in 1480 is depicted in this painting taken from the Gestorum Rhodiae obsidionis commentarii, published in 1481, the year after the failed attack. The foreground of the painting shows the Hospitallers occupying the Tower of St Nicholas.

At length the Turks, overcome, wearied, and panic-stricken, and covered with wounds, turned their backs, and took flight with such vehement haste that they became an impediment to one another, and added to their losses. In that flight there fell 3,500 Turks, or thereabouts, as was known by the corpses which were found within the city, and upon the walls, and in the ditches as also in the camp of the enemy, and in the sea; and which we afterwards burnt, to prevent disease; the spoils of which corpses fell into the possession of our men, who, following the flying Turks, even to their camp on the plain, slew them vigorously, and afterwards returned safely into the town. In which battle many of our bailiffs and brave soldiers fell, fighting most valiantly in the midst of the hostile battalions.

We ourselves, and many of our brothers in arms, having received many wounds, having returned thanks to God, and placed a strong guard on the walls, returned home; nor was so great a calamity averted from us save by the Divine assistance. For we could not doubt but that God had sent assistance from heaven, lest His Poor Christian people should become infected with the filth of Mahometanism [Islam]. Turkish women had prepared ropes, under the hopes of obtaining possession of the city, wherewith to bind the captives, and huge stakes, wherewith to impale them whilst living. For they had decreed that every soul, both male and female, above ten years of age, was to be killed and impaled; but the children under that age were to be led into captivity and compelled to renounce their faith; and all booty was to be given over to plunder, the city being reserved for Turkish governance. But being frustrated in their evil designs, they fled like a flock of sheep. During these battles, and the attacks made on different days, as also in defending the approaches, and clearing the ditches, and in the general defence of the town by means of our artillery, which played constantly on their army, we killed, as the Turkish deserters revealed to us, 9,000 of them, and an innumerable quantity more were wounded; amongst whom Gusman Balse and a certain son-in-law of the sultan's died of their wounds. The struggle being ended, they first burnt all their stores, and retired to their camp, a little distance from the city, where embarking their artillery and heavy baggage,

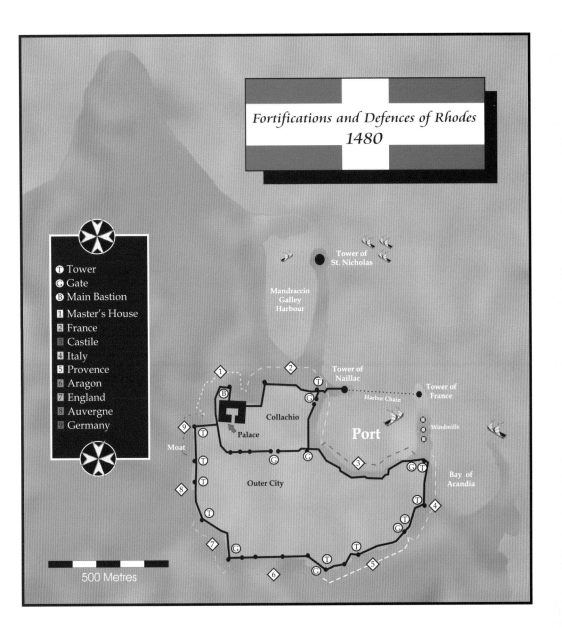

Fortifications and Defences of Rhodes 1480

- **T** Tower
- **G** Gate
- **B** Main Bastion
- **1** Master's House
- **2** France
- **3** Castile
- **4** Italy
- **5** Provence
- **6** Aragon
- **7** England
- **8** Auvergne
- **9** Germany

Tower of St. Nicholas

Mandraccio Galley Harbour

Tower of Naillac

Tower of France

Harbor Chain

Collachio

Palace

Port

Windmills

Moat

Outer City

Bay of Acandia

500 Metres

and consuming a few days in transporting some of their army to Lycia, they left the Rhodian shore, and retired to Phiscus [Marmarice], an ancient city on the mainland: thus they retired beaten, with ignominy. May the omnipotent God happily preserve your Imperial Majesty to our prayers!'

Given at Rhodes, on the 13th day of September, in the year of the incarnation of our redeemer MCCCCLXXX. [1480]

Your Imperial Majesty's humble servant,

PETER D'AUBUSSON,
Master of the Hospital of Jerusalem.

Although d'Aubusson's brief account gives us the substantial details of the siege and its various stages – the failed attempt to take the Fort of St Nicholas, the subsequent assault on the city walls on several fronts, and the final hand-to-hand battle on the city walls and in the Jewish quarter that ultimately drove the aggressors from the city and island – it leaves out some of the more interesting details concerning spies and intrigue. Whether d'Aubusson left these portions of the story out for reasons of brevity or shame is uncertain. What is certain is that the Janissaries were not the first Turks to gain ground on the

Hospitaller side of Rhodes' fortified walls.

Five days after the Turks landed at Trianda, a defector arrived at the city gates looking to be let into the city. His story was plausible enough: a former Christian who had converted to Islam and spent many years in the service of Mehmed II helping him develop cannon of all variety and power, he could no longer countenance his betrayal of his former faith, particularly since his talents

details about the Turkish army: its size and organisation, the depth of the provisions and stores they had brought to the siege and the destructive power of its artillery. In relation to the last point, George was certainly in possession of inside knowledge, having founded the cannon himself. But Master George's unwillingness to provide accurate information that would benefit the Hospitallers soon confirmed what d'Aubusson had suspected from the moment the German arrived at his gates. Information about the army's standing or the best place to station the Hospitallers' cannon proved ineffectual.

The so-called defector was tortured for further information which disclosed that he was indeed a spy and that he had been sent by Pellagrous Pasha. Although the fate of the

Above: **Cem, the son of Mehmed II, shown in this painting by Pinturicchio Bernardo di Betto, became entangled in a territorial dispute with his brother, Bayezid, and sought asylum at the Hospitaller castle at Bodrum. He would later find himself a prisoner of the Pope.**

Right: **The Castle of St Peter or Petronium, now known as Bodrum Castle, is located in southwest Turkey and was built by the Hospitallers in 1402 as a mainland stronghold to stave off a possible invasion of Rhodes by Seljuk Turks. The site was selected by Grand Master Philibert de Naillac.**
Bigstoc

Far right: **The French Tower of the Castle of St Peter at Bodrum towered over the other turrets maintained by the various Langues of the Hospitaller Order.**
Bigstock/ Valery Shanink

were now being used to attack Christians. His choice was a limited one, he told d'Aubusson. Defection outside the city walls would mean a certain death, but within the walls he could help the Hospitallers drive back the Turks. Despite the apparent sincerity of his claims, d'Aubusson regarded the man with a great deal of suspicion, but let him into the city in the hope of learning as much as he could from this peculiar German called Master George, particularly his genius in the art of war. But if George expected a free run of the city, he was quickly disappointed. The Grand Master assigned six knights to act as a bodyguard with the dual role of watching his every move both day and night. Under interrogation, Master George confided in the Grand Master all the

Templars in France 173 years earlier had shown that a tortured man would disclose whatever one wished to hear, there is little doubt that Master George was precisely what he had confessed through pain-filled cries. Wasting no more time on the pretender, d'Aubusson had him publicly hanged and a message telling the pasha that his master artillery craftsmen was dead was shot into the enemy lines.

Master George was not the only Turkish subject to appeal to the Grand Master for protection. In the years that followed the siege, a power struggle for the Ottoman throne broke out between Mehmed's sons Bayezid and Cem soon after the sultan's death in 1481. Mehmed originally had three sons, but the eldest, named Mustapha, was strangled on his father's orders for committing adultery with the wife of his chief vizier, Achmet Pasha. This left Bayezid as the surviving eldest son, which, under Muslim tradition, entitled him to inherit his father's throne, but Bayezid had been born prior to Mehmed's ascendency to the Ottoman throne. As such, Cem, who had been born when his father was already sultan, felt the Empire was his to inherit. He was not without his supporters, including the chief vizier, ultimately murdered by the Janissaries, who supported Bayezid. After Bayezid's installation on the throne, the conflict continued to escalate with Cem launching a campaign to capture pieces of the Ottoman Empire for himself. Despite a number of victories, Cem was ultimately defeated at Bursa and fled to Mamluk-controlled Egypt.

Cem was not content to concede the throne and returned the following spring to launch an attack in Anatolia. Again he was defeated by his elder brother, this time at Konya, and prepared to return to Cairo; however, Bayezid had ensured that his path was blocked. Trapped in hostile territory, Cem travelled to the Hospitaller castle at Bodrum seeking asylum. It was not long after being taken into the protection of the Order that Cem was invited to Rhodes as the guest of the Grand Master himself.

D'Aubusson's victory over Cem's father two years earlier had restored the Hospitallers to a prominence in Europe that they had not enjoyed since before the loss of Acre in 1291. Suddenly, the almost forgotten Order was important to Christendom once again. Of course this had more to do with the realities brought to light by the fall of Constantinople and the Ottoman Empire's expansion ever closer to European territory than the good news of d'Aubusson's ability to hold onto a tiny island in the Aegean. But neither the Pope nor the collected crowned heads of Christendom could ignore the fact that this tiny band of remaining crusaders was Europe's last best hope on the eastern frontier – if not for recapturing eastern territory, then certainly for helping to ensure that the Turks made no further inroads west. Had Sultan Mehmed captured Rhodes, the sea road to Italy would have been wide open to him to see, as he so desired, the standard of Islam flying over the walls of papal Rome; but his death, falling less than a year after his defeat at Rhodes, robbed him of the opportunity to besiege the city once again while its fortifications were still weak.

On the other hand, the direct result of d'Aubusson's victory over Mehmed was the influx of gifts and supplies from across Europe, all of which proved of great value in refortifying the city from any future siege that the new sultan might bring upon them, but now d'Aubusson had a weapon against the Turks of greater value than the most solid of mortar or the most efficient cannon: the new sultan's disgruntled younger brother.

It was believed by many on the council that so long as the sultan's brother was a resident

BAJAZET I.

Bayezid was the son of Mehmed II who succeeded his father on the throne. He grew increasingly concerned that his brother, Cem, was a guest of the Hospitallers and signed a truce with the Order.
Jupiter Images

of the island and could assist the Hospitallers in taking action against Bayezid, that he would never himself take action on the island. However, not all were in favour of the Turkish prince's presence. Opposing viewpoints saw him as a liability rather than an asset because there was a high risk of Cem being assassinated and the efforts needed to guard against such an event were not worth the rewards. The final decision was to transport him, as he himself wished, to France, where he would be out of the reach of his older brother. However as preparations were being made to put the exiled Ottoman prince aboard one of the Order's ships, ambassadors from Constantinople arrived at Rhodes requesting a party of Hospitallers to return to the capital to negotiate a truce. As many in the council suspected and believed, Cem's presence at Rhodes in the company of the one standing army that had been able to drive off his father's advances had caused Bayezid concern about the future of his place on the throne. Bayezid's uneasiness at the proximity of his younger brother increased Cem's own uneasiness of the same and prompted him to push the matter of being transported to France. D'Aubusson granted the request, and on 1 September 1482, Cem set sail for Europe aboard a Hospitaller galley.

The following year Sultan Bayezid signed two treaties with the Hospitallers: the first was an agreement to pay an annual compensation of 10,000 ducats for the damages that had been caused during the siege of 1480, and the second was a larger annual payment of 35,000 ducats for Cem's maintenance while housed in France. Cem remained under the Hospitallers' direct protection until March of 1488 when he was transferred to the custody of Pope Innocent VIII. He had long wanted to get the Ottoman prince into his hands in the hopes that Cem could assist him with an expedition against Bayezid.

Although reluctant to make the transfer to the Pope, allegations were made against d'Aubusson and the Hospitallers that they had sold the Turk to the Holy See in return for some papal favours, but the favours, though granted, were hardly a bargaining chip and more likely a gift of appreciation for reluctantly doing as the Pope desired. Among the benefits was the merging of the inferior

Orders of the Holy Sepulchre and St Lazarus with that of St John, as well as a promise from the Pope never to interfere with commandery nominations, which was merely a return to the way things had been in the past. But the gifts were not the only ones the Pope had bestowed upon the Grand Master as three years earlier he had made d'Aubusson a cardinal in the Catholic Church, a position which in reality was below the rank he enjoyed as Master of the Hospitaller Order. Although the cardinalship allowed d'Aubusson some ecclesiastical privileges, the real motivation for granting the honour was that Pope Innocent wanted d'Aubusson's talents as a diplomat and political force. The cardinalship came with the secondary title of papal legate and with d'Aubusson carrying such a title, the Pope was ensured of having a talented diplomatic puppet to deal with the Ottoman court. However, Pope Innocent died before he could make proper use of either d'Aubusson or Cem in his designs for an eastern reconquest.

Life for Cem under the new Pope, Alexander VI, was quite different. He was placed in the Castle of St Angelo, effectively a prisoner, and deprived of the company of the Hospitallers whom Pope Innocent had allowed to live with him during his stay in Rome. He died three years later in 1495. Although both the Pope and the Hospitallers were accused of poisoning the Ottoman prince, it seems unlikely, certainly from the Hospitallers' standpoint. Alive, Cem had provided a bargaining chip that had generated a decade and a half of peace and prosperity for the island of Rhodes. Dead, he was of no value and his demise could offer the Order nothing except difficulties with their neighbours in Constantinople. Fortunately for d'Aubusson and his Hospitallers, Cem's death coincided with a period of deteriorating relationships between the Mamluks of Egypt and the Ottoman Empire. Notwithstanding teaming with the papal fleet for a few minor naval raids against the Turks in the northern Aegean, the remainder of d'Aubusson's reign as Grand Master was spent reinforcing the city walls for the attack that always seemed imminent. He died on 3 July 1503, nearly two decades before his beloved island would be lost to the Order for good.

CHAPTER 10
Siege of Rhodes 1522

The nineteen years between the death of d'Aubusson in 1503 and the second siege of Rhodes in 1522 saw the Hospitallers under the influence of four Grand Masters as their ever-larger ships steered through the harbour d'Aubusson's leadership had safeguarded nearly two decades earlier. During this period the Order expanded its naval prowess in the Aegean to include both the oared and lateen-sailed galleys that had served them well for the past three centuries, but also the heavier ocean-going ships and carracks that had been developed by the Portuguese in the fifteenth century.

Hospitaller successes at sea, particularly a victory over the combined efforts of the Ottomans and Mamluks at Laiazzo (Yumurtalik) in 1510, built upon the pedestal on which the Order had been placed following the Turkish defeat in 1480. This inflated opinion of the Hospitallers' situation belied the fact that, despite their seemingly remarkable ability to hold their own, Rhodes was but a small dot of Christendom surrounded by Islamic forces on all sides. The conflicts with the Turks and Mamluks were hostilities the Order could anticipate and prepare for. Harder to anticipate and counter were the conflicts within the Order born of ego, jealousy and revenge, seeds that were planted during the naval engagement at Laiazzo and that would bear sinister fruit many years later.

The Muslims had a good business trading spice in the East Indies, a trade that was being disturbed by Portuguese sailors disrupting Muslim ships in the Indian Ocean. To counter the situation, Sultan Bayezid made an alliance with the Mamluk Sultan Qānsūh al-Ghūrī to undertake the building of a fleet in the Red Sea to guard against further Portuguese incursions. Although many miles away from the proposed shipyards, Laiazzo which lay northeast of Cyprus, was a key port for the transhipment of timber from Asia Minor.

When word arrived on Rhodes that a Mamluk fleet under the direction of the sultan's nephew was en route from Egypt to Laiazzo, the Order's fleet was sent east to intercept it. As the Order was by this time operating both galleys and sailing ships, the vessels were commanded by two different men: the oared galleys by a Portuguese Hospitaller named Andrea d'Amaral and the sailing vessels by a French Hospitaller named Philippe Villiers de L'Isle Adam. The reason for two separate commanders was that the two types of ships operated differently, but moreover, were most effective in contrary weather conditions. The larger, heavy-masted sailing ships were at their best with the wind at full force, something that diminished the effectiveness of the slave-powered galleys, which were far more effective in calm weather, when they could pass in and out of the harbour with ease.

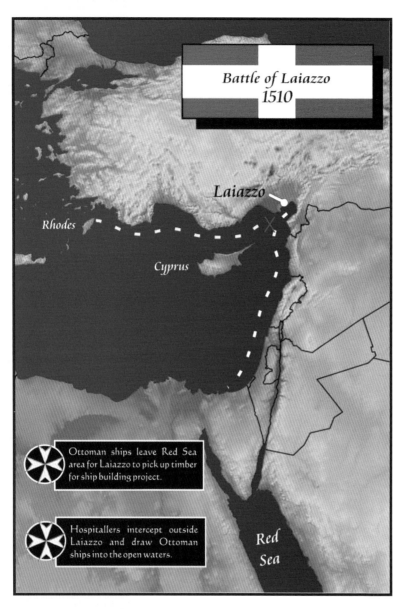

Battle of Laiazzo
1510

Laiazzo

Rhodes

Cyprus

Red Sea

Ottoman ships leave Red Sea area for Laiazzo to pick up timber for ship building project.

Hospitallers intercept outside Laiazzo and draw Ottoman ships into the open waters.

Base terrain:
*Bigstock/
Barbara Fordyce*

them in the port. It was here in the open waters of the Mediterranean that the Hospitallers' true naval superiority allowed them to capture fifteen Egyptian ships, eleven of which were large sailing vessels like those commanded by the hero of the day, L'Isle Adam. With the captured vessels sailing back to Rhodes with the Hospitaller fleet, all could look back to port and see the flames rising from the lumber that had once been destined for the Red Sea.

However, the freshly hewn timbers were not the only thing burning that day. D'Amaral felt slighted over decisions made during the battle and harboured bitter feelings for his French counterpart, feelings that would only fester and grow when years later it was L'Isle Adam, and not he, who was selected to be the Order's next Grand Master. When Fabrizio del Carretto died in 1521, the three candidates for succession included d'Amaral, who was then Chancellor of the Order, and the Grand Priors of England and France, Thomas Docwra and Philippe Villiers de L'Isle Adam. Although a contender in principle, d'Amaral's reputation as an arrogant man with a quick and haughty temper had earned him enough enemies that he really did not stand a chance of being promoted any further, certainly not to the highest post within the Order. This left Docwra and L'Isle Adam as the only possible options. Docwra was a career Hospitaller, having been admitted to the Order at the age of sixteen, spending his fist half decade as a novitiate. He had been one of the knights present during the first siege of Rhodes in 1480 and in the closing years of the century had been promoted as Prior of Ireland and then Captain of the Hospitallers' castle at Bodrum. By the turn of the century he had been further elevated to the post of Grand Prior of England. Although his diplomatic and military experience were in his favour, not to mention the size of his personal wealth, L'Isle Adam's support among the French led to his being selected as the Order's next Grand Master. Docwra, a legitimate contender for the office, was among the first to congratulate the new Grand Master on his return to Rhodes, as he had been in France during the election. However, d'Amaral's distaste for his rival's preferment was so great that he was unable to hide it and is alleged to have remarked that

When the fleet arrived in the Mediterranean the weather was calm. As such, d'Amaral wanted to move into the harbour where the Muslim ships were anchored and launch an immediate attack, something L'Isle Adam was staunchly opposed to: he felt it better to play upon the Mamluks' false sense of security that lay in their superior number. For L'Isle Adam, the best strategy was to stay put at the edge of the harbour, the fleet dangling like a piece of meat before a pack of hungry dogs. The strategy proved effective. The Mamluk ships weighed anchor and moved out to sea, away from the defensive mechanisms available to

L'Isle Adam would be the last Grand Master of Rhodes. It is entirely probable, as will be seen in due course, that the remark was ascribed to him apocryphally in light of the role he would play the following year.

L'Isle Adam was not the only new leader in the region. A year earlier the Ottoman Empire had installed a new sultan in the person of Suleiman, the only son of Sultan Selim, who had succeeded Bayezid in 1512. Like Mehmed II, the 26-year-old Suleiman envisioned himself as becoming the greatest ruler the Ottoman Empire ever known. But where Mehmed had failed, Suleiman would succeed, removing the crusaders from the island of Rhodes. Fresh from his conquest of Belgrade (something his father had advised him would be necessary for his sultanic success) Suleiman made his first overtures towards Rhodes by way of a letter of victory sent to L'Isle Adam shortly after he had taken the reins of the Hospitaller Order. Porter provides us with a translation of the letter, which apprised the new Grand Master of the sultan's military successes in the past year:

'Suleiman the sultan, by the grace of God, king of kings, sovereign of sovereigns, most high emperor of Byzantium and Trebizond, very powerful king of Persia, of Arabia, of Syria, and of Egypt, supreme Lord of Europe and of Asia, prince of Mecca and Aleppo, lord of Jerusalem and ruler of the universal sea, to Philippe Villiers de L'Isle Adam, Grand-Master of the island of Rhodes, greeting. I congratulate you upon your new dignity and upon your arrival within your territories. I trust that you will rule there prosperously and with even more glory than your predecessors. I also mean to cultivate your favour. Rejoice then with me as a very dear friend that, following in the footsteps of my father, who conquered Persia, Jerusalem, Arabia, and

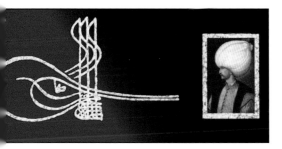

Egypt, I have captured that most powerful of fortresses, Belgrade, during the late autumn, after which, having offered battle to the Giaours [non-Muslims], which they had not the courage to accept, I took many other beautiful and well-fortified cities, and destroyed most of their inhabitants either by sword or fire, the remainder being reduced to slavery. Now, after sending my numerous and victorious army into their winter quarters, I myself have returned in triumph to my court at Constantinople.'

Philippe Villiers de L'Isle Adam
1521 - 1534

There could be no mistaking the intent of the sultan's letter, no matter how veiled the threat was. Suleiman had designs upon L'Isle Adam's island. Wasting no time in replying, the Grand Master sent his own message that was far from diplomatic and let the new head of the Ottoman Empire know that he not only understood the intent of his message, but that he was not without his own successes:

'Brother Philippe Villiers de L'Isle Adam, Grand Master of Rhodes, to Suleiman, sultan of the Turks, I have right well comprehended the meaning of your letter, which has been presented to me by your ambassador. Your propositions for a peace between us are as pleasing to me as they will be obnoxious to Cortoglu. This pirate, during my voyage from France, tried to capture me unawares, in which, when he failed, owing to my having passed into the Rhodian Sea by night, he endeavoured to plunder certain merchantmen that were being navigated by the Venetians; but scarcely had my fleet left their port than he had to fly and to abandon the plunder which he had seized from the Cretan merchants. Farewell.'

Although the sultan wrote to L'Isle Adam again requesting that a Hospitaller dignitary be sent to Constantinople, the Grand Master chose instead to send envoys to Europe seeking assistance against the inevitable attack, which could fall upon the island at any time. As was the case with his predecessor

Suleiman is shown in this Agostino Veneziano engraving created in 1535 wearing a four-tiered helmet, a head covering that exceeded the papal tiara by one level.

d'Aubusson's letters to the west, no ships were forthcoming from European ports, at least none dispatched by those who wore the royal crown. Both the French King Francis I and the Holy Roman Emperor Charles V were too preoccupied with their conflicts with one another to be of assistance, and England's Henry VIII was already viewing the Order's possessions with the same avarice that Philip IV had shown in the early fourteenth century. Even the Order's own houses were limited in the numbers of men they could send, leaving L'Isle Adam's only support in the coming conflict as those already on the island and the 500 Cretan archers who Anthony Bosio, a simple serving brother of the Order, was able to recruit from the neighbouring island.

But Bosio was successful in attracting one additional volunteer, a Venetian engineer named Gabriel Tadini Martinigo, who was so impressed with the Hospitallers' zeal that he solicited the Grand Master to join the Order. Martinigo was admitted and immediately placed in charge of the city's fortifications. Under Matinigo's expertise a number of improvements were made to strengthen the fortress's defensive and offensive capabilities: the city's gates were covered with demi-lunes, ironically crescent-shaped outworks that would allow the Hospitallers to sweep their cannon in an arc to fire upon any enemies who were running along the fortifications; casements were also added to the fortress's bastions for similar reasons. Inside the city, Martinigo ordered the erection of barricades through the city streets so that should the ramparts be breached, the assault upon the city could be protracted. This was a similar concept to the maze-like corridors at Krak des Chevaliers which the Order had called home until it was captured by the Mamluk Sultan Baibars in 1271.

On 14 June 1522, L'Isle Adam received word that Martinigo's preparations were about to be put to the test, for the sultan had sent another letter. This time, however, the missive was not merely a thinly veiled threat. It was direct and to the point: surrender was the only option. Again Porter provides us with a translation of the letter:

'The sultan Suleiman, to Villiers de L'Isle Adam, Grand Master of Rhodes, to his knights and to the people at large. Your monstrous injuries against my most afflicted people have aroused my pity and indignation. I command you, therefore, instantly to surrender the island and fortress of Rhodes, and I give you my gracious permission to depart in safety with the most precious of your effects, or if you desire to remain under my government I shall not require of you any tribute, or do aught in diminution of your liberties or against your religion. If you are wise you will prefer friendship and peace to a cruel war. Since, if you are conquered, you will have to undergo all such miseries as are usually inflicted by those that are victorious, from which you will not be protected, either by your own forces, or by external aid, or by the strength of your fortifications, which I will overthrow to their foundations. If, therefore, you prefer my friendship to war there shall be neither fraud nor stratagem used against you. I swear this by the God of heaven, the Creator of the earth, by the four Evangelists, by the 4,000 prophets who have descended from heaven, chief amongst whom stands Mohammed, most worthy to be worshipped, by the shades of my grandfather and father, and by my own sacred, august, and imperial head.'

L'Isle Adam read the letter to the council the day it was received, but there was to be no response save that issued from Hospitaller cannon. Whether surrendered or captured, Suleiman wanted the island. Mustapha Pasha had assembled his troops and Cortoglu had been appointed admiral of the Ottoman fleet. For the Hospitallers at Rhodes, it was merely a matter of waiting for the appearance of Turkish sails coming over the horizon.

Vertot, in his history of the Order, tells us that Suleiman sent a force 200,000 strong, made up of 140,000 men-at-arms, supported

Kos Castle withstood an Ottoman invasion during the second siege of Rhodes in 1522.
Bigstock/Olga Lipatova

by an additional 60,000 peasants from recently captured territory. Although this number was repeated by many other European historians, it is almost certainly an exaggerated figure. A letter written by the English Hospitaller Sir Nicholas Roberts to the Earl of Surrey shortly after the loss of Rhodes tells us that the sultan sent 15,000 men by sea and another 100,000 fighting men by land. These soldiers were then transported in groups from Marmarice to Rhodes. Additionally, Roberts claims that an additional '50,000 labourers with spades and pikes' were sent to assist in the operation, but even Roberts' numbers seem larger than probable. The Turkish account of Ahmed Hafiz gives a number of 65,000 men made up of 25,000 infantry and 40,000 rowing the galleys to bring them to the island. But this number only represents the initial landing force and not the reinforcements who arrived later with the sultan. Given that this later party was said to be 100,000 strong, Hafiz's numbers are in harmony with Roberts. But Christian and Muslim accounts of the battle place a different figure on the size and breakdown of the Ottoman fleet. Hafiz gives a figure of 700 vessels of which 500 were galleys, while Christian accounts number the fleet at 400 vessels, of which only 100 were galleys.

What is more certain, however, is that the strength of L'Isle Adam's garrison was about 4,500 men-at-arms including the 500 Cretan archers Bosio had recruited to the cause. These men combined with the 600 knights of the Order gave the Hospitallers a force of a little more than 5,000 men plus the Rhodians themselves. Regardless of the true size of the Turkish forces, it is certain that the Hospitallers were vastly outnumbered; the degree to which this was so is unimportant to the final result.

The assault in the Dodecanese began in late June with a small advance detachment marauding its way down the Aegean in the same way that Saladin had worked his way down the Palestinian coast in 1187 before turning inland to take Jerusalem. Pouring out onto the smaller of the islands the Turks found no Hospitaller steel or shot to block their path, and had free rein to wreak as much destruction as they cared to. However, their disembarkation on Lango (Kos) delivered them an entirely different result. Here the Hospitaller fortress was still maintained and competently commanded by the French knight Prejan de Bidoux who led his men in a rush counterattack at the Turks as they came ashore, driving them back onboard as quickly as they had disembarked. Being repulsed on

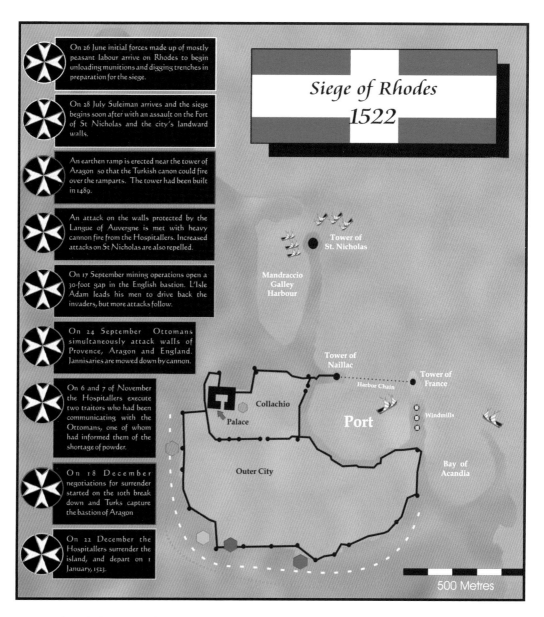

On 26 June initial forces made up of mostly peasant labour arrive on Rhodes to begin unloading munitions and digging trenches in preparation for the siege.

On 28 July Suleiman arrives and the siege begins soon after with an assault on the Fort of St Nicholas and the city's landward walls.

An earthen ramp is erected near the tower of Aragon so that the Turkish canon could fire over the ramparts. The tower had been built in 1489.

An attack on the walls protected by the Langue of Auvergne is met with heavy cannon fire from the Hospitallers. Increased attacks on St Nicholas are also repelled.

On 17 September mining operations open a 30-foot gap in the English bastion. L'Isle Adam leads his men to drive back the invaders, but more attacks follow.

On 24 September Ottomans simultaneously attack walls of Provence, Aragon and England. Jannisaries are mowed down by cannon.

On 6 and 7 of November the Hospitallers execute two traitors who had been communicating with the Ottomans, one of whom had informed them of the shortage of powder.

On 18 December negotiations for surrender started on the 10th break down and Turks capture the bastion of Aragon.

On 22 December the Hospitallers surrender the island, and depart on 1 January, 1523.

Siege of Rhodes
1522

Tower of St. Nicholas

Mandraccio Galley Harbour

Tower of Naillac

Tower of France

Harbor Chain

Collachio

Palace

Port

Windmills

Outer City

Bay of Acandia

500 Metres

Lango the Turks pressed on towards their main destination, the island of Rhodes.

As the Turkish sails fluttered into view on the morning of 26 June 1522, L'Isle Adam and his knights were completing religious ceremonies in connection with the Feast of St John the Baptist, a ceremony that had taken on an even greater importance on the precipice of battle. The annual observance concluded, the Grand Master ordered his men to their posts as the city's gates were closed and barred, its bridges raised and secured, and everywhere the standards and banners of the Order and its Langues were hoisted high above the ramparts and bastions in proud contrast to those of the Turks advancing towards them by sea. As the Master of the Order led his guards, accompanied by three knights and all on horseback, he could see that not a soul had taken refuge in their homes. Rather, men, women and children alike had stationed themselves in every crack where the advancing Turks could be seen. For some, the present conflict had been the first they had experienced; for others more advanced in years the sails of the Ottoman Empire that grew ever larger on the blue waters were a reminder of a similar scene forty-two years earlier when the Order had been able to repel the Turks. Over the past four decades the older Rhodians had seen the fortifications of their city constantly strengthened and many had broken their backs hauling materials to prepare for the assault that the knights felt was always imminent. The wise among the veterans knew that, although the Rhodes they now lived in was far stronger defensively and offensively than that of 1480, the Turks had not been negligent in strengthening their own martial prowess. News of Suleiman's victories in Belgrade had shown that they too had advanced. There simply was no guarantee that the Hospitallers would be able to repel another invasion.

The advance force sailed past the Akra Milos, past the Fortress of St Nicholas on the mole of the Mandraccio harbour where the Order's galleys and ships were docked, and past the city's southeasternmost point which bordered the Bay of Acandia. The small fleet continued down the Rhodian coast to Kallithea Bay where the disembarkation and initial preparations for the siege took place over several days, unhindered by the Hospitallers. De Bidoux may have been able to repel the Turks on Lango by storming the beach, but L'Isle Adam could not suffer the inevitable casualties a full-on land battle would cause, for he simply did not have the men to spare. This did not prevent his men from launching small sorties from the city to harass the Wallachian peasants Mustapha Pasha had brought to Rhodes to dig trenches in preparation for the siege. Unprotected and unarmed, the Turks' labourers were whittled down by Hospitaller steel with each run.

According to the Christian accounts of the battle, the deaths of the common workers led to dissatisfaction throughout the whole of the advance force, leading to a message being sent to Constantinople apprising Suleiman of the low state of morale in the camp. From the beginning the sultan had planned to take part in the siege himself, believing, as many did, that the main reason for the failure in 1480 was that Sultan Mehmed II had not been on the front lines to provide his leadership. Turkish accounts suggest that the initial force consisted only of the peasant labourers and what troops would normally travel aboard the galleys. David Nicolle in his book *Knights*

Hospitaller 1306 – 1565 indicates that Venetian galleys of the fourteenth century carried up to fifty swordsmen and another twenty archers. Given that these figures are likely to have been similar among the Turkish vessels, even into the next century, it would give a total of seventy troops per ship. With twenty ships in the initial landing force, that would make for roughly 2,100 soldiers. In the Turkish accounts Suleiman was not summoned early, but led the land forces to Marmarice in Asia Minor and then travelled to Rhodes by ship.

Regardless of which account of the sultan's arrival is true, both sources agree that he arrived on 28 July 1522 accompanied by the uniquely intimidating music of the Janissary troops which always preceded them into battle, a sure sign that the siege was about to begin. The Ottomans wasted no time in attacking the Fortress of St Nicholas on the seaward side or spreading their forces out along the city's landside walls from one end to the other. The Muslims had assembled an impressive train of artillery including six brass guns with a calibre circumference of 10 inches, another fifteen of 29 inches and two others of almost 32 inches. Additionally the Ottoman arsenal consisted of twelve basilisks with a calibre circumference of almost two feet and fifteen double cannon for throwing iron shot. Their combined power was intended to reduce the Hospitallers' Rhodian walls to rubble. Under the cannon's roar, the Turks worked diligently to erect an earthen ramp facing the Tower of Spain so that their cannon could be taken to the top of the walls to fire directly into the city. This tower was located at the midpoint of the city's crescent-shaped landside walls and was constructed in 1489 as part of d'Aubusson's strengthening of the city fortress after the first siege.

However, the Turks were not the only ones trying to make use of the city's towers. The Hospitallers stationed themselves in the bell tower next to St John's Church, from which point they were able to overlook the Turkish camp in all directions and follow their progress through the trenches, something they had been deprived of when L'Isle Adam suspended the sorties against the labourers. One evening a group of Rhodian sailors dressed as Turks were sent by sea into the enemy camp where,

Above: **The bastions, ramparts and towers proved difficult to breach during the siege of 1522, but repeated bombardment from Turkish cannon wore down the Hospitallers' ability to resist.**
*Bigstock/
Fernando Barozza*

Right: **The Palace of the Grand Master was built by the Hospitallers in the fourteenth century. Here is shown the entrance to the current palace that was rebuilt in the twentieth century, the original structure having been damaged in 1856.**
*Bigstock/
Frank Kebschull*

great value to L'Isle Adam. Not only did the Turks reveal the order of troops from the Bay of Acandia to the Amboise Gate, but that Sultan Suleiman had based his headquarters on St Stephen's Hill. Of greater importance was the information on the strength and number of the Ottoman artillery. Soon after the revelations, the St John's bell tower was destroyed by the Turks who had discovered that the value of its high altitude was not being wasted by L'Isle Adam and his men.

The sultan also realised that just as the elevated height of the tower had helped the Hospitallers, the low elevation of his trenches was hindering his own progress. He ordered another two ramps of earth to be built by his peasant labour force. The first was to be constructed against the Bastion of Italy; the other was to be built near the St George Gate between the Auvergne and German posts. However, these were not undefended posts but heavily armed outposts with their own cannon, more than capable of raining down on the Turkish camp. The scurrying of Wallachian peasants like so many ants below the walls told the Hospitallers that their movements must be important to the sultan's plans, which led to the Hospitallers moving every cannon they could spare to the location. Despite the constant roar of the Hospitallers' cannon and

through their ability to speak the language, they succeeded in enticing two Muslims to return to their boat. The Turks were taken into the city to the bell tower where Martinigo proceeded to interrogate them as to just whose troops were stationed where. Procuring the answers was not difficult. Martinigo told them that should they fail to answer or hesitate too long, the two Hospitaller knights who stood by his side would be only too happy to toss them out the window to the streets below. They quickly disclosed information that was of

the destructive effect it had on the unprotected peasants, their superior number allowed the ramps to scale to the summit of the city's parapets where the Turks were able to return fire into the city itself.

Although the Turks had succeeded in gaining a front in their landside strategy, an assault from the sea on the Fortress of St Nicholas and a separate landside assault against the Auvergne-protected walls on the city's western side proved ineffective due to Martinigo's expertise in directing Hospitaller artillery against them. Despite the successes of the Order's guns in driving off the attackers on most fronts, by the end of August, the walls were beginning to show damage from the constant pummelling delivered by the Turks' cannon. Wherever there was a danger of a breach, the Order worked hard digging interior trenches to support the retrenchments necessary to hold the walls together.

Realising that the aerial assault of his powerful projectiles were having a limited effect in bringing down the walls, Suleiman switched gears to methods that had worked well for hundreds of years and ordered the city's walls to be mined. On 17 September, the Turks exploded a mine under the English Bastion which opened a 30-foot gap in the wall. Although the Turks immediately poured through the breach and succeeded in planting their standard on the ramparts, L'Isle Adam, who had been in a nearby church and was roused by the explosion, left his devotions, along with his bodyguards, and joined his heavily armoured English knights in repelling the Turks. But Mustapha Pasha, seeing the first wave retreating from the breach, drew his scimitar and cut down those who led the retreat. The pasha rallied the remainder and led a second wave of attackers who, perhaps fearing the pasha's scimitar more than the Hospitallers' pikes and battle axes, carried on the battle against the Christians for two hours, until, their energies spent trying to regain entry through the breach, they plodded over the corpses of their co-religionists back to the trenches from whence they came. Unfortunately for the Hospitallers, the turcopolier John Buck was killed during the battle.

Similar scenes were played out through the month of September as the vastly outnumbered Hospitallers held out against the Turkish cannon and mining operations with their own cannon and countermining efforts. The Hospitallers did have a valuable asset in this endeavour, for Martinigo was not only adept at showing the Hospitallers how to place and angle their cannon for the best results,

The Grand Master's palace from behind the city's walls.
Bigstock/ Fernando Barozza

he also had an impressive bag of tools to aid in countermining. Among them was a new technique involving a diaphragm of parchment drawn tight like a drumhead which responded to the pick and shovel of the peasants by triggering bells in the direction of the Turks' mining operations. On 24 September, it was decided by the Ottomans to simultaneously attack the posts of Italy, Provence, Aragon and England, but even this proved unsuccessful. Despite a short-term foothold on the Bastion of Aragon during which the Turkish flag was planted, the Hospitallers quickly mowed down the Janissaries with their cannon fire and repelled the Turks who were ready to follow them, something their leader Sultan Suleiman had been able to witness first-hand from the pinnacle of the scaffold he had erected for the purpose of watching over his victory.

Enraged at the failure of his superior numbers, Suleiman ordered the death of his two generals, Mustapha and Pir Mehmed, the latter of whom had lobbied for the assault on all sides. However, their lives were spared when the other Turkish leaders were able to convince the sultan that it was not in the best interest of the campaign. Instead of taking their lives, Suleiman banished them from the camp and sent them home, but still wishing to appease his rage, he had his admiral, Cortoglu, whipped on the poop deck of his own ship for having neglected to assist the land forces with a naval diversion. He was subsequently expelled from the fleet.

While the sultan was admonishing his commanding officers, L'Isle Adam learned that his store of gunpowder was rapidly diminishing and that the present rate of consumption would leave the magazines empty within a month. This was problematic not only for their defences against the Turks, but because prior to the siege the Grand Master had been assured by three of his men, including the Grand Chancellor Andrea d'Amaral, that there was sufficient gunpowder to withstand a year-long siege. L'Isle Adam assigned two of his knights and a number of townspeople to begin manufacturing more using the existing stores of saltpetre within the city. Despite the assurances of a fresh supply of gunpowder, it became necessary to conserve what little remained, a situation that did little to help the Hospitaller cause. Their efforts

were further hindered when Martinigo was shot in the head. Although the wound was not fatal, it hospitalised him for several weeks, during which time the Order was deprived of his expertise in countermining operations. This lack of ammunition and advice allowed the Turks to undermine the fortress at a greater rate than ever before.

However, the Turkish peasant sappers were not the only ones engaged in undermining the city. A Jewish doctor whose name has been lost to history was caught firing a message into the Turkish lines and, under torture, he confessed to telling the Turks about the scarcity of gunpowder. The execution of the doctor for treason opened the city, now feeling the effects of four months of siege, and its defenders, now greatly reduced in number to about half, to all sorts of suspicions and fears that those around them may also be traitors, even the armoured knights themselves. The fears of the worst proved to be true when a Spanish knight named Blaise Diaz was arrested on the Bastion of Auvergne, freshly fired bow in hand. Diaz, who had been seen more than once on the bastion with his bow, was brought before L'Isle Adam. Like Master George and the Jewish doctor, Diaz was put to torture to assist with the interrogation, during which he confessed that he had indeed fired valuable information into the enemy camp, but that it had been at the insistence of his master, the Grand Chancellor Andrea D'Amaral, the Prior of Castile.

D'Amaral, who had been in competition for the leadership of the Order in 1521, was arrested and brought before his old rival L'Isle Adam, where he was confronted by his accuser Diaz, who repeated to his master's face what he had confessed to the Grand Master under torture. The Spaniard was not the only one to levy accusations against the Grand Chancellor; a Greek priest said he too had seen Diaz and d'Amaral at that location in the past, where the former had launched a letter-laden arrow into enemy lines. To support d'Amaral's alleged treachery the judges were reminded that upon L'Isle Adam's election, d'Amaral had said that the newly elected Grand Master would be the island's last. D'Amaral was put to torture, but refused to confirm the lies just to save himself from pain. His resistance was futile and both he and his underling were put to death. Diaz was publicly hanged, drawn and quartered on 6 November. D'Amaral's execution was less degrading due to his rank. On 7 November, the Grand Chancellor was taken to the Church of St John and stripped of his habit; the following day he was stripped of his head. Although Diaz's guilt was certain, that of d'Amaral is less definite, something that even the contemporary chronicles were at odds about. But d'Amaral's old rivalry with the Grand Master, his unpopularity due to his character and temper, and the fact that he had underestimated or over-reported the stores of gunpowder, combined with the all-too-convenient accusations of Diaz and the priest, led to his demise.

However, although the Hospitallers may have doubted their Master, they certainly could be in no doubt whatsoever about Sultan Suleiman's willingness to keep up the siege on the city. More than four months had passed and he remained on the outside of the walls. In fact, had it not been for the assurances of a deserter that the city was on the verge of collapse, Suleiman may well have done as Mehmed II had in 1480 and set sail for other opportunities. Although the assault that followed under the direction of Achmet Pasha, who had been given command of the troops, gained no victory, it was certain that the city's walls were becoming weaker, its ramparts harder to defend, and its defenders fewer in number, their ability to resist slowly being worn down by a lack of food and ammunition. This situation was recounted in a letter from Sir Nicholas Roberts, an English Hospitaller who was present at the battle, to the Earl of Surrey and has been recorded in the histories of both Whitworth Porter and John Taafe. The ellipses indicate places where the ancient document has been damaged by time. Writes Roberts:

'...and at such tyme as we saw yt theyr come
no succours, nor no succours reddy to come,
and considering that the most of our men

The city of Rhodes and its fortifications are shown in this old illustration. Between the sieges of 1480 and 1522, the Hospitallers spent considerable time increasing the strength of their ramparts and towers.

were slain, we had no powther nor ... manner
of munycone, nor vitalles, but all on by brede
and water, we wer as men desperat ...
determined to dye upon them in the felde,
rather than be put upon the stakes...'

Achmet Pasha approached the sultan with the suggestion that instead of firing cannon balls over the ramparts, perhaps it was time to fire a request for surrender instead. Suleiman conceded to the wisdom of the idea, but was unwilling to let it appear that the suggestion had come directly from him. Instead, a Genoese by the name of Monilio was given the task of negotiating with the Hospitallers. Accordingly, letters requesting the town to capitulate were fired into the city, time was allowed to pass in order for the content of the letters to gain its full effect, and then Monilio was sent to the Bastion of Auvergne looking to talk not to the Grand Master but to one of Rhodes' leading citizens, Matteo de Via. The request was at once denied, but Monilio pushed his agenda with those he was able to communicate with, the armoured knights who guarded the bastion, who assured the messenger that the Knights of Rhodes' only negotiations with the Muslims would be at the point of the sword.

Two days later the messenger returned to the city gates with a letter for L'Isle Adam from Suleiman himself, which the Grand Master refused to accept. Monilio informed L'Isle Adam that dragging the matter on any further would only cause the Turks to relight their cannon. The threat, no matter how sincere or certain, did not concern the Grand Master; he was willing and prepared to be buried beneath the ruins of Rhodes should it come to that. It is doubtless that most of his knights would have been willing to suffer the same fate, rather than let their beloved island become an Aegean port for the Ottoman Empire, but the Hospitallers were not the only residents of the city or island, and the other residents were willing to hear what the sultan was offering.

As Roberts wrote in his letter, Suleiman was prepared to exchange the citizenry's lives and goods for possession of the town, something the Rhodians were more than prepared to accept. However, it was not as acceptable to L'Isle Adam, and Roberts wrote: 'The lord master hering the opinion of the hole commonalty resolved to take that partido, fell downe allmost ded, and what time he recoveryd himsel in sort, he seeing them contenue in the same, at last consented to the same.'

It had been a long and drawn-out battle during which, according to Roberts, 703 Hospitallers had been killed in the twenty-two battles that had been fought in five different parts of the town. Despite his personal objections to surrendering, L'Isle Adam held a council to discuss the matter further, calling on Martinigo and the Prior of St Gilles to give him their assessment of the condition of the town's fortifications. Both men gave their honest and grim opinion: the city was no longer tenable because they no longer had sufficient manpower left to move the cannon from place to place, let alone keep repairing damaged walls. The debate that followed was passionate, with many men siding with their Grand Master and his willingness to fight to the death if need be. However, a greater number of Rhodians were simply not prepared to go down with the fortress after having stood by the Hospitallers for so many months. Surely they would fare better if surrender could be negotiated than they would once the

Turks had scaled the ramparts after the last Hospitaller was dead? The Rhodians won out.

On 10 December, two white flags rose above a church and a windmill, signalling the Order's willingness to talk. Martinigo and the Prior of St Gilles met with two Turkish representatives and the group discussed the terms of surrender. If the Grand Master surrendered the town immediately, he, his knights and those citizens who wished to leave could do so, taking with them all their belongings. Those who wished to remain on the island as citizens of the Ottoman Empire could do so with the full assurance that they could continue to exercise their religion unhindered and that they would be free of tithes for a period of five years. However, while the treaty was being negotiated an unexplained conflict occurred between some Hospitallers and a contingent of Turks, which saw several of the latter killed. The result was the immediate end of the truce and the immediate reinstatement of the previous assault on the town, and by 18 December, the Turks had succeeded in gaining control of the Spanish bastion. The raising of Turkish standards on the walls aroused panic among the citizens, causing L'Isle Adam to fear that if he did not act immediately, he may have his own citizens turning on his men. New negotiators were sent to the sultan's camp with full permission to surrender the city on whatever terms they could secure. The sultan offered the same terms that had been previously agreed to and the Grand Master's envoy was only too happy to accept them. The knights were free to leave in their own galleys, taking with them all their property, including their sacred relics, and they were given twelve days to do so. To accommodate the transfer of ownership, the Turkish army was to withdraw from the town, while a hand-picked group of Janissaries would take possession of the city on the sultan's behalf. Not only would the Hospitallers give up Rhodes, but also the dependant islands, as well as the castle of St Peter at Bodrum on the mainland. To ensure that the terms of the treaty were upheld, twenty-five knights and twenty-five Rhodians were held as hostages until the transfer was completed. For the first time in more than two centuries, the Hospitaller ships sailing across the Aegean were doing so without a home port to return to.

CHAPTER 11

Knights Without a Home

A Hospitaller knight circa 1400-1450 is shown in this original image by David Naughton Shires after a depiction of knights of the era found in the Grand Master's Palace at Rhodes. The Hospitallers were presented the islands of Malta, Gozo and Comino in 1530 by the Holy Roman Emperor Charles V. Although armour had evolved by this time, the Hospitallers would have been a mixture of older and newer units.
David Naughton Shires

L'Isle Adam's first port of call for his homeless Hospitallers was the dock at Chania on the northwest coast of Crete, then known as Candia. Word had been sent to the garrisons stationed at Lango and St Peter's Castle at Bodrum on the Turkish mainland to withdraw from their posts and set sail for Chania. It was here that the reunited Hospitaller survivors would take to shore for food and water and to tend to their sick and wounded, before setting off for Messina on the eastern tip of Sicily.

The Hospitallers left Rhodes with as many of their ships that were still seaworthy after nearly six months of battle. Among them was the Order's great carrack, the *Santa Maria*, commanded by an English Hospitaller named William Weston. The *Santa Maria* was originally called the *Mogarbina* and had been part of the fleet of the Mamluk Sultan of Egypt until it was captured by the Hospitallers along with several others near Kos in 1507, three years before the Order's great victory over the combined Mamluk-Ottoman fleet at Laiazzo. Rechristened the *Santa Maria* after its capture, the great carrack would continue to fly the white-crossed banner of the Order for many years after the Hospitallers had found a new home for themselves.

As the Hospitallers made their way towards Italy in the winter of 1523, it was not the traditional red and white banner of the Hospitallers that flew from L'Isle Adam's galley, but a banner depicting a weeping Virgin Mary holding a dead Jesus in her arms. The image was surrounded by the Latin motto *Afflictis tu spes unica rebus* or 'in all which afflicts us thou art our only hope'. The Grand Master's selection of banners represented two of his thoughts at the time: the great loss the Order and Christendom had suffered through the sacrifice of Rhodes, and the sense of abandonment L'Isle Adam undoubtedly felt by the lack of support from Christendom in defending the island in the first place.

As William Weston, who had been made turcopolier at Crete, replaced John Buck who was killed at Rhodes, led the *Santa Maria* and the Hospitaller fleet – including L'Isle Adam's galley of sorrows – towards the Ionian Sea, an even larger and more modern carrack was being built for the Order at Nice: a new state-of-the-art, metal-clad warship. However, it was completed too late to be of any service in the struggles that the Order had endured, but would go on to become the most powerful fighting ship in the Mediterranean.

The theological world that the Hospitallers were now sailing towards had changed considerably since the knights had taken possession of Rhodes more than two centuries earlier, and those changes would affect the Hospitallers as greatly as the technologies present in their two great ships. Five years before the Hospitallers surrendered their island, a German theologian named Martin

Map showing the Hospitallers' route during their period of exile between 1522 and 1530 and their theatre of operation after that time.
Author's diagram/ Base Map
Bigstock/ Barbara Fordyce

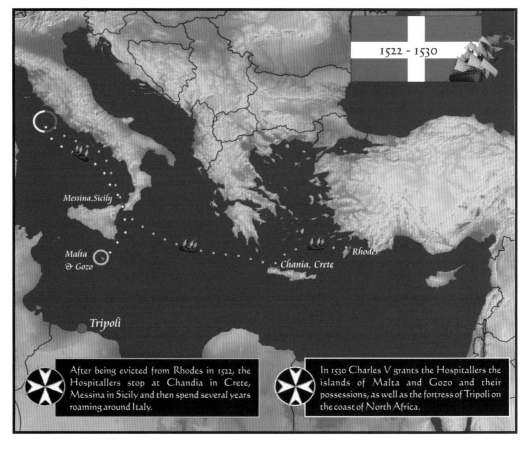

1522 - 1530

Messina, Sicily

Malta & Gozo

Chania, Crete

Rhodes

Tripoli

After being evicted from Rhodes in 1522, the Hospitallers stop at Chandia in Crete, Messina in Sicily and then spend several years roaming around Italy.

In 1530 Charles V grants the Hospitallers the islands of Malta and Gozo and their possessions, as well as the fortress of Tripoli on the coast of North Africa.

Below: **The German theologian Martin Luther is shown here in this monument in front of the Frauenkirche in Dresden. Luther began challenging Catholic beliefs and traditions with his Ninety-Five Theses on the Power and Efficacy of Indulgences.**
Bigstock/Uwe Bumann

Luther had begun challenging Catholic beliefs and traditions with his *Ninety-Five Theses on the Power and Efficacy of Indulgences*, which he nailed to the door of the Castle Church in Wittenberg, Germany, on All Saints' Eve in 1517. Luther's central complaint against the Catholic Church involved the selling of indulgences as a means of getting into heaven. While Catholicism held that man could avoid punishment for his sins through good works, particularly good works that involved the donation of money to the Church, Luther argued that only God had the power to forgive sin.

Luther's refusal in 1521 to retract his writings, which had been ordered by Pope Leo X and the Holy Roman Emperor Charles V, resulted in his being excommunicated by the Pope and regarded a criminal of the state by the emperor. Not only was Luther excommunicated, but any place where he resided fell under a local interdict, which meant that the sacraments of the Church, including the burial rite, would not be granted. A few months after his excommunication, Luther's writings were banned by the Church altogether, and he was taken prisoner for a time in the same city into which he had first released his criticisms of Catholic theology. The Catholic response did little to stop him from continuing his work. Luther translated the New Testament from Latin to German and continued to pen his attacks on the Church, all of which were published in pamphlet form, thanks to the widespread use of the printing press.

By the time the Hospitallers landed at Messina in the spring of 1523, Luther's writings were stirring up reformers in Germany to the point of revolt and war. While the Hospitallers were still clinging to the power of the medieval relics that they had brought with them from Rhodes – the mummified right hand of St John the Baptist, fragments of the True Cross, a thorn from the Crown of Thorns, the body of St Euphemia and the icon of Our Lady of Philerimos – Christianity was beginning to reach out for new ideas about faith. In many regards the Hospitallers were as much an anachronism as the relics of their Holy Religion: warriors loyal to a Church that no longer wielded the power it once did, and an army of men loyal to the medieval idea of crusading, a cause that once united entire nations towards a common enemy, but had lost most of its appeal by the middle of the Renaissance. Granted, there was still an

ideological war between Christendom and Islam, but the Ottoman Empire's greatest threat to Europe was the further capture of territory rather than the danger of gaining converts. The Order's defeat of the Mamluk fleet in 1510 at Laiazzo had destroyed the relationship between the Hospitallers and the Mamluks, and the latter's subsequent defeat by the Ottomans in 1517 ended the possibility of any future alliance with the Egyptian Muslims.

The Muslims were not the only ones who had been at war with one another. By 1523, the Habsburg-Valois wars had been under way in Italy for a couple of years, having reignited

in 1521 from ill feelings caused by the election of Charles V as Holy Roman Emperor over Francis I of France, who, along with Henry VIII of England, had been a contender for the honour. The war, started when France invaded Navarre in the autumn of 1521, ultimately pitted France and Venice against the combined imperial forces of Charles V, Spain, England and the Papal States. The battles would continue in Italy, France and Spain with shifting allegiances between the various European powers throughout L'Isle Adam's remaining years as Grand Master, and it is a testament to his leadership abilities that he was able to hold together and lead to a new home an Order that comprised members from countries who were now at war with one another. Until that time the Hospitallers would make stops at Messina, Cumae, Cita Vecchia, Viterbo, Cornetto, Villefranche and finally Nice, before settling on their new island home of Malta.

L'Isle Adam had requested an audience with Leo X's successor, Pope Adrian VI, to discuss where that home would be, soon after dropping anchor at the papal naval base of Cita Vecchia. Adrian delayed the meeting, instructing L'Isle Adam to sit tight in port until further notice. The delay had nothing to do with not knowing where to establish the Hospitallers next; there had been talk of Majorca, Malta, Crete or even Elba, closer to Rome. Rather, Adrian's stalling concerned the ongoing struggles between his alliance with Henry VIII and Charles V against Francis I. It was not until 1 September that Adrian held an audience with the Hospitaller Grand Master, by which time the Pope was on his deathbed. Outside of proclaiming the Grand Master an Athlete of Christ and a Defender of the Faith, the meeting produced little harvest for the Order. Pope Adrian died two weeks later on 14 September and L'Isle Adam was appointed guardian over the conclave that elected Adrian's successor, Pope Clement VII.

The Hospitallers had a kindred spirit in Clement. Born Giulio de Medici in 1478, Clement had spent part of his 45 years of life as a member of the Order.

Pope Leo X is shown with Cardinals Giulio de Medici and Luigi de Rossi in this Raphael painting. Leo excommunicated Martin Luther for challenging the church.

Holy Roman Emperor and King of Spain Charles V (left) fought with Francis I of France (right) throughout the 1520s, putting further strain on the Hospitallers whose Order consisted of men from both nations.
Jupiter Images

Not only had de Medici been a Hospitaller, he had gone on to serve the Order as Prior of Capua. However, being the cousin of Giovanni de Medici, better known as Pope Leo X, Clement had been made a cardinal and became the right-hand man to his cousin, influencing papal policy throughout Leo's term. But when Clement assumed the throne of St Peter a decade later, the strongest parts of Christendom were at war with one another, and Clement's tendency towards irresolute decision making would ultimately put him at odds with the Holy Roman Emperor.

However, in 1523 when the Hospitallers were still looking for a home and Clement was still on good terms with the man most able to help them, the Pope petitioned the emperor to offer his aid to the homeless knights. Charles responded to the request in 1524 by offering the Hospitallers the islands of Malta and Gozo, both of which were and had been part of the Kingdom of Sicily for centuries. The offer was certainly of benefit to Charles who would have a well-trained and well-armed military force to act as a barrier between the advancing Ottoman Empire and his own territorial interests in the Mediterranean. This benefit was further ensured by the emperor's two conditions attached to the offer. In addition to Malta and Gozo, the Hospitallers would become responsible for garrisoning the city of Tripoli on the North African coast, and the Order would offer its complete fealty to the emperor. Taking on the responsibility of Tripoli was problematic in itself because, being an isolated outpost surrounded by Muslim enemies, it would occupy more of the Hospitallers' resources than they could afford, but the greater obstacle to the offer was the oath of allegiance to Charles V, which would put the Order at odds with the sovereigns of the other nations in which it held priories and from which it drew members. Given that some of those lands were at war with one another, the acceptance of the condition could only strain matters further.

For the next three years the Hospitallers continued to base the headquarters of their weakening Order at Viterbo, 100 kilometres north of Rome, during which time the Order faced a greater threat from the expansion of the Lutheran Reformation than it did the expansion of the Ottoman Empire. Hospitaller properties were being lost throughout Christendom, if not to the Protestant Reformation in England and Scandinavia, then to raids by Anabaptists and even Catholics in other countries. In Germany, where Lutheranism had begun while the Hospitallers were still fighting for Rhodes, some of the Order's priests became Lutheran and converted many of the Order's knights to their new religion. With the continued and growing strife between Spain and France, and the Pope's desire to make the Hospitallers little more than an extension of his papal guard, it is little wonder that L'Isle Adam had not given up on the idea of reconquering Rhodes, if only to be back where the Order's enemies were a little more clearly defined. But the falling revenues and recruitment numbers of the Order, combined with improbability of assistance from warring nations, ensured that if the Hospitallers were to plant their feet on firm ground, it would not again be found in the eastern Aegean. Despite the unfavourable conditions attached to the offer, L'Isle Adam sent a commission of eight Hospitallers, one from each of the Order's eight Langues, to investigate the feasibility of accepting Charles's offer of Malta and Gozo.

As the Hospitallers contemplated expanding their territory with Malta, a Spanish-imperial army was battling troops under the command of Francis I at Pavia in Northern Italy. Four hours after the battle commenced on the morning of 24 February 1525, the French had suffered another defeat and their king was in chains, a prisoner of the Holy Roman Emperor. Francis remained Charles's prisoner in Madrid for more than a year until he signed a treaty conceding Burgundy to the emperor. Soon after his release in the spring of 1526, Francis reneged on his word to Charles and signed another treaty, a pact with the Pope, Venice and Florence, to unite against the Holy Roman Emperor. Henry VIII was to be part of the agreement, but, incensed that the treaty was signed at Cognac instead of in England, refused to be a part of it, a decision he would stick to until 1527.

Henry did not just feel snubbed by the Pope, he felt snubbed by the Hospitallers. Concurrent with the strife between Spain and France, L'Isle Adam had been to both countries in the hopes of drumming up

support for his Order's fanciful plan to retake Rhodes. However, he failed to drop in on the English king, preferring to return directly to Italy. Infuriated by the slight, Henry made rumblings about seizing the Order's assets in England and making the English Hospitallers a separate knighthood that would serve his garrison at Calais. To remedy the situation, L'Isle Adam travelled to England to visit the king, proclaimed him a Protector of the Religion, and was pleased to have the king withdraw his proceedings against his Hospitallers and promise to give the Order 20,000 crowns for their efforts. It would be five years before the king would make good on his promise, and even then it would be goods in kind that would be gifted, rather than the cash he had promised.

Having smoothed things over with the King of England, the Grand Master returned to Italy to discover that the Order's chief ally, Pope Clement, was in trouble. From the time Clement had formed the pact with his allies, he had bounced back and forth between his allegiance to his League of Cognac and the emperor, finally signing a truce with Charles promising the emperor an immediate payment of 60,000 ducats or roughly 415 pounds of gold. When Charles's German mercenaries operating in Northern Italy learned of the promised indemnity, and having not been paid in some time, they threatened mutiny, which led to the Pope increasing his offering to 100,000 ducats. The increase in Pope Clement's promise did little to appease the angry underpaid Landsknecht mercenaries, most of whom were Lutherans. They forced their imperial commander to lead them in an attack on Rome, and by 6 May 1527, the assault of Rome began. Although the rampage lasted only days, Clement would be a veritable prisoner in the Castle of Sant' Angelo, where he had taken refuge when the conflict began. A month later on 6 June, the Pope surrendered to Charles and offered a ransom of 400,000 ducats for the security of his life, as well as the surrender of the papal cities of Ostia, Modena, Parma, Piacenza and the naval base at Cita Vecchia. Pope Clement remained at Sant' Angelo until December when he retired to Orvieto.

Pope Clement would not return to Rome until 1529, and although truces of peace would be signed by the Pope at Barcelona in June and by Francis at Cambria in August that would settle the political strife in Western Europe for several years, it was far from the end of the conflicts between Charles and Francis. However, the renewed friendship between the Pope and the emperor, solidified by the Pope's coronation of Charles at Bologna on 24 February 1530, made it easier for Charles to soften the terms of his original offer of Malta and Gozo to the Hospitallers that he had made six years earlier. After nearly a decade of bouncing from place to place, surrounded by the political machinations of their western co-religionists, the Religion, as they referred to themselves, were about to take possession of their new home.

The document penned a month after Charles's coronation on 23 March granted 'the Grand Master of the Religion and Order of St John of Jerusalem, in feudal perpetuity, noble, free, and uncontrolled', the cities and fortifications of Malta, Gozo and Tripoli. Although the requirement that the Hospitallers would swear fealty to the emperor had been removed, the condition concerning the isolated North African outpost, located 320 kilometres south of Malta, remained a necessary element of the agreement and was of great importance to the emperor. Despite spending the better part of the previous decade warring with fellow Christians, Charles was not ignorant of the victories Suleiman had achieved during that time: Belgrade in 1521, Rhodes in 1522, and finally Mohács in 1526, a Turkish victory that had allowed the Ottomans to occupy a large part of Hungary, thus opening a doorway to Vienna, which they attacked unsuccessfully in 1529. Beyond the Ottoman landward toehold into Europe, the sultan's ally Yakupoğlu Hızır, the Khair al-Dīn, better known as the pirate Barbarossa, had established himself along the North African coast and was successfully wreaking maritime havoc along the coasts of Italy and Spain. To further tax the struggling Order's occupation of Tripoli, the artillery and ammunition at the garrison was to be inventoried and granted to the Hospitallers' use for a period of three years, but the expectation was that they would replace what was there with their own equipment.

While the Grand Master had but temporary control over the arms and armaments of Tripoli, the grant made L'Isle Adam the feudal lord over the new territories with absolute power over the life and death of every male and female residing in the lands. Once the citizens had taken their oath to the Grand Master they would be released from their previous oaths to

Charles V. With the passing of the lands, so too passed the import and export duties, feudal rents, and other taxes the residents were still required to pay, but would now pay into the Hospitallers' greatly depleted coffers.

In exchange for the lands and revenues, the Hospitallers were to pay the annual tribute of one hawk or falcon to be given on the Festival of All Saints. Of course there were other conditions attached to Charles's gift than the annual passing of a single Maltese falcon. The Order vowed not to attack any of the lands under Charles's control, by land or by sea, or to offer their assistance to any who were. On the contrary, they were to do all in their power to avert the attack, and although not an oath of fealty, the condition assured Charles that the Hospitallers would not act against his interests. To further secure his territorial interests and those of the empire, provisions were made to return Malta and the other possessions to Charles, or his successor, should the Hospitallers succeed in reconquering Rhodes or if they left the islands for any other reason. Additionally, the Order was to give Charles support by expelling any fugitives or criminals who sought refuge from the Kingdom of Sicily on any of the Hospitallers' newly granted territory, unless they were accused of treason or heresy, in which case they were to be arrested and turned over to the authorities.

As the Maltese citizens were given no say in the transfer of land, the transfer document outlined the procedure for dealing with the inevitable land disputes that might arise between the new occupiers and individuals who had been granted land or property in the territories now gifted to the Hospitallers. Two judges were to be selected: one by the viceroy of Sicily, the other by the Grand Master of the Hospitallers. In the event that the two judges' opinions were at odds a third judge was to be selected to break the tie. It is hard to imagine that anyone would want to take legal action to secure property on a barren, unattractive, little rock of an island just 27 kilometres long by 14 wide, but despite the largely unfavourable report of L'Isle Adam's commissioners, Malta would become the Order's home for the next two and a half centuries, largely because of its two fine harbours, something the Order had been without for nearly a decade.

When Rome was sacked by mercenaries in the army of Charles V on 6 May, Pope Clement VII was forced to flee to the Castle of St Angelo.
Bigstock/Lorenzo Rossi

CHAPTER 12

An Island with Two Fine Harbours

Life on Malta differed vastly from the Hospitallers' life on Rhodes, not least because of the differences in the landscape itself. Unlike the Levantine garden that was the island of Rhodes, Malta was incapable of growing crops other than cotton and some fruit; its rocky surface and thin soil was unable to produce the timbers the now entirely naval-based warriors would need to expand and maintain their fleet. As the Hospitaller commissioners learned on investigating the island, wood was so rare that it was sold by the pound, leaving the locals no option but to use thistles and dried cow dung to light their cooking fires. Indeed, with few trees and no natural water supply outside a couple of springs located in the centre of the island, there was little surface appeal to the Hospitallers' new home. Gozo was better suited for crops but had no harbours for the fleet, and the other Maltese islands, including Comino, situated between Malta and Gozo, were nothing more than rocks jutting out of the Mediterranean, part of the archipelago that had risen up out of the water from the shifting of the African and European tectonic plates millions of years earlier.

And yet this fallow chunk of land had been occupied since prehistoric times and been important to Christendom for many centuries. Although at various times occupied by the Greeks, Phoenicians and Romans, Malta became part of the Byzantine Empire in the late fourth century when the Roman Empire split into eastern and western divisions. With the exception of brief occupations by the Goths and Vandals in the fifth century, the island remained in Byzantine hands until AD870 when it came under Arab rule. During the Norman conquest of Sicily, Malta was wrested from Muslim hands by Roger I and the island again fell under Christian rule, part of the newly formed Kingdom of Sicily. Despite several attempts to gain control of the island during the crusades, Malta had remained in Christian hands for more than four centuries, a patch of land more important for its strategic location poised between three continents than for any other reason. Geographically positioned midway between Sicily and North Africa and centred in the Mediterranean, Malta was uniquely situated to serve as a military outpost or port of commerce. Although the island's western coastline was of little use militarily or commercially, its eastern coastline was indented by a number of capes, bays and coves, including, as L'Isle Adam's commissioners had reported, 'two particularly fine, large harbours, big enough to accommodate any size of fleet'.

The island's suitability to that purpose could easily be seen by the Grand Master and his Hospitallers as soon as they sailed into the harbour, which was divided into two parts by a high ridge of rock jutting out in a

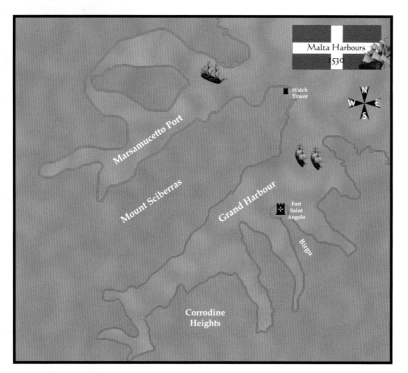

northeasterly direction into the bay. The easternmost harbour's shoreline was further indented by three smaller harbours running in a northwesterly direction. Although the westernmost harbour was considerably smaller than the one to the east, due to a small island dominating the harbour, it was nonetheless suitable for the Hospitallers' purpose, being naturally shielded from the often violent winds that cross the Mediterranean from the northeast.

As pleasing as the great strips of waterway that comprised the Order's new twin harbours were, L'Isle Adam could not but be disappointed by the existing fortifications. The island's sole protection along the sea was located on a promontory that separated the first two small indentations of the easternmost harbour. Here the Hospitallers found a small fort defended by three cannon and a few mortars, surrounded by the huts of fisherman who had settled around the island's only real firepower. Although its main town, Citta Notabile, located in the centre of the island, was protected by ramparts rather than the earthen works found at the fishing hamlet the locals referred to as the Birgu, it could hardly be considered well defended. That the island had not been attacked by Khair al-Dīn, other than to occasionally find fresh galley slaves to

man his oars, was further proof that it was utterly devoid of anything worth stepping off a ship for. Now that the Hospitallers had taken possession of Malta with its 12,000 inhabitants and Gozo with its 5,000 citizens, that could change at any moment, if only as a pre-emptive strike against the Hospitallers.

Although L'Isle Adam made strengthening Fort St Angelo, as the little fortress was called, his first order of business, no great energies were to be expended on the fortress beyond repairing its decaying walls and improving upon its existing minimal fortifications. The Hospitallers saw Malta as a temporary refuge and a base from which they could facilitate recapturing Rhodes, something that was always in the back of the Grand Master's mind. Even the Order's convent was a makeshift affair during the Hospitallers' first year on the islands, with the younger knights sharing dormitories in existing facilities and the Order's commanders expected to fend for themselves by buying their accommodations with their own money or from their share of the spoils of war. Although still bound by vows of poverty in principle, Hospitallers were by this point allowed to keep a portion of what they captured. Although conventual life still required the hearing of Mass and eating communally, it was a far cry from the luxurious Auberges the Order's Langues had enjoyed on Rhodes, and the contrast in living conditions between their former and current island homes inevitably led to conflicts between the knights and their rule, and even between the knights themselves. Fighting amongst the knights and the Langues was not unknown.

As strange, alien and demoralising as their new home was to the Hospitallers, it was equally foreign to the largely Arabic-speaking, peasant population of the islands who undoubtedly saw the armour and multi-coloured trappings of the Hospitallers and their great ships of war as extremely opulent compared to the far more austere trappings they had to show for a life of breaking their backs under a Mediterranean sun. If the peasantry felt any uneasiness or bitterness at the Hospitallers being on the island, it paled in comparison to the local aristocracy who were not at all pleased with what they saw as an overbearing Order occupying their island. For both groups of nobility – the local aristocracy and the

Hospitallers themselves – nothing could be better than to see the Order's fleet leaving for Rhodes.

The Hospitallers took their first chance towards that end in 1531 when they set sail for Modon (Methoni) on the southwestern coast of Greece to assist the Venetians in recapturing the port town that had been conquered by the Ottomans in 1500. Although they briefly captured the town, they just as quickly lost it, rendering the military expedition wasted. The Hospitallers would return a year later with four galleys to assist Andrea Doria in the capture of Coron (Koroni), southeast of Modon, returning again in 1533 to assist in its defence against the Turks who were eager to take it back.

Although ships had evolved considerably since the Hospitallers first took to sea, sleek, oared galleys powered by a combination of Muslim slaves and insubordinate Hospitallers continued to be the main component of the fleet. As early as the fifteenth century, Hospitaller galleys were generally larger than those found in other fleets; however, the smaller galliots consisting of between twelve and twenty-two sweeps of oars proved effective in assisting the Hospitallers in the hit-and-run tactics used in coastal raids. Other smaller vessels, including brigantines, feluccas

and saettas rounded out the Hospitallers' fleet of ships suitable for coastal raids. Speed and manoeuvrability were of great importance in coastal raids because, unlike modern naval vessels, soldiers disembarked from the stern rather than the bow of the ship. As such, a coastal raiding party would travel in tight formation so that all the boats arrived at the same time, then turn around near the shore and backwater to allow the landing party to take to shore. Larger ships, including the *Santa Maria* and *Santa Anna*, although they both often accompanied the fleet, were primarily defensive ships. To this end, the *Santa Anna* was remarkable – a four-masted, six-decked warship with 3,000 tonnes of displacement to keep afloat the fifty large cannon and numerous smaller guns she was capable of carrying. The splendour of the *Santa Anna* is given in an account by John Taaffe in Volume III of his 1852 work, *The History of the Holy, Military, Sovereign Order of St. John of Jerusalem*:

'The great karack of Rhodes having been burned down by accident, the new one built at Nice came off Barbary, and was examined with wonderful admiration, not only by the Moors, but by Charles V. himself; for it truly was a

The Hospitallers assisted Andrea Doria, shown here in this portrait by Sebastiano del Piombo, in capturing Coron (Koroni), Greece in 1532.
Jupiter Images

A small galliot similar to the type the Hospitallers would have used with their oared galleys is shown between a frigate (left) and a galleon (right).
Jupiter Images

no water could sink it. When the plague was at Nice, and the mortality so frightfully huge that the stench of the corrupted air made the birds of the sky drop down dead, not a man was ever sick on board it, which is attributed to the great quantity of fires kept by the workmen – chiefly the quantity of smiths – to supply the requisite screws, nails and other irons, while vessels full of earth had cypress, or orange and lemon trees, and flowers, like small, but delicious gardens, in that ship, which had eight decks or floors, and such space for warehouse and stores, that it could keep at sea for six months without once having occasion to touch land for any sort of provision, not even water; for it had a monstrous supply for all that time of water, the freshest and most limpid; nor did the crew eat biscuit, but excellent white bread, baked every day, the corn being ground by a multitude of handmills, and an oven so capacious, that it baked two thousand large loaves at a time.

That ship was sheathed with six several sheathings of metal, two of which under water, were lead with bronze screws (which do not consume the lead like iron screws), and with such consummate art was it built, that it never could sink, no human power could submerge it. Magnificent rooms, an armoury for five hundred men; but of the quantity of cannon of every kind, no need say anything, save that fifty of them were of extraordinary dimensions; but what crowned all is that the

Above: **The Santa Anna was built for the Hospitallers at Nice in 1530 and was decommissioned a decade later. At the time of its building it was the largest ship in the world.**

Right: **Comparison between a twelfth- and sixteenth-century helmet.**
Jupiter Images

marvel, and would be even now for many things, its salubrity particularly, and that it rivalled with our life-boats in this, that however pierced with multitudinous holes,

enormous vessel was of incomparable swiftness and agility, and that its sails were astonishingly manageable; that it required little toil to veer or reef, and perform all nautical evolutions, not to speak of fighting people, but the mere mariners amounted to three hundred; as likewise two galleys of fifteen benches each, one galley lying in tow off the stern, and the other galley drawn aboard; not to mention various boats of divers sizes, also drawn aboard; and truly of such strength her sides, that though she had often been in action, and perforated by many cannon balls, not one of them ever went directly through her, or even passed her *deadworks*.'

Although the Order's admiral was in charge of the carracks, galleys and other ships equipped for war, the chain of command for the men who rode the waves along with those ships had changed little from when the Hospitallers were primarily a land-based army. On board the ships the knights still fell under the command of the Marshal, and when Hospitaller boots hit the shore, it was the commander of knights who took control of their movements.

Armour and the arms the Hospitallers used to fight had changed vastly by the sixteenth century. Plate armour had evolved considerably from its reintroduction in the late thirteenth century when it complemented existing mail armour. By the time the Hospitallers had surrendered Rhodes in 1522, knights were wearing full suits of plate armour and had been for some time. Although design varied by nation, by the middle of the fifteenth century a full suit of armour constructed in Milan typically consisted of a rounded breastplate that ended at the waist, overlapped with a lower plate called a plackart that covered the lower part of the torso, usually to the groin area. A similar set-up covered the knight's back, and the individual pieces were connected to one another by a series of straps, buckles and belts. The rest of the body was protected with individual units covering the shoulders, arms, thighs and lower legs. The shields that had once offered the knight his first line of defence were now long gone, his protection now provided by an assortment of plate steel from his head to his toes. However, advances in ballistics over the next two centuries, particularly the improvements of the

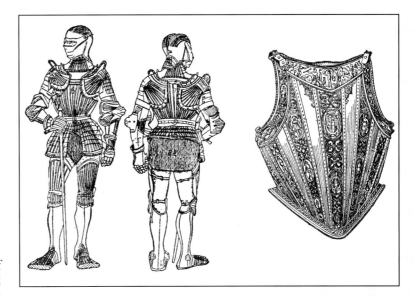

musket through the sixteenth and seventeenth centuries, would render plate armour ineffective, and it would disappear very quickly from the knights' battledress. Even while it was still in common use, Hospitaller armour was far removed from the romantic depictions of mirror-polished armour so heavy that a knight had to be hoisted onto his horse, images found only in oil paintings and Hollywood movies. The reality of Hospitaller armour can be gleaned from the items they left behind when Rhodes was evacuated in 1522. Artefacts show that the Order's armour was not the elegant jousting or parade armour used by the nobility, but a motley assortment, largely comprised of munitions-grade armour, a mass-produced armour consisting of interchangeable pieces, usually forged from iron with some phosphorus added to increase its hardness. Even then it hardly possessed the uniformity so often depicted in paintings and woodcuts showing the Order in action.

Hospitaller arms were also a mixed bag in their early years on Malta. Although Suleiman had permitted the Order to leave with their most important possessions, cannon were not among them, and given L'Isle Adam's limited success in procuring assistance for the Order in their eight years of roaming Europe, it is unlikely that the Hospitallers would have accumulated a mass of weaponry during that time. In 1531, the same year the Order attacked Modon, Henry VIII sent a ship to Malta with a number of cannon for the

Left: **Front and back images of a fifteenth-century suit of armour.** *Right:* **an example of a sixteenth-century ornamental breastplate. The majority of Hospitallers' armour would have been less detailed than either of these examples.** *Jupiter Images*

Hospitallers in lieu of the 20,000 crowns he had promised the Grand Master five years previously. Rose Kingsley in her 1845 work *The Order of St. John of Jerusalem* records the donation from the English king as consisting of 'nineteen great cannon and 1,023 balls'. Modern historians generally note that Henry's donation consisted of a quantity of cannon ranging from large to small, but if Kingsley's figures are correct, the addition of even nineteen cannon would have been of considerable benefit to an Order who, upon the acceptance of their new lands, had added but six cannon and a few mortars to replace those they had lost at Rhodes and, to supplement what they had been able to obtain, a small amount of fire power to distribute between two locations some 350 miles apart.

As the Hospitallers were accumulating cannon and cannon balls, galleys and galliots, and generally refilling their coffers to prepare for war with the Ottomans that could come at any time, Khair al-Dīn was overseeing the construction of some seventy new galleys at Constantinople at the request of Suleiman. The Ottoman defeat at Coron in 1532 – and near-miss at Modon a year earlier – had made the sultan painfully aware of the weakness of the Ottoman fleet and the increasing naval prowess of Andrea Doria. Khair al-Dīn was the one man capable of rectifying the situation, and in the autumn of 1533, Suleiman summoned the Barbary pirate from Algiers to aid him in his designs. The following spring Khair al-Dīn left Constantinople the admiral of an Ottoman fleet consisting of 100 ships, 10,000 soldiers and a regiment of the sultan's Janissaries. In April, he recaptured, by force or by treaty, Coron, Patras and Lepanto (Naupactus). In July and August, the Ottoman fleet made its way along the western coast of Italy, plundering and burning to within 160 kilometres of Rome, causing Pope Clement

VII to fear that he would leave the Vatican. A force of 6,000 soldiers was rounded up and sent to intercept the Muslims, but by the time the army arrived, all Khair al-Dīn had left behind was havoc, his fleet vanishing over the southern horizon. One of the admiral's objectives along the Italian coast had been the capture of Giulia Gonzaga as a prize for Suleiman's harem; however, the beautiful Italian widow eluded the Muslims, and in his frustrated rage, Khair al-Dīn had her village of Fondi destroyed, massacring many of its citizens and forcing others to flee.

The subsequent appearance of the fleet near Bizerta a week later put Muley Hassan, the Hafsid ruler of Tunis, and his family to flight, allowing Khair al-Dīn to sail into the port unopposed. On 16 August 1534, less than a week before L'Isle Adam breathed his last breath, Khair al-Dīn arrived at his new North African naval base. No longer was this merely a successful pirate operating out of a nest in Western Africa, but the admiral of a greatly improved and expanded Ottoman fleet, operating 500 kilometres from Tripoli and less than 400 kilometres from Malta. The situation was a wake-up call for Europe which had been preoccupied with secular and religious infighting for more than a decade and felt no real urgency in dealing with Ottoman expansion after the Turks were beaten back at Vienna in 1529 and Suleiman's subsequent eastward push into Persia. But the capture of Tunis had planted the Ottoman Empire in the midst of the Mediterranean, a short distance from Sicily, and suddenly the Hospitallers, under their new Grand Master Piero del Ponte, were about to enter a fight to ensure that the two fine harbours of Malta remained theirs.

CHAPTER 13
Troubles on Land and Sea

L'Isle Adam's death left his successor, Piero del Ponte, a fellow veteran of Rhodes, with the problem of holding Malta, Gozo and Tripoli at a time when the Ottoman Empire was on the move. The donation of Tripoli to the Hospitallers had been largely to save King Charles from the expense of defending the port, but also because Charles truly believed that the presence of the Hospitallers would help to curb the growing problem of piracy in the area. With the Mediterranean's foremost pirate now admiral of the Turkish fleet and many of his ships now anchored at Tunis, the possibility of the Hospitallers garrisoned at Tripoli seeing a flotilla of Ottoman ships coming towards them increased with each passing day, and the best they would be able to do was to try and maintain a beachhead against such an attack.

Although the Ottoman position was of concern to the Hospitallers, both at Tripoli and on Malta, it was of equal if not greater concern to Charles. No longer was the battle against Islam an offensive campaign such as that which his predecessor Frederick II had travelled to the Holy Land to fight more than three centuries earlier; this was a defensive campaign to protect Western Europe and its Christian faith, even if that faith was knee deep in a period of schism. As a Spaniard (for Charles was first and foremost the King of Spain) the importance of his situation was not

hard to comprehend. Spain and the whole of the Iberian peninsula had endured centuries of warfare in its struggle to retake land that had been captured for Islam in the eighth century. In fact, it had been just over a generation earlier, in 1492, that Spain expelled the Muslims from the country altogether. The prospect of Suleiman gaining control of portions of the Holy Roman Empire was unacceptable to Charles, and in his capacity of King of Spain, the emperor led the charge to remove the Ottomans from Tunis. The expedition was funded largely by the Spanish conquest of Peru four years earlier, during which time Francisco Pizarro had managed to accumulate a huge ransom for the Sapa Inca ruler Atahualpa. Charles spent one million ducats of gold on his expedition, and, although Spain provided the bulk of the fleet and the majority of soldiers, Portugal, Genoa, the Papal States and the Hospitallers all contributed ships and men for the campaign.

In all some 30,000 men boarded more than 300 ships that gathered at Sardinia in the spring of 1535 and prepared to sail on Tunis under the command of Andrea Doria. On 12 June, the Hospitaller contingent of 700 knights pulled out of port with a fleet of fifty-four ships, including the *Santa Anna*, twenty-five large galleys and eighteen smaller vessels, joining the Christian navy on its eight-day voyage to Tunis. The Hospitallers' *Santa Anna*, although the largest ship at the time of

Frederick II was the Holy Roman Emperor from 1220 until 1250 and went on crusade in 1227, securing a truce in 1229 that allowed Christians to return to Jerusalem. *Jupiter Images*

its construction, was not the only big gun to coast the Mediterranean during the campaign. The Portuguese had sent the *São João Baptista* (*St John the Baptist*), a massive galleon capable of carrying hundreds of cannon, and better known as *Botafogo*, or 'fire-maker'. The ship, launched in 1534, was commanded by the Infante Louis, the 5th Duke of Beja, the brother of King John III of Portugal, and therefore the brother-in-law of Charles V, who had married Louis's sister Isabella in 1525. In addition to his connection with the Holy Roman Emperor, Louis had been a prior of the Hospitaller holdings in Crato, and therefore a member of the Order. In the battle that lay ahead, although the Hospitallers would serve an important role in securing the fortress, it would be their former prior and his ship that would give them the opportunity to do so.

Tunis would prove to be no easy conquest for the Christians, nor would it have been for Khair al-Dīn had Muley Hassan fought to defend his city instead of fleeing at the first sight of Turkish sails. The city of some 80,000 inhabitants, made up of a combination of Arabs and Moors, was uniquely situated to be well secured. Although located on a large gulf in the Mediterranean, the city was buffered inland by the Lake of Tunis, a ten-kilometre diameter body of water whose access was through a narrow canal leading from the gulf. To get to Tunis, Charles and his men would have to get to Lake Tunis, and to get to Lake Tunis, they would have to gain control of La Goletta, the fortress that guarded the canal.

Anticipating a Christian attack on his recently captured prize, Khair al-Dīn had put La Goletta in the command of a Jewish lieutenant named Sinan, who gathered together some 6,000 Turks and Moors to man its ramparts. Although the *Botafogo*'s spur ram made short work of the chains that blocked the entrance to the canal, gaining access to the fortress proved another matter. The Christian forces began their assault on La Goletta on 20 June and came under intense cannon fire as well as frequent attacks from native defenders who were sent out in small boats to fight the attackers. The battle raged for two weeks, during which time Charles's forces were thwarted by the enemy, the weather and internal conflicts among the various nations which had gathered for the campaign: the

Spaniards distrusted the Italians, and the German Protestants had little respect for anyone who was Catholic. Things could only have been worse among the multinational enterprise had France and England participated in the battle; however, Francis and Charles were hardly the best of friends after their recent battles and Charles's advocacy of his aunt Catherine, whom King Henry had divorced two years earlier, ran the risk of pushing the English king towards an alliance with France. Matters with France were further complicated by the king's growing closeness to the Ottoman Empire.

Soon after Khair al-Dīn had captured Tunis, an embassy of Janissaries was sent from Constantinople to France to meet with the king. Arriving in the autumn of 1534, the delegation remained until February of the following year, and spent their four-month stay planning joint military campaigns between the empire and their French allies. However, Francis's plans were to be put on hold by Pope Paul III, who issued an edict forbidding Christians from warring with one another until the conclusion of Charles's campaign in Tunis. The edict would not, however, prevent Francis from supplying the Ottomans with cannon balls, which would later be discovered in the ruins of La Goletta, their fleur-de-lis markings clearly disclosing the fact that the French were already working with the Ottomans.

Christian animosity and the threat of war among western nations was not the only parasite to undermine the campaign; a lack of suitable drinking water led to many of the invaders falling to dysentery before their objective could be achieved. Despite the odds, Charles pushed onward with his plans, launching a full-out assault on the ramparts of La Goletta on 14 July, three weeks after the assault had begun. At dawn the silence of night was replaced by the cannon's roar as the seventy-two ships Andrea Doria had lined up against the fortress let loose their bombardment, a succession of fire that did not stop until midday, when one of La Goletta's towers began to fall. No sooner had the crumbling masonry hit the shore than the Spanish and Hospitaller forces followed suit. The Hospitallers waded to shore with siege ladders, forming the vanguard of the assault on the ramparts. That the Hospitallers were chosen to form the vanguard of the assault shows the confidence Charles had in their abilities. The emperor's trust proved well placed, for after a heavy battle along the ramparts, the Hospitallers succeeded in pouring over the walls and storming through the breaches, sending the defenders fleeing as Muley Hassan had a year earlier. But now the exiled Tunisian ruler was not running, at least not with Charles by his side. The emperor entered the fortress with the Muslim ruler, telling him, "Here is the gate open to you by which you shall return to take possession of your kingdom." Of course, that dignity would be returned to Hassan only after Charles had captured Tunis and Hassan had pledged his loyalty to Spain, but before either requirement could be accomplished, the Christians would need to gain control of Lake Tunis, which had eighty-four pirate ships floating in its midst, a number that was easily captured by the Christians.

With the Christian fleet now in clear control of the lake, Khair al-Dīn decided to press the battle on land rather than wait for Charles and his troops to arrive at the city's gates. He would not have much time, as the enemy ships were already backing their sterns to the shoreline for the troops to disembark. It would not be long before Christian cannon would be dragged across the Tunisian sands to fire upon the city's walls. But there was more to Khair al-Dīn's plan than merely wishing to engage the Christians with boots and hooves. The city's walls were weak and the force of Arabs and Moors Khair al-Dīn had assembled from the various tribes in the neighbouring regions even weaker, giving him a fortification and an army he didn't have a great deal of confidence in, but leaving the city also posed its own share of problems because there were thousands of Christian slaves (10-20,000 according to various accounts) confined to the prison. Khair al-Dīn was afraid that if he did not leave a large force behind to guard them, they might use the absence of power to revolt and regain their freedom, particularly since word had spread that their co-religionists were on the lake and would soon be scaling the walls of Tunis to free them. Although Khair al-Dīn suggested slaughtering the slaves by burning the prison that housed them, Sinan and many others in his council convinced him to spare their lives, leaving a small contingent

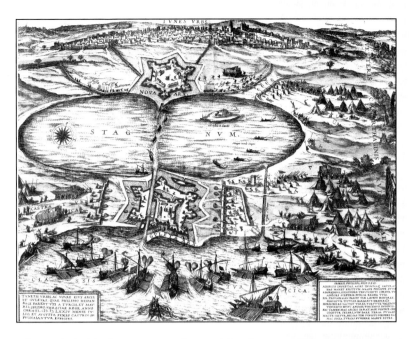

Sixteenth-century map of the conquest of Tunis in 1535, showing the position of La Goletta.

of guards behind to oversee them while the main forces met Charles and his troops along the plain between the city and lake. Despite large numbers of desertions from the forces Khair al-Dīn had assembled, the Muslims still outnumbered their Christian opponents.

Where the Ottomans had strength of number, the Christians met them with the power of the heavy cavalry charge, a destructive force that held as much bone-crushing power as it did in the battles of the Levant centuries earlier. Still, those of Khair al-Dīn's men who still remained did not merely lie down on the sands and surrender; they fought fiercely to repel the Christians. During the conflict, Charles's horse was shot from under him and one of his pages was killed in the melee. Still the Christians fought on, motivated in part by their desire to capture the city, but in a larger sense by a desire to reach a fresh supply of water, as the crusaders had during the Battle of Hattin three and a half centuries earlier. Unlike that fateful battle that ended in tragedy, the Christians would succeed, not because of the efforts of those who battled their way across the hot sands, but because of the prisoners who, as Khair al-Dīn had feared, rose up against their oppressors and took control of the city. Among the revolting slaves was a Hospitaller named Simeoni who had been a veteran of Rhodes and took command of the slaves once they had freed themselves. Simeoni was among the first to greet the emperor when he entered Tunis on 21 July without the need to unsheathe his sword against Khair al-Dīn, who, along with his remaining troops, had long since fled the city and was en route to Bône (Annaba) in the northeast of Algeria.

If the inhabitants of Tunis felt that the capture of the city from within would spare them the customary bloodshed that occurred whenever a city changed hands, they were mistaken. The three days of plunder the Christian commanders permitted their men resulted in the massacre of some 30,000 civilians and the enslavement of thousands more, an unnecessary act of aggression that increased the height of the heroic pedestal on which the city's capture had placed the Holy Roman Emperor. Not only had Charles succeeded in destroying a large portion of Khair al-Dīn's fleet and driven the Ottomans from Tunis, but Muley Hassan was restored to his former throne, now a tributary of Spain. Throughout Europe the Christian conquest of Tunis was seen as a great achievement for Christendom and the emperor was regarded as a conquering hero and Defender of the Faith. Wherever he went, Charles was lavished with high praise and even honoured by Pope Paul III in a special ceremony of thanksgiving. Not everyone was pleased with the outcome at Tunis. The Ottoman defeat prompted Suleiman to enter into more aggressive negotiations for an alliance with Francis I against their mutual adversary Charles V in a pooling of efforts that would last well after all three men were dead.

As for the Hospitallers, they returned to Malta pleased with their involvement in the Christian successes at Tunis. Although numerically small in terms of their contribution to the conquest, their pivotal roles in capturing La Goletta and Tunis had not only earned them praise from the Holy Roman Emperor, but more importantly from

their own Grand Master Piero del Ponte, who died four months after the knights returned to Malta, having served at the Hospitaller helm for but fifteen months. This, however, was longer than his successor, Didier de Saint-Jaille, who was elected to the office but died in 1536 before ever reaching Malta. De Saint-Jaille was succeeded by Juan de Homedes y Coscón, a Spanish knight, who was chosen largely through the Spanish influence in the convent. De Homedes's competition consisted of two Hospitaller commanders, de Grolée and Botigella, one of whom had led the charge up the assault ladders at La Goletta in the summer of 1535. Although less notable than de Grolée and Botigella, de Homedes had been an active participant during the siege of Rhodes 23 years earlier and had a missing eye to prove it. In the end it was he who would lead the Order through a period of time that would see the Hospitallers assaulted by Muslim and Christian alike.

The first of these attacks would come in 1540 at a time when Muley Hassan – who was regarded a traitor to Islam by his subjects, had been dethroned, imprisoned and blinded by his son – and the Spanish garrison at La Goletta had abandoned their posts, leaving the Mediterranean open to the returning spectre of Khair al-Dīn, and the greater threat of the Franco-Ottoman alliance, now in its second year. But the attack against the Hospitallers was not from Islam but from Henry VIII, the very king who had honoured his commitment to help the Hospitallers when they had first moved to Malta a decade earlier. Henry had been supportive of the Order since his early days as King of England. In fact, when Thomas Docwra was the Grand Prior of England he had a prominent place within the House of Lords as the head of the Temporal Barons. Docwra had been one of the candidates for Grand Master after the death of Fabrizio del Carretto in 1521, and it was Docwra himself who received L'Isle Adam when he visited England seeking Henry's support when the Order was without a home and when the English king had felt snubbed that the Hospitaller Grand Master had not visited him sooner. On Docwra's death in 1527, Henry tried to force the Order to accept his own candidate for England's new Grand Prior as well as seeking to extract an annual tribute of

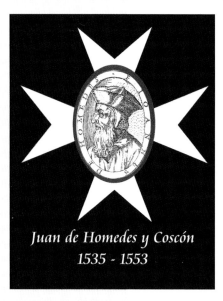

Juan de Homedes y Coscón
1535 - 1553

Juan de Homedes y Coscón, shown in this Antonio F. Lucini engraving, was Grand Master from 1536 to 1553.

£4,000 from the Order. However, Henry's movements met with little success, and the Hospitallers replaced Docwra with their own choice, William Weston, who had commanded the *Santa Maria* when the Order had been evicted from Rhodes and who went on to command their greatest ship, the *Santa Anna*.

Following his troubles with the Catholic Church over his divorce from Catherine of Aragon in 1533, Henry established his own Church with himself as the supreme head. This put the English Hospitallers in an awkward position because their allegiance to the papacy made them a sure target for a king who had broken all ties with the Catholic Church, and who had begun disbanding the monasteries, nunneries and friaries throughout the country, disposing of their assets and appropriating their income in the process. Henry went after the Hospitallers with the same passion with which Philip IV had gone after the Templars in France two centuries earlier, the difference being that the English king needed neither trumped-up charges nor torture to do so. He made his first move towards that end in July of 1538 through a letter addressed to the Grand Master, identifying himself as head of the Anglican Church and protector of the Knights of St John. Henry informed Grand Master de Homedes that he authorised William Weston to confer the Hospitaller habit and receive English subjects into the Order, provided applicants had first professed their allegiance to the king as their supreme lord. Henry went on to inform de Homedes that henceforth any candidate he nominated to an English commandery had to first meet with the king's approval, and had to swear allegiance to the King of England before his appointment could be ratified. Appointees would be forbidden from recognising, supporting or promoting the jurisdiction or authority of the Bishop of Rome. Once approved and sworn, the commander would be required to pay the first year of commandery revenues directly to the king's treasury. As if those requirements were not enough, Henry forbade the Order from taking up any charitable collections within his domains unless a warrant was produced to prove that such collections were issued from the king and not in response to any bull from the Holy See. To ensure that the Hospitallers followed his orders, an annual chapter was to be held to try and punish any member of the Order guilty of crimes against the state.

For centuries the Hospitallers had existed without tax or tithes and remained bound to none save the Church and the Grand Master. With some carefully crafted paragraphs, Henry sought to change all of that, securing for himself and his kingdom rights that no Pope had ever assumed. Despite the dismantling of the Catholic institutions around them, the Hospitallers declined Henry's request, a decision that sealed their fate in England. Like Pope Clement V at the Council of Vienne in 1312, Henry dissolved the Order of St John with the stroke of a pen in April 1540, seizing its assets in the process. Not only did all castles, manors, churches and houses belonging to the Hospitallers transfer to the crown, the Hospitallers were no longer permitted to wear the regalia of the Order or use any of its titles. Although William Weston was granted an annual pension of £1,000, he did not live long enough to receive it. The Grand Prior died on 7 May, soon after learning that the king was seizing the Order's assets. Similar confiscations took place in Ireland. However, the Order's preceptory at Torphichen remained in Hospitaller hands until the Reformation, when, in 1563, its last preceptor, Sir James Sandilands, surrendered Torphichen to Mary Queen of Scots and

King Henry VIII, shown in this Hans Holbein painting circa 1535, attacked the Hospitallers in 1540, seizing their assets and dissolving the English Langue.

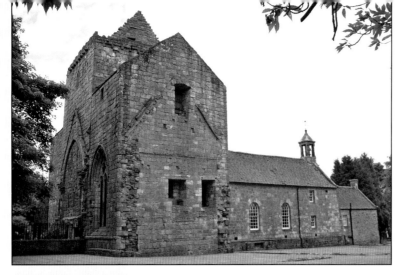

immediately bought it back privately, along with the title Lord Torphichen.

There were no such concessions in 1540 England, and for many English Hospitallers, the answer to the troubles with King Henry was to board a ship for Malta, where the Order's victory at Tunis five years earlier still garnered them the respect they felt they deserved. For the few that remained behind, an unfortunate end was in store, something they had witnessed first hand a year earlier when Adrian Fortescue was beheaded. Fortescue had entered the Order in 1532 at the age of 56, probably more in recognition of his status in English society than any service he could have been to the Hospitallers. Like Thomas Docwra before him, Fortescue once held a prominent place in King Henry's court, serving as the king's courtier. However, in 1534, he had done something to irritate the king and spent several months in jail. Five years later, he was once again arrested, this time along with sixteen others, charged with treason, incarcerated in the Tower of London for two months, and beheaded without benefit of trial.

The Hospitallers suffered other losses as well. The great carrack, the *Santa Anna*, which had served the Order well since being launched from Nice more than a decade earlier, and had been victorious in several naval engagements, including the conquest of Tunis, proved too taxing to operate in the financial crisis caused in large part by the situation in England.

As such, the Mediterranean's most menacing vessel was anchored in harbour and eventually torn apart. Even after things improved, the Hospitallers would never again launch a ship as large or impressive as the *Santa Anna*, instead commissioning ordinary galleons once every decade or so. Despite the loss of their great carrack, the Hospitallers did take part in King Charles's next naval expedition against Khair al-Dīn and the Ottomans.

Since taking on the possession and responsibility of Tripoli, the Hospitallers had appealed to Charles for assistance, either in fortifying the burden or allowing them to remove it from their backs altogether. Although the Order spent some of its resources to fortify it, the destruction of the English Langue had greatly reduced the Order's revenues and made Tripoli an even greater millstone around the Grand Master's neck. Charles, for all his successes at Tunis, had failed in his objective of killing the Barbary pirate, Khair al-Dīn, who had escaped back to Algiers, which he had originally captured in 1529. In the past half-decade since his escape, Khair al-Dīn had once again become a shark in treacherous waters, keeping the whole of the Mediterranean coast in a state of constant alarm. For Charles, the answer to both his and the Hospitallers' problems in the Mediterranean lay in crushing the pirate in his nest.

As had been the case in Tunis, Charles assembled an international army and armada composed of ships and soldiers from Spain, Genoa, Naples, Sicily, the Holy Roman Empire and the Papal States, as well as the Hospitallers, who supplied 700 men for the mission, as they had in the Tunisian campaign. Once again, Andrea Doria commanded the fleet, which set sail from Majorca in late September with some 500 ships and 24,000 soldiers, the latter under the overall command of Fernando Álvarez de Toledo. Álvarez was assisted by a number of commanders, including Hernán Cortés, who had conquered Mexico while the Hospitallers were struggling to prevent the conquest of Rhodes. The Ottomans were not without accomplished commanders to defend their position. The Algerian Governor Hassan Agha had the assistance of Sinan, who had defended La Goletta for Khair al-Dīn at Tunis, Salih Reis and Turgut Reis, the latter of whom would give the Hospitallers considerable trouble in the years to come.

As formidable as the Ottoman commanders were, Charles's admiral had another reason for not wanting to go through with the mission. Doria was reluctant to undertake the expedition due to the weather conditions present so late in the season and tried to talk Charles out of setting sail; however, the emperor was still riding high from his victory five years earlier and driven forward by the recent news that his brother Ferdinand of Austria had lost Buda to the Ottomans, a defeat that allowed the Muslim empire to spread further into Western Europe.

Proceeding on towards Algiers, the fleet arrived on 23 October and, as he had at Tunis, Charles again became an active participant in the campaign, establishing his camp surrounded by soldiers from his empire. Once camp had been established, 150 Hospitallers joined the initial assault, largely composed of Italians, Germans and Spaniards who surrounded the city on the east, south and western sides. As certain as victory may have seemed, as the soldiers were encircling the city, storm clouds were encircling the Mediterranean. As Andrea Doria had warned, the fleet was now exposed to bad weather.

Two days after disembarking at Algiers, strong winds began to blow in from the northeast, halting the land operations with heavy rains and driving many of the fleet's ships to shore and sinking others. In total the Christian fleet lost fifteen galleys and another 140 of its transport and stores ships. Many who attempted to seek land were slaughtered by Algerians, who made repeated sorties from the city's gates.

Doria, meanwhile, was able to save some of the ships by weighing anchor and setting sail for Cape Matifu, where the surviving ships could get a respite from the fierce winds. The admiral sent messengers to let the emperor know of the fleet's whereabouts, and Charles and his surviving troops made the 15-kilometre march around the Bay of Algiers to rendezvous with them, harassed along the way by the enemy they had come to conquer. It was during this long march through inclement weather that the Hospitallers would play their greatest role in the campaign and suffer the most losses. Although they had hoped to form the vanguard of the assault on the city, as they had at Tunis, the Order was now given the responsibility of forming the rearguard in the retreat from the city. Few of the knights who had taken to shore during the campaign would live to see Malta again, and those who did survive returned to a Malta that was in the midst of a hornet's nest stirred up by the Christians' aggression towards Algiers.

With Charles's defeat at Algiers, the fate of Tripoli was sealed; however, it would not be Khair al-Dīn who would assume the victory. The Ottoman admiral was 63 when he repelled the Christians from Algiers. In 1545, at the age of 67, Khair al-Dīn retired to Constantinople and remained in his palace by the sea until his death on 4 July 1546. His position as admiral of the Turkish fleet was assumed by Turgut Reis who had assisted at Algiers five years earlier.

One of his first moves as admiral was to capture the port town of Mahdia, midway between Tunis and Tripoli, thus putting his ships a little closer to his twin prizes of Tripoli and Malta. The situation did not escape the eye of either Grand Master de Homedes or King Charles, and in June of 1550, the Hospitallers supplied 140 knights and 500 mercenaries to the mission to take Mahdia from Turgut Reis. Where Charles had failed miserably at Algiers, he now had a victory in the Mediterranean to redeem himself. Although the Ottomans put up a strong resistance, in the end the Christian forces were victorious. But the conquest was not without its own problems, for now the Hospitallers were faced with the prospects of having two coastal ports to defend for Christendom. That possibility was removed when it was decided that they would destroy the town's fortifications and abandon the port, leaving it as useless to the Christians as it would be to the Muslims, should they return.

The loss of Mahdia did not diminish Turgut Reis's enthusiasm for removing the Christian knights from the Mediterranean, and in July of the following year he anchored a small fleet of galleys and galliots off Marsamuscetto harbour, the northwestern of the two fine

A cannon sits on the bastion of the citadel of Gozo. In 1551, Turgut Reis raided Gozo and took the islanders as slaves before capturing Tripoli from the Hospitallers.
Bigstock/ Liam McCarthy

harbours the Hospitallers had acquired along with the rocky island. Turgut and his commanders landed at Mount Sceberras from where they could look down upon and study the Hospitallers' fortifications at Birgu, which had evolved a great deal from the time they had assumed control of the island. Withdrawing from their elevated position, Turgut Reis had his men press on across land to assault Citta Notabile, which would have resulted in a victory had the admiral not believed that Andrea Doria and a large fleet were en route to defend the island. Withdrawing immediately, Turgut returned to his ships and set sail for Gozo, which capitulated without resistance, allowing the Turks to ravish the village and its citizens, carrying thousands off to a life as galley slaves.

As pleased as he may have been with the conquest of the undefended island of Gozo, Turgut did not want to return to Constantinople with nothing to show Suleiman other than some recently captured and inexperienced oarsman. If he could not tell the sultan that Malta now belonged to the empire, he could at least tell him that Tripoli was at last theirs. As his ruler had at Rhodes, Turgut sent word to the Governor of Tripoli, a French knight named Gaspard la Vallier, that he would accept nothing less than the surrender of the city. La Vallier, who was also Marshal of the Order, returned a negative reply, and the siege of Tripoli began in earnest.

Matters were complicated by the arrival of the French Ambassador to the Ottoman Empire, Gabriel d'Aramon, who attempted to dissuade the Ottomans from continuing the siege on the grounds that the Hospitallers were not considered an enemy of the Franco-Ottoman alliance, at least not from France's position. However, Turgut was determined to wipe the Hospitallers from the African coast and when d'Aramon threatened to settle the matter with the sultan at Constantinople, he was taken prisoner until the siege was completed. D'Aramon did not have long to wait. After six days of Turkish bombardment, the small number of Hospitallers garrisoned at Tripoli surrendered and after two decades of effort to maintain it, the burden had finally been lifted from the Hospitallers' backs.

For all his inability to help the Hospitallers while the cannon balls were flying, d'Aramon did manage to secure the release of those who had been taken prisoner, returning with them and Marshal la Vallier to Malta, where he hoped to be thanked for his efforts on the Order's behalf, rather than criticised for his failure in staving off the siege. It was the latter that greeted the ambassador as he made shore at Malta. It was here that the distrust and even hatred towards him and the Franco-Ottoman alliance prompted him to set sail for Constantinople soon after he had arrived. If de Homedes felt powerless in being unable to take out his anger at the loss of Tripoli on D'Aramon, he felt no such restrictions with his own members, particularly those who had allowed Charles's troublesome gift to fall into Ottoman hands. The sacrifice of land needed a sacrifice of men, a scapegoat to purge the sins of the Order and to quell the popular clamour. La Vallier and three of his men were arrested and stripped of their habits. For the Marshal who had fought to defend the city, even though vastly outnumbered by the Turks, a greater punishment was in store: la Vallier was imprisoned and would remain there until released two years later by de Homedes's successor, Claude de la Sengle. It would not be until the time of la Sengle's successor that la Vallier would be readmitted to the Order. But Jean Parisot de la Valette was a unique man, and one who knew well what it was like to be a prisoner, both to the Ottomans and to his own Order.

CHAPTER 14
The Shield of Europe

Jean Parisot de la Valette was born into a noble family at Quercy in the south of France in 1494 and entered the Order at the age of 20. A career Hospitaller who was a survivor of the siege of Rhodes in 1522, la Valette followed his Order throughout its eight years of transience and subsequent settlement on Malta in 1530. Around the time of the failed campaign against Algiers, la Valette was captured by a Turkish corsair named Abda Racman, operating under the command of Turgut Reis. La Valette spent the next year of his life as a galley slave until he was released in a prisoner exchange, enduring the same hardships that those beneath the Hospitaller ships had faced. Although the custom of executing captured members of the Military Orders was the order of the day during Saladin's reign, by the time Suleiman was battling Christendom captured Hospitallers were often put to work manning their enemy's galleys. Such was the nature of life in the Mediterranean: prisoners could swiftly become captors. If la Valette's incarceration aboard an Ottoman galley had been gruelling, it was certainly well matched by the two years he spent as Governor of Tripoli, in charge of Charles's extra gift to the Hospitallers.

Neither burden broke la Valette's back and in 1554, three years after Tripoli had been stripped from the Order, he was appointed admiral of the Hospitaller fleet. The honour was a particularly important one, more so for the Langue of Provence than for la Valette himself, because it had been customary for the Order's admirals to be selected from the Langue of Italy; in fact, it had been one of the conditions outlined in Charles's agreement to give Malta to the Hospitallers. In his capacity as admiral, la Valette had the opportunity to capture a Turkish galley commanded by Abda Racman, the very man who had imprisoned him years earlier. Although it is not known what la Valette thought of the man personally, the capture was undoubtedly pleasing. However, in the autumn of 1555, a hurricane all but destroyed the Hospitaller fleet anchored at Malta and the sunken galleys took with them many of their slaves.

It was under la Valette that the Order rebuilt its fleet, due largely to the charity of its most wealthy members and patrons. Charles's son Philip immediately sent two of his galleys on the news of the Hospitallers' loss, and Grand Master Claude de la Sengle, who had

Jean Parisot de la Valette (1494-1568), who was Grand Master of the Order from 1557 until his death in 1568, is shown in full armour in this nineteenth-century painting by François-Xavier Dupré.

succeeded de Homedes two years earlier, financed the construction of a new galley at Messina, a ship whose oars would be powered by galley slaves provided by Pope Paul IV. Within the Order itself, the Prior of St Gilles offered his assistance by providing a fully armed and trooped galleon, and the Grand Prior of France arrived in person to deliver two galleys for his eastern Brethren. The arrival of the Grand Prior of France prompted la Valette to selflessly abdicate the admiralship of the fleet in favour of his superior officer. It was an act that was observed by la Sengle, who, impressed with la Valette's noble gesture, made the former admiral his lieutenant, a position la Valette would hold for the next two years.

On la Sengle's death in August of 1557, la Valette was unanimously elected the Order's forty-eighth Grand Master, the sixth to command the Order from Malta. Like his immediate predecessor, la Valette would govern from an island constantly under the threat of impending Ottoman attack, and like la Sengle, he would spend much of his administration strengthening his fortifications, Order and its alliances. One of his first moves was to re-establish his authority over the German and Venetian provinces whose commanderies had for many years been refusing to pay the taxes levied by the general chapter. However, his attempts to restore the commanderies that had been lost in Protestant lands proved less successful. Where his efforts to return lost parts of the Order to the Hospitaller enterprise met with mixed success, la Valette succeeded in restoring one Hospitaller to the Order whom he felt never should have been removed from the fold. Gaspard la Vallier, who had been imprisoned by Grand Master de Homedes in 1551 and released by his successor la Sengle, was still exiled from the Order, having been stripped of

his habit by de Homedes. Not only did la Valette readmit the former Marshal and Governor of Tripoli to the Order, he publicly proclaimed his innocence of the crimes with which he had been charged, crimes that had been alleged for no other reason than to provide a suitable scapegoat for the loss of Tripoli. La Valette had more in mind than simply restoring the former governor; he had designs to recapture the North African city itself. It was a mission he would not accomplish alone, if at all.

Charles V abdicated the Spanish throne in 1556 in favour of his son Philip, who had been King of England by right of his wife Mary I since 1554. Like his father, Philip was concerned with Suleiman's rising power in the Mediterranean. Things became of greater concern for the new king when the Turks attacked the Balearic Islands of Majorca and Minorca in 1558 and ran further coastal raids along the Spanish mainland. As had been the case when the Hospitallers were on Rhodes, great stories circulated about the invincibility of the fleet. However, in the mid-sixteenth century, particularly after the fiascos at Preveza

and Algiers between 1538 and 1541 and the subsequent loss of Tripoli a decade later, the prevalent myth about the fleet was that the undefeatable navy now belonged to the Ottoman Empire. As such, the major players in the waters of the Mediterranean were reluctant to challenge Muslim ships. However, Philip had no such compunctions and assembled, as his father had before him, an international force to recapture Tripoli.

In February of 1560, the Hospitallers travelled to Messina to join the combined naval and military forces of Spain, Venice, Genoa, Savoy and the Papal States, all of whom would once again fall under the general command of Andrea Doria. Accounts of the size of the fleet and the men aboard vary considerably between writers; however, the Christian ships numbered probably no more than 120, of which 54 are believed to have been galleys. Although there seems to be no accurate assessment of how many ships the Hospitallers contributed to the campaign, Whitworth Porter suggests that 2,000 men were supplied by the Order, but that only 400 of these were knights. Given that the total number of men was probably around 10,000, it seems unlikely that the Hospitallers would have contributed 20 per cent of the fighting forces of the campaign. Whatever the true numbers, the Christian fleet eventually dropped anchor near Tripoli. Bad weather, sickness and the lack of drinkable water forced the fleet to weigh anchor and withdraw to the island of Djerba off the Gulf of Gabès in Tunisia. The Christians quickly conquered the island and Juan de la Cerda, the Viceroy of Sicily, ordered that a fortress be constructed on the island. It soon became apparent to the Hospitallers that la Cerda's work project was more for his own vanity than the advancement of the Tripoli mission. By order of Grand Master la Valette, the Hospitallers boarded their ships and returned to Malta, sparing them the fate that awaited those who stayed behind. Two months after the Christians had begun building la Cerda's fortress, Pyali Pasha and Turgut Reis arrived from Constantinople with an Ottoman fleet of some eighty galleys and an equal number of galliots. On 11 May, the Turks then began the quick task of capturing or sinking the majority of the Christian fleet. Although the naval portion of the battle took but a few hours, the Ottomans would lay siege to the fortress for three months, until the garrison finally surrendered, accepting servitude as Ottoman galley slaves in exchange for their lives.

Although the Battle of Djerba can be seen as but a blip on the timeline of Hospitaller history, it is nonetheless a key and critical point in the naval history of the Mediterranean and the conflicts between the Ottoman Empire and Europe. Although as battles go Djerba pales in comparison to the Rhodian sieges, the conquest of Tunis or even the loss of Tripoli, the conflict nonetheless marked the high point of Ottoman domination of the Mediterranean. For more than two decades the Christians had suffered defeat after defeat, as they watched their ships sink along with their hopes of stopping the spread of Islam into Europe. But the myth of Ottoman invincibility, that had enjoyed a generation of

travel over the waves, was about to be put to rest by perhaps the Order's greatest naval commander, Mathurin d'Aux de Lescout, better known as Romégas.

Romégas, like la Valette, was born in the south of France and came from a noble family. In 1542, at the age of 17, he became attached to the Hospitaller Order, but did not become a full knight until the age of 21. Like all knights, Romégas served his mandatory caravan, an obligatory period of time aboard the Order's ships. The young sailor was adept at the ways of the oar and sail and in 1555 he came to prominence, not through a victory at sea, but through an almost miraculous escape while shipwrecked at home. Romégas had been on board one of the ships that capsized in the harbour at Malta during the hurricane that autumn. When the knights were assessing the damage after the storm, they heard a tapping from one of the overturned hulls. Smashing a hole through the bottom of the ship, they were surprised to find the ship's monkey emerging from the hole, followed by Romégas, who had managed to survive in an air pocket. Although shaken by the experience, the Hospitaller sailor

The Battle of Djerba took place on 11 May 1560 and had started as a joint effort between the Hospitallers and Philip II of Spain to retake Tripoli from the Ottomans. The mission went off course and met with failure.

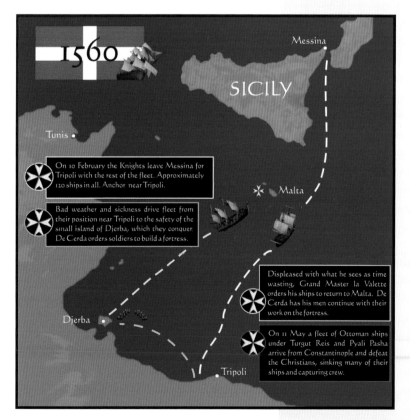

On 10 February the Knights leave Messina for Tripoli with the rest of the fleet. Approximately 120 ships in all. Anchor near Tripoli.

Bad weather and sickness drive fleet from their position near Tripoli to the safety of the small island of Djerba, which they conquer. De Cerda orders soldiers to build a fortress.

Displeased with what he sees as time wasting, Grand Master la Valette orders his ships to return to Malta. De Cerda has his men continue with their work on the fortress.

On 11 May a fleet of Ottoman ships under Turgut Reis and Pyali Pasha arrive from Constantinople and defeat the Christians, sinking many of their ships and capturing crew.

Seven of the Order's galleys under Romégas come across an Ottoman merchant ship near the Greek islands of Kafalonia and Zakynthos. It would be the capture and plunder of this ship that would lead Suleiman to finally launch a full scale attack on Malta the following year.

1564

was soon feeling the wind at his back, once again travelling the Mediterranean in search of new conquests for his Order. Whether it was because of his life-long career as a Hospitaller, his many experiences at sea, or his second chance at life, Romégas's nautical manoeuvres on the Mediterranean showed him as a man without fear. Of Romégas's prowess on the seas and personal character, Vertot wrote in Volume III of his history of the Order:

'No body was so well acquainted as he himself with all the coasts, the ports, and even the smallest creeks and bays in the Mediterranean: he was brave and intrepid, was fearless of danger, and would never suffer any officers or soldiers to be aboard of him that had not as much courage and resolution as himself.'

Romégas's bravery and fearlessness would manifest itself many times throughout 1564. While operating under the Hospitallers' general of galleys, Gozon de Melac, Romégas would engage in several battles and skirmishes with Turgut Reis. Additionally, he assisted the Viceroy of Sicily, Don Garcia de Toledo, who was also King Philip II's admiral, in capturing Peñón de Vélez de la Gomera for Spain. Lying on the North African coast opposite Malaga, the fortress had long been a place of refuge and base for the Ottomans' corsair allies. It was to be Romégas's subsequent capture of a single Ottoman galleon that would set off the powder keg beneath Suleiman, finally provoking him to a full-out assault on Malta.

Soon after capturing the pirate stronghold of Peñón de Vélez, seven Hospitaller galleys sailing near the Greek islands of Zakynthos and Kefalonia came upon and captured a large merchant ship armed with twenty brass cannon, manned by 200 Ottoman Janissaries

and loaded with 80,000 ducats' worth of eastern merchandise. This was not merely another Ottoman merchant vessel: it was owned by the Kızlar Ağası, the chief eunuch of Suleiman's seraglio or imperial harem. Eunuchs were a common component of the Ottoman court and were procured from either Egypt or the Balkans. The Kızlar Ağası, or black eunuchs, looked after the harem, while the white eunuchs were, from the late sixteenth century onwards, forbidden from even entering the harem. Within the Ottoman court, the Kızlar Ağası took on an important political role, rivalling the grand vizier in power. Although this power would begin to wane by the mid-seventeenth century, at the time Romégas captured the chief eunuch's galley the position was an important one, and any outrage the Kızlar Ağası expressed to Suleiman would have been listened to. Complicating the matter was the fact that several of the sultan's harem favourites had a financial interest in the goods captured along with the ship.

At the time of the capture of the Kızlar Ağası's galleon, Suleiman, like la Valette, was 70 years of age, both men having been born in 1494. If either man would have preferred peace to war in their remaining years it was simply not to be. For Suleiman, the pleas of his seraglio for revenge against the Christian dogs whose piracy had cost them so much could not be ignored. Nor could la Valette and his knights ignore the Ottoman fleet Suleiman sent to punish the Hospitallers for their misdeeds. Suleiman had begun his reign by driving the knights from Rhodes; he would now end it with one last campaign against his long-standing enemies.

Right: **Located on the seaward shore of the Mount Sceberras peninsula is Fort St Elmo. When the Hospitallers arrived in 1530 the point had but a watch tower. Over the years the Hospitallers evolved the area into a well-fortified star-shaped fortress.**
Bigstock/Steve Reineck

CHAPTER 15
The Siege of Malta

Although advance intelligence had allowed la Valette to seek help from his European allies, only Pope Pius IV and King Philip supplied immediate aid, and even then it was only 10,000 crowns from the Holy

See and a small number of troops from Spain. As was the case for L'Isle Adam in 1522, Grand Master la Valette would have to put his trust in the tenacity and skill of his own men if he were to survive against the sultan. No matter how much faith he had in his knights, the precedent had not been a good one, and the very reason he now prepared to defend Malta was because L'Isle Adam had failed to secure Rhodes forty-three years earlier. It was a situation he knew well, for he had been there and had looked back on the island as the Order's ships sailed for Candia, uncertain of where their next home would be. Soon after the battle's completion, Grand Master la Valette wrote to Brother George of Hohenheim, the Grand Prior of Germany, appealing for his assistance. The letter, dated 9 October 1565, was originally published in *Caeli Augustini Curionis Saracenis Historia libri tres* and was republished in Porter's 1883 history of the Order and gives la Valette's reminiscences of the conflict:

'Brother John la Valette, Master of the Hospital of St. John of Jerusalem, to his venerable and dear brother in Christ, George of Hohenheim, called 'Bombast', the prior of our priory in Germany.
'Greeting,
'Although we doubt not from the letters and verbal reports of many you have already heard of the coming of the Turkish fleet to invade and utterly destroy these islands and our

Pope Pius IV is depicted in this monument to his honour in Milan Cathedral. Pius donated 10,000 crowns to the Hospitallers to help finance their defences prior to the siege of Malta in 1565. *Giovanni Dall'Orto*

Order, and the glorious victory we, by the Divine aid, have gained over it, yet we have thought that these things would give you still greater pleasure if they were brought to your knowledge by a letter from ourselves.

'For whereas we are firmly persuaded that in this our most happy and opportune success thou wilt render due thanks to Almighty God for the same, and that by reason of the high position that thou holdest in our Order, thou wilt reap the full reward of our good fortune, we are therefore minded to rejoice with thee with a common joy, and clearly to bear witness that we ascribe the most admirable and glorious victory to our Lord Jesus Christ, the King of kings, and the author of all good things, and in order that this may be done worthily and willingly, we will narrate the whole matter in as few words as possible, and at no great length, for that would be to write a history of it.

'Sultan Solyman, the bitter enemy of the name of Christian, and of our Order especially, not satisfied with already having taken from us our noble island of Rhodes and the fortress of Tripoli, and with having plundered us of nearly all our worldly goods, dreaming only of utterly destroying, and above all extinguishing our Order by any means in his power, ordered a well-appointed and numerous fleet to be fitted out, which sailed from Byzantium on

March 21st, and reached Malta on May 17th. 'The fleet was composed of three-banked and two-banked galleys, and about 250 vessels of other kinds. The number of fighting men on board was approximately 40,000; the land forces under Mustapha Bassa [Pasha], the fleet under Pyali Bassa.

'After a few days spent in unloading stores, reconnoitring, pitching tents, and making such other preparations as are usual, the attack commenced with a violent assault and bombardment of Fort St. Elmo, at the mouth of the harbour. Having continued this for many days without intermission, and having opened a great breach in the walls, they assailed it with all kinds of missiles; but the valour and energy of our knights and other soldiers held it for thirty-five days, with great slaughter of the enemy, although the fort itself, in the opinion of many, was deemed tenable against so vast a force only for a few days.

'At length, on the 23rd of June, when we could no longer repel the attack and withstand the overwhelming number of the besiegers, the fort itself, surrounded and shut in as it was by sea and land, and deprived of all succour, was taken by the Turks, and the few survivors of our men were put to the sword.

'Elated by this success, they then commenced the attack on the fort and town of St. Michele, and on this newly-built town (the Bourg),

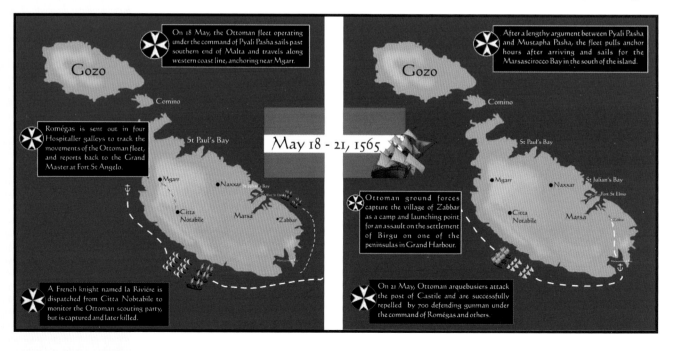

On 18 May, the Ottoman fleet operating under the command of Pyali Pasha sails past southern end of Malta and travels along western coast line, anchoring near Mgarr.

Romégas is sent out in four Hospitaller galleys to track the movements of the Ottoman fleet, and reports back to the Grand Master at Fort St Angelo.

A French knight named la Rivière is dispatched from Citta Nobtabile to monitor the Ottoman scouting party, but is captured and later killed.

May 18 - 21, 1565

After a lengthy argument between Pyali Pasha and Mustapha Pasha, the fleet pulls anchor hours after arriving and sails for the Marsascirocco Bay in the south of the island.

Ottoman ground forces capture the village of Zabbar as a camp and launching point for an assault on the settlement of Birgu on one of the peninsulas in Grand Harbour.

On 21 May, Ottoman arquebusiers attack the post of Castile and are successfully repelled by 700 defending gunman under the command of Romégas and others.

especially directing it on the bastions of Castella and Lusitania (Castile and Portugal). According to their usual custom, they began with the greatest activity, and an increased strength of artillery, to batter and breach the walls in many places.

'This terrible and furious attack was made by the whole of the Turkish force, equally powerful by land and sea, and then by huge engines of vast size and fearful power, throwing, day and night, stone and iron balls of from five to seven palms circumference, large enough to destroy not only walls, but to overturn even mountains; and by their force the walls themselves were so breached in many places that it was easy to walk up them. The infidels frequently assaulted these with much noise and fury, but as often as they came on they were driven back with great defeat and loss in killed and wounded.

'Their leaders, both naval and military, having in vain delivered many attacks at different points with all their forces during a space of nearly four months, and having sustained great losses of their old soldiers, and all the more as winter was now drawing on, when, by the law of nations, all warfare rightly ceases, now meditated withdrawal, or rather flight, which was accelerated by the arrival of Don Garcia de Toledo, viceroy of Sicily, and admiral of the king of Spain's fleet, who brought a reinforcement of 10,000 soldiers and picked men, among whom were at least 214 of our knights, and many other noble and well-born men, who, stirred by Christian piety alone, had voluntarily assembled from various parts of the world to bring us aid.

'You have now shortly, and in a few words, the account of the arrival and flight of the Turkish fleet, and of the victory which by God's help we gained over it.

'It will be for you to consider and imagine in what a state the Order and island now are, and would be found to be, to what poverty we are reduced, and of how many things we are in want; and unless we are relieved by the assistance of our brethren, especially of those like yourself, as we hope and believe we shall be, we must be undone.

Farewell!'

Although a faithful overview of the nearly four-month-long siege, la Valette's letter was clearly written for the purpose of appealing to his Grand Prior's sense of charity in order that he would offer his assistance in rebuilding and re-establishing what had been destroyed. As such, the Grand Master leaves out many of the details of what can be considered the Hospitallers' most important battle, a conflict of which Voltaire would write two centuries later, stating 'Nothing is better known than the siege of Malta.'

It is important to understand that the siege of Malta in 1565 was considerably different from the siege of Rhodes in 1522; for in the former conflict the knights had invested two centuries of work on its fortifications to prepare for the siege, whereas at the time of Suleiman's attack on Malta in 1565, the Hospitallers had been on the island for only three decades, and little had been done in the early years due to L'Isle Adam's belief that Malta was but a launching point for the Order's reconquest of Rhodes. Although subsequent Grand Masters had sought to strengthen the island's defences, there was still much to do if the Hospitallers were to repel the Turks Suleiman would send. Every available body was put to work – knight, native and slave – on strengthening the Order's three fortresses of Fort St Angelo, located on the tip of Birgu, Fort St Michael located on the tip of Senglea, and the star-shaped Fort St Elmo on the tip of Mount Sceberras.

But there were other differences between their two island homes that would work in the Order's favour. Rhodes had been a lush island in the Aegean, well capable of sustaining the sultan's armies with food, water and materials. Malta, on the other hand, was but a barren rock barely capable of sustaining the lives of its inhabitants, let alone the tens of thousands of soldiers Suleiman would send to capture it. At the first sign of Ottoman sails on the horizon, the island's limited water supply would be spoiled with bitter herbs and animal carcasses to make any combatant sick who tried to drink from it.

Although la Valette's account of the battle indicates that an additional 214 knights accompanied de Toledo as part of the reinforcement party, he makes no mention of how many knights were present on the island when the Ottomans arrived in May. Another eyewitness to the siege was Francesco Balbi di Correggio, a Spanish arquebusier who kept a journalistic account of the conflict which he published in 1568. In di Correggio's account of the siege we see that there were 500 knights from the Langues. This is similar to the number offered by Whitworth Porter who tells us that an inventory of knights and sergeants-at-arms taken prior to the battle numbered 474 knights and 67 servants-at-arms. Of the knights, 164 were from Italy, 85 from Aragon, 68 from Castile, 61 from Provence, 57 from France, 25 from Auvergne, 13 from Germany, and la Valette's Latin secretary, Oliver Starkey, representing the suppressed Langue of England. Although the island was further defended by a combination of Spanish, Italian and Greek soldiers, it was 3,000 Maltese natives that made up the bulk of the 5,500 defenders di Correggio lists in his account.

La Valette's letter provides us with greater detail on the number of enemy combatants; however, his numbers are higher than those of di Correggio, who says there were 29,500, of whom 6,000 were Janissaries, 9,000 were Spahis cavalry from various regions, and another 4,000 were Iayalars, religious fanatics who sought glory in death, and who formed the vanguard in many attacks. The remainder was composed of adventurers, corsairs and volunteers. Other accounts indicate that the Ottomans numbered closer to 20,000, but whatever the true number on either side, the ratios always indicate that the Hospitallers and their allies were greatly outnumbered.

On 18 May 1565, the Ottoman fleet operating under the command of Pyali Pasha was spotted by the lookouts of Fort St Elmo and Fort St Angelo, but rather than pulling north, the fleet appeared to be heading south.

The arquebusier were soldiers who fired an arquebus, a smoothbore firearm with a range of around 200 metres. The arquebus was the first shoulder-fired gun.

Grand Master la Valette dispatched two shots from the Order's cannon and four galleys from the Great Harbour; the former to let those at Citta Notabile and Gozo know that the enemy had arrived, the latter to follow the movements of the same. Romégas, whom la Valette had put in charge of the galleys, returned with the report that the Ottomans had bypassed the Marsascirocco Bay on the southern tip of the island and continued along its western coast. With the Turkish fleet out of sight, la Valette took the opportunity to dispatch a swift boat from the Grand Harbour bound for Sicily with the message to send help as quickly as possible.

Although it was not apparent at the time, the reason for the cruise along the western coast of the island was to drop anchor near Mgarr in the northwest. As the commander of the armies, Mustapha Pasha had intended to initiate his attack with Citta Notabile in the centre of the island and then push on to capture the whole north of the island. However, Pyali Pasha had completely different ideas about where the fleet should drop anchor and where Mustapha should concentrate his attack. For the naval commander, Fort St Elmo was where the assault should begin, something Mustapha Pasha felt was unnecessary to achieve victory. Having been humiliated by the Hospitallers in 1522 and nearly killed for his inability to capture the island early on, Mustapha still had a strong desire to redeem himself for his earlier failure. However, several hours of debate did not go in his favour and the fleet weighed anchor and returned southward towards Marsascirocco Bay, which would have still allowed Mustapha to carry out his designs.

Three days after arriving in the Mediterranean, the Ottomans began their debarkations, and by 21 May, they had worked their way northeast, capturing the village of Zabbar as a base of operations and pressed on to the landward end of the Birgu, which was defended by the Langue of Castile. Although there had been a skirmish near Mgarr in which the French knight la Rivière had been killed after being captured on a scouting mission, Birgu would be the point of the first real battle. La Valette dispatched the Marshal and several of his leading commanders, including Romégas, to lead approximately 700 arquebusiers against the Ottoman advance.

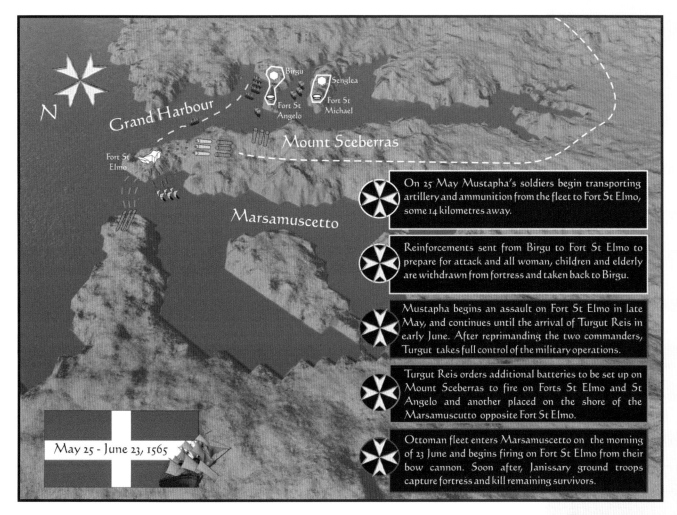

On 25 May Mustapha's soldiers begin transporting artillery and ammunition from the fleet to Fort St Elmo, some 14 kilometres away.

Reinforcements sent from Birgu to Fort St Elmo to prepare for attack and all woman, children and elderly are withdrawn from fortress and taken back to Birgu.

Mustapha begins an assault on Fort St Elmo in late May, and continues until the arrival of Turgut Reis in early June. After reprimanding the two commanders, Turgut takes full control of the military operations.

Turgut Reis orders additional batteries to be set up on Mount Sceberras to fire on Forts St Elmo and St Angelo and another placed on the shore of the Marsamuscutto opposite Fort St Elmo.

Ottoman fleet enters Marsamuscetto on the morning of 23 June and begins firing on Fort St Elmo from their bow cannon. Soon after, Janissary ground troops capture fortress and kill remaining survivors.

May 25 - June 23, 1565

The arquebus was a precursor to the musket and the first gun fired from the shoulder. Similar in design to a modern-day rifle, the arquebus was a smoothbore firearm that operated on a matchlock system and had a range of about 200 metres. Although the Ottomans also had muzzle-loading weapons, di Correggio tells us in his account of the battle that the Turkish weapons were seven to nine palms long, considerably longer than the Christians' weapons. Although the attackers had more guns to fire, the defenders were able to reload theirs quicker and get off more shots. Accuracy seems to have been problematic for both sides because the five-hour battle that ensued saw the death of one hundred Ottomans and about twenty-two defenders. Of the latter casualties, the majority had been killed when a Spanish knight was distributing gunpowder to his men

and a barrel exploded, killing him and a dozen of his soldiers.

Mustapha and Pyali were once again at odds over what to do next. Pyali, unfamiliar with weather patterns in the Mediterranean, felt that the fleet was not safe in Marsascirocco and wanted to move north to take harbour in Marsamuscetto. Before that could take place, Mustapha's army would have to take control of Fort St Elmo which was well positioned to sink any enemy ship pulling into the northern harbour. Again the younger Pyali won the approval of the war council and on 25 May, Mustapha's soldiers began transporting the heavy and awkward artillery over the 14 kilometres between the fleet and Fort St Elmo.

To prepare for the imminent attack la Valette sent an additional 100 knights and 60 galley slaves from Birgu to Fort St Elmo and ordered all women, children and elderly who

Stephen Dafoe and Stephen McKim map (Base terrain *Bigstock/Christian Formosa)*

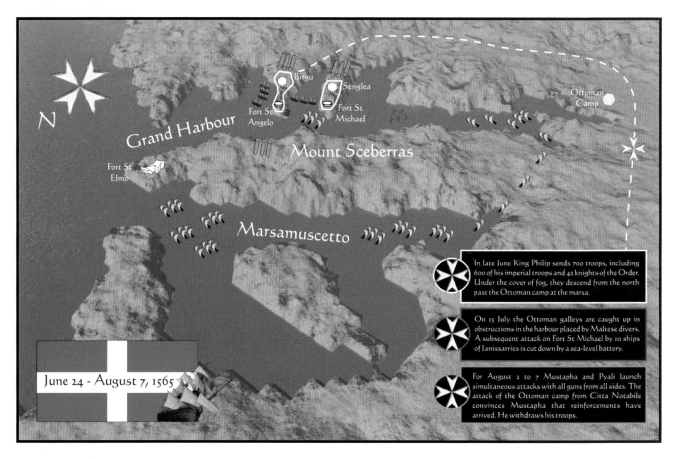

Within the map image:

N

Grand Harbour

Birgu

Senglea

Fort St Angelo

Fort St Michael

Ottoman Camp

Mount Sceberras

Fort St Elmo

Marsamuscetto

In late June King Philip sends 700 troops, including 600 of his imperial troops and 42 knights of the Order. Under the cover of fog, they descend from the north past the Ottoman camp at the marsa.

On 15 July the Ottoman galleys are caught up in obstructions in the harbour placed by Maltese divers. A subsequent attack on Fort St Michael by 10 ships of Janissaries is cut down by a sea-level battery.

For August 2 to 7 Mustapha and Pyali launch simultaneous attacks with all guns from all sides. The attack of the Ottoman camp from Citta Notabile convinces Mustapha that reinforcements have arrived. He withdraws his troops.

June 24 - August 7, 1565

Stephen Dafoe and Stephen McKim map (Base terrain *Bigstock/ Christian Formosa)*

were at the soon-to-be-besieged fort to return to Birgu. By the time the Turks arrived at Mount Sceberras, la Valette had, according to di Correggio, assembled some 800 men to defend the fortress. But the arrival of Turkish forces on the peninsula did not mark the start of cannon fire; first they would have to create trenches for troop protection. The lack of soil on the rocky outcropping delayed the procedure, as men transported earth and other materials from where the fleet was anchored to the front line. La Valette matched the Ottomans' work with efforts of his own, namely securing Birgu and Senglea as much as possible and heightening the cavalier at Fort St Angelo so that a pair of cannon could effectively fire on the Ottomans on Mount Sceberras, something they did ceaselessly while the Ottomans prepared their defences. Once the trenches were completed, the Turks assembled their battery of artillery about 180 metres from the fortress. There lined up against Fort St Elmo's walls were ten cannon and three colubrines capable of firing 80lb and

60lb shot respectively, as well as one basilisk capable of hurling 160lb shot. It was not long before debris from the fortress walls and the ravelin were filling the ditches between.

By early June, some of the defenders were feeling the gnawing fear of impending doom and slipped away by night to seek council with la Valette at St Angelo. The delegation, led by a Spanish knight named la Cerda, told the Grand Master that St Elmo was untenable and would surely fall within a few days. When la Valette asked the Spanish knight what the extent of his casualties were, the knight sheepishly admitted that they were minimal, that the real purpose of his request for aid or abandonment was that the walls were so breached from Ottoman bombardment that it was taking an increasing amount of manpower to prevent them from crumbling altogether. Having fought at Rhodes and lived to tell of it, la Valette saw la Cerda's moaning as the worst form of cowardice. The Grand Master assured the young knight that he need not return to Fort St Elmo. Instead, la Valette and a hand-picked group of knights would return to fight in la Cerda and his fellows' places. The Grand Master's point had been made and la Cerda and his companions apologetically returned to the fort, their heads hanging lower than when they had come. After their return, la Valette sent some additional troops over to the fortress and continued to do so each night, returning St Elmo's wounded back to the Order's hospital at Birgu.

The arrival of Turgut Reis with thirteen galleys and 1,500 soldiers provided relief to the Ottomans' own wounded and replacement for their dead. But the arrival also marked a change in command. Whatever position Mustapha and Pyali truly held in the campaign's hierarchy, both men had been instructed by Suleiman that when Turgut arrived from Tripoli, he was to take supreme command. It was a situation neither leader could argue with, for Turgut knew Malta well, both from having sailed numerous times around it over the years, but also from having attempted its capture in 1551. Turgut was not long in criticising both commanders for their efforts thus far. It was his opinion that they should have captured Gozo first and foremost, followed by Citta Notabile, which, as Mustapha had originally argued, would give the Ottomans control of the north of the island. From there, an attack on the Hospitallers' main fortifications on Birgu would have been protected from the rear, preventing reinforcements from landing to offer the Christians assistance.

Now that cannon were firing on the walls of Fort St Elmo, it would sap Turkish morale to withdraw from the siege and Turgut ordered the attack to continue in earnest, placing himself on the front lines of the battle. He ordered a second battery of artillery to be positioned on Mount Sceberras so that it could fire on either St Elmo or St Angelo, and a third battery of four cannon was positioned on the opposite side of Marsamuscetto on the northernmost point of land. Despite the constant bombardment from three sides, the fortress held out for another three weeks, hanging on by its last tenuous grasp until 23 June when the Turkish fleet entered Marsamuscetto and began firing on the fort with their bow cannon, while the landward batteries continued their forward assault on the crumbling fortress. With little left but rubble, the Janissaries followed the Iayalars into the breach to slaughter the hundred or so remaining, and mostly wounded, defenders.

Fort St Elmo was now in Ottoman hands, but the price had been dear; not only had the Turks lost countless men, but also Turgut Reis himself. The supreme commander had been struck in the head by a rock fragment the previous week when a shot from Fort St Angelo had landed near to the front line battery he was personally commanding. Although mortally wounded, Turgut hung on for six days, long enough to learn the news that the star-shaped fortress had been secured.

With the death of Turgut Reis, command of the operation returned to Pyali and Mustapha, who undoubtedly took pleasure in capturing Fort St Elmo on the eve of the Festival of St John the Baptist, the patron of the Order they had come to crush. Searching the ruins of the captured fortress for the bodies of fallen knights, Mustapha ordered their heads to be struck off and mounted on poles facing their Grand Master at St Angelo, a mockery of the fate of their patron. Their bodies were nailed to makeshift crosses in a mockery of the crucifixion of Christ and were then dumped into the Grand Harbour. Whatever Mustapha's message was in mutilating la Valette's knights, the Grand Master sent the Ottoman commander one of his own. After decapitating every Turkish prisoner in his possession, he had their heads loaded into the two cannon on the cavalier above Fort St Angelo and fired across the Grand Harbour into the Ottomans' camp.

Now that St Elmo had been lost, all defences turned on the twin towns of Birgu and Senglea, which were connected by a makeshift bridge across the waterway between them. La Valette instructed his men that no further prisoners were to be taken; no quarter would be given in the battle that lay ahead, and the prisoners who were held at Citta Notabile were publicly hanged one per day throughout the remainder of the siege. As the prisoners were trotted out for execution, reinforcements arrived on the northern shore of the island, and made their way across land to Birgu. These fresh troops consisted of forty-two knights, thirty-five volunteers, sixty gunners and six hundred of King Philip's imperial troops. The arrival of more than seven hundred additional soldiers raised the morale in both of the Grand Harbour's towns.

Although the Ottomans still greatly outnumbered the Christians, the arrival of reinforcements, combined with the arduous task of dragging arms and armaments from Marsamuscetto around the Grand Harbour and along the heavily fortified towns of Birgu and Senglea, prompted Mustapha to offer la Valette the same terms of surrender that Suleiman had offered L'Isle Adam four decades earlier at Rhodes. La Valette was unprepared to accept them and personally led Mustapha's messenger to the edge of the ditches surrounding St Angelo where he pointed down to them and told him that they were the only part of Malta he was prepared to let the Ottoman Empire have, and only then as a grave for Janissaries.

Failing in his negotiations, Mustapha ramped up his efforts to simultaneously besiege the two towns by land and sea, and by the first week of July a fleet of eighty small galleys had been dragged across the narrow land passage between the two harbours and launched at the landward point of the Grand Harbour. This would allow Mustapha to attack Fort St Michael on the tip of Senglea from the water and then launch an assault from the landward side once it had been sufficiently reduced in its ability to resist, but the efforts in the Grand Harbour were a failure. Unknown to the Turks, Maltese divers created a series of underwater obstructions to halt the galleys. On 15 July, when the ships moved in for an attack, they were scuttled on the obstructions and easily picked off by the Maltese swimmers who took to the water for that purpose. A subsequent attempt to get ten boats loaded with 1,000 Janissaries past Fort St Angelo to attack Fort St Michael also met with failure. Although the ships evaded both fortresses'

Vincenzo Anastagi, shown in this oil painting by El Greco, was an Italian knight who joined the Order in 1563, two years prior to the siege of Malta. Leading a group of horsemen from Citta Notabile to attack and burn the Ottoman camp, Anastagi fooled Mustapha Pasha into believing that an army of reinforcements had arrived, a deception that prompted the Turkish commander to withdraw his troops from a successful attack on the Hospitallers' fortress.

main batteries and many of the Janissaries made ground at Fort St Michael, they and nine of their ships were cut down by three cannon hidden at the foot of St Angelo, a sea-level battery that had been positioned by la Valette to protect the spur of the Senglea peninsula. The loss of 400 to 800 Janissaries combined with nearly 3,000 who were cut down in a simultaneous attack on the fortress from the land side, prompted Mustapha to take a different tactic than simply sending his men to their deaths.

Putting Pyali in charge of an assault on Birgu, Mustapha focused his efforts on Senglea. On 2 August, the air filled with smoke as every available cannon, basilisk and mortar fired on the two fortifications, a cacophony that could be heard as far away as Syracuse and Catania, and was mistaken for the sound of distant thunder. The two commanders kept up the cannonade for five straight days, pausing only to allow the troops to attack the breaches when they thought they had been sufficiently opened for a proper assault. Despite the repeated blasts, the walls held fast and where openings had appeared, the defenders held in maintaining the security of the breaches.

On 7 August, while Mustapha personally oversaw a renewed assault on Senglea, he ordered a full assault on the post guarded by the Langue of Castile on Birgu. This is where the initial land assault had taken place after the fleet had landed at Marsascirocco. The fortifications had taken a considerable pounding since that initial attack, and after nearly three months were beginning to show the effects of Turkish shot. Like Rhodes, the settlement had double walls; the breach of the outer walls presented attackers with the double problem of breaking through the second, while being confined within the first. For those who defended the position, the presence of combatants between the walls allowed many to be mowed down before they could escape back through the breach. It was a price many would pay after breaking through Birgu's outer walls. Meanwhile, Mustapha's efforts at Senglea were more favourable and his men had not only broken through the outer walls but had reached as far as the citadel. But as Mustapha's men continued to assault the fortifications, they heard the sound of trumpets, an unmistakable signal that their commander was ordering a full retreat.

Word had reached Mustapha's ears that further reinforcements had arrived from the north and that Christian horsemen were setting fire to the Ottoman camp and slaughtering everyone who was there. The reality of the matter was that the Turkish camp was being attacked. However, the assault was led by Vincenzo Anastagi, an Italian knight who had joined the Hospitallers two years prior to the siege, and who had been stationed at Citta Notabile. Anastagi, unaware of the assault on Senglea, was leading a small party of horsemen on a routine patrol looking for stragglers when he learned of the renewed assault. Hoping to help by creating some kind of diversion, he ordered his men to attack the Turkish camp, which at the time was populated with the enemy's sick and wounded, as well as other non-combatants. The diversion succeeded well beyond what Anastagi had hoped for, but it would not halt Mustapha for long.

With the summer nearing its close, Mustapha knew that prolonging the siege through the autumn and into the approaching winter would not work in the empire's favour. It was a reality that la Valette would use in his own decisions when the attacks inevitably resumed. Both men knew that the general paucity of crops on the island would only be increased as winter approached and that the Ottomans' supplies would be further reduced. Although temperatures would not hamper the siege, winter rains and gale-force winds certainly would.

It was for these reasons that Mustapha made a concerted effort to bring down the two fronts through mining and artillery operations. As the sappers dug beneath the walls and the Turkish cannonade did the same, a suggestion was made to la Valette to abandon Birgu and withdraw his troops into the Fortress of St Angelo. La Valette would have no part in the idea. He had meant what he had said to Mustapha's messenger in June; the only land he was prepared to offer the Turk was the ditches that surrounded his stronghold, which would be filled with Mustapha's men. Despite his determination to be buried beneath the rubble of the fortress, if it should come to that, the Grand Master knew that the chances

of survival were slim if the Ottomans were not driven away by the approach of winter. Also slim were the chances of reinforcements from Sicily. Don Garcia de Toledo had assured him that he would send an army of reinforcements before the end of August, but he had made similar promises throughout the siege, usually with some conditions attached. It was not that de Toledo was reluctant to help as he had left his own illegitimate son with the Grand Master before the battle began, a young man who was killed despite la Valette's best efforts to keep him from open conflict. Whether de Toledo arrived as he had repeatedly promised or not, one thing was clear in la Valette's mind – as his earlier predecessor had learned on Rhodes many years ago – if he had any faith in the chance of survival it rested solely with his men and his God. It was his duty as Grand Master to ensure that his men had the same confidence in him that he had in them.

La Valette soon got this opportunity on 18 August when a Turkish mine was exploded in a tunnel beneath a Castile-defended bastion. The unexpected breach took the defenders by surprise and by the time the smoke had cleared the Ottomans had taken the post, putting some of la Valette's knights to flight. The sudden appearance of their aged Grand Master, protected with but a simple helmet and a long pike, and leading a contingent of knights to offer aid to the defenders, prompted and inspired the men to return to

An eighteenth-century engraving romantically depicts the whole of the four-month siege in one epic display.

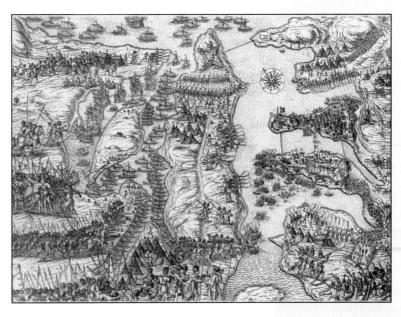

the front line. During the battle that followed, la Valette's leg was wounded by an exploding grenade. For the next three days the Turks continued the assault, and although the Hospitallers held their position, their numbers were steadily reduced.

The slow movement of the siege led the two Turkish commanders to an impasse over what to do next. For Mustapha, Malta must be conquered at all costs. He was 65 years old, had already failed once in his attempts to exterminate the Hospitallers, and knew that if he failed Suleiman again he would not live to get a third opportunity. For the much younger Pyali Pasha, the fleet Suleiman had entrusted to his care was of far greater importance than the conquest of the island. When Mustapha suggested that arrangements be made to secure enough provisions and supplies from Tripoli and Constantinople to continue the siege into the winter, Pyali assured him that when summer was over, so too was his involvement in the siege. With or without the army, Pyali would return the sultan's fleet to Constantinople. It was a point of view shared by a large number of the army; they had been on Malta for more than three months, seen large numbers of their fellow soldiers killed in battle, and were rapidly losing all enthusiasm for continued fighting.

Despite their misgivings, Mustapha rallied the troops for another full-out assault on the morning of 23 August, knowing that perhaps it was their last chance to obtain the victory that had become his obsession. Again the Hospitallers – bloodied, wounded, tired and greatly reduced in number – maintained the breaches. Withdrawing his troops, Mustapha remained content to spend his remaining time assailing the fortress's walls with his cannonade alone, but as August ended he knew that his time was ending along with it. He ordered his men once again to launch an assault, but their lack of enthusiasm resulted in a failed attack and a greater desire to withdraw from the island.

Spending the next week in his tent, despondent over his second failure with the Hospitallers, Mustapha was moved again to action by the news that troops were on the way from the north to give aid to the Christians. This was not a false alarm caused by a handful of horseman launching a minor raid from Citta Notabile, but the arrival of 8,000 troops under Don Garcia de Toledo, who was on his return to collect another 4,000 who were camped at port and ready to join the battle. Accepting at long last that he would have to return to Constantinople to accept his fate with Suleiman, Mustapha ordered the full

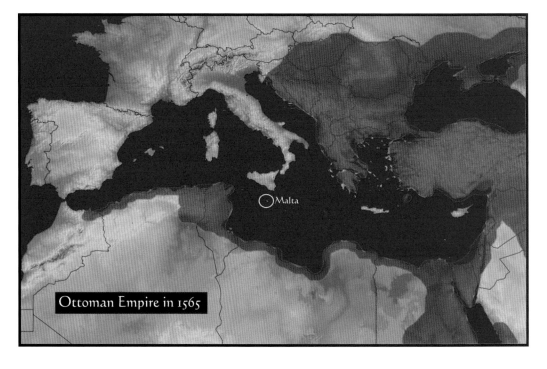

The extent of Suleiman's Ottoman Empire at the time of his death in 1566 shows the true import of the Hospitallers' success in defending Malta. Had the sultan been victorious, he would have had a base of operations to press an attack on Sicily and Italy, taking a larger portion of Europe than he already had.
Author graphic (Base map Bigstock/ Barbara Fordyce)

Ottoman Empire in 1565

Malta

withdrawal of the army. Throughout the night of 7 September 1565, the Turks moved their arms and ammunition from the tip of the Grand Harbour and across land to the fleet at Marsamuscetto. The next morning the troops began their embarkation and voyage back to Constantinople. As the ships left the harbour, the white crossed banner of the Order could be seen once again flying over the ruins of Fort St Elmo. The Hospitallers had emerged victorious in their greatest and most important battle since leaving Rhodes.

The siege of Malta was similar to the Battle of Djerba in that the Ottomans wasted considerable time attacking Fort St Elmo, just as the Christians had in building a fortress on the tiny island of Djerba instead of advancing on Tripoli. Had Pyali listened to Mustapha and taken Citta Notabile early on, the Muslims would have been able to sweep out and capture the whole of the north, effectively cutting off all communications in that direction. Having failed to do so, it was easy for the Hospitallers to maintain contact with the forces assembling at Sicily, who eventually landed in the north, a point of debarkation that would have been difficult had it been previously captured by the Ottomans. After having their energy sapped by the efforts to take St Elmo, the arrival of Don Garcia de Toledo's reinforcements had been the catalyst to force the Ottomans to retreat.

The importance of this great siege, a combination of Hospitaller unity and Ottoman disunity, cannot be underestimated. This was not merely another in a long line of battles between east and west, between Christianity and Islam. Nor was it a last hurrah for those who clung to long-dead Crusader ideals. Had this small speck of an island, given as a gift to an archaic Military Order, actually fallen to the Turks, the Ottoman Empire would have gained a powerful base from which to launch an assault upon Sicily, and from there Italy. Once the crescent banner was flying from the

St John's Co-Cathedral was commenced after the great siege as a conventual church for the Hospitallers. Construction began in 1573 and completed in 1578 under Grand Master Jean de la Cassière. Although la Valette was originally buried in Our Lady of the Victories, his remains are currently housed in St John's, along with many of his fellow Grand Masters.
Bigstock/Pawel Osinski

ramparts of Rome, the Catholic faith would face a greater demoralisation than it had faced from the rise in Protestantism, and the rest of Europe, whether Catholic or Protestant, would have been open to the attacks of the powerful Muslim empire advancing from land and sea. Had it not been for Jean Parisot de la Valette, his Hospitallers and the Maltese people, the whole of Europe may have looked very different than it does today.

But the sultan's commanders had failed in their mission and the one commander who had the military skill to succeed was killed by a fragment of rock. As far as fragments of rock went, Malta was one that the sultan would not return to, although upon learning of Mustapha and Pyali's failure, he vowed to lead the mission personally as he had at Rhodes in 1522.

Suleiman the Magnificent would die the September after his troops returned from Malta, leaving behind an empire that was a sixteenth-century superpower, built steadily over his 46-year-long reign. Although his armies had extended his empire throughout North Africa and into Persia, where he was able to capture the many sacred cities where his faith had begun, his penetration into Europe remained largely land-based, ending in modern-day Croatia and Austria. The sultan's hopes of using Malta as a base from which to take Europe, starting from the boot of Italy, had been repelled by Jean Parisot de la Valette,

the shield of Europe, whose Hospitaller brethren had taken a barren rock in the Mediterranean and saved Europe from being ruled by the crescent.

La Valette followed his old adversary to the afterlife two years later, dying at Malta on 21 August 1568. The Grand Master had suffered a stroke after returning from a hunting expedition and spent his remaining weeks in his palace. Before his death he freed his slaves and enjoined his brethren to return to the unity they had shown during the great siege three years earlier, something that had fallen apart in the interim. La Valette was buried in the city that to this day bears his name – Valletta – a city whose cornerstone was laid on 28 March 1566 by the Grand Master's own hand, and was still being built when he died peacefully, to the sound of hammer striking chisel. Inscribed upon his tomb are words written by his secretary and long-time friend, Sir Oliver Starkey, that summarise his prominence in Hospitaller and European history:

'Here lies La Valette.
Worthy of eternal honour,
He who was once the scourge of Africa and Asia,
And the shield of Europe,
Whence he expelled the barbarians by his Holy Arms,
Is the first to be buried in this beloved city,
Whose founder he was.'

CHAPTER 16
Lepanto and Beyond

Many modern histories of the Knights Hospitaller end with the siege of Malta in 1565, and although this book has largely followed that model, the victory over Suleiman was by no means the end of the story. There are a few key events that occurred over the next four centuries that are worthy of at least a few words.

The completion of Valletta gave the Hospitallers a fortified home which was even more impregnable than it had been when Ottoman sails had come to capture it in 1565. Francesco Laparelli, the papal engineer sent to oversee the construction, had created a city unlike anything the Order had occupied in its 500-year history. Once again the Hospitallers felt confident to sally forth into the waters of the Mediterranean, certain that in their absence their island home could withstand anything the Ottoman Empire, or any other potential enemy, could hurl at it. La Valette's successor Pierre de Monte permitted the knights to launch missions against Turkish corsairs. These piracy voyages often brought the Hospitaller ships back to port loaded with booty, but one unsuccessful mission resulted in a catastrophic disaster for the fleet.

In 1570, Saint-Clement was commanding four galleys that were returning provisions to Malta when he was overtaken by a corsair named Ochiali. The pirate captured two of the fleet's ships, caused Saint-Clement's to run aground and Saint-Clement himself to run for cover. Sixty-two Hospitallers were killed in the conflict. On his return to Malta, Saint-Clement was put on trial, found guilty of fleeing in the face of the enemy and stripped of his habit. But public indignation was high, reminiscent of the outrage shown towards Gaspard la Vallier after the loss of Tripoli in 1551. To satiate the outrage, Saint-Clement was turned over to the public courts who decided that the best punishment to fit his heinous crime was to have him strangled, loaded into a sack and dumped into the sea. Although this sentence may seem barbaric and

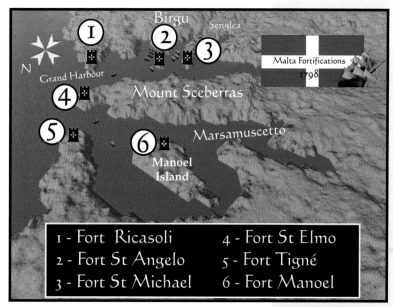

1 - Fort Ricasoli   4 - Fort St Elmo
2 - Fort St Angelo   5 - Fort Tigné
3 - Fort St Michael   6 - Fort Manoel

inhumane to modern eyes, it is important to remember that without ships, the Hospitallers were prisoners on their own island, and the siege of 1565 had deprived the Order of a part of its fleet. The loss of three more due to Saint-Clement's carelessness and cowardice was one that had to be properly paid for. But despite the losses and diminished size of the remaining fleet, Grand Master de Monte did not hesitate to commit them to attacking the Ottoman fleet.

In October 1571, three of the Order's galleys (*Capitana*, *San Pietro* and *San Giovanni*) took part in a major naval battle in the gulf of Patras in the Ionian Sea. Although the Hospitallers' contribution to the Battle of Lepanto was but a fraction of the 282 vessels the Holy League of the Papal States, Spain, Venice, Genoa and Savoy had put in the water, it nonetheless showed the Order's continued dedication to protecting Europe from an Ottoman invasion. During the expedition, the Hospitaller vessels were under the command of Pietro Giustiniana and formed the far right side of the central division of ships. This division was flanked by a left and right wing, and the whole supported by a rearguard and vanguard of ships.

Alof de Wignacourt, shown in this painting by Michelangelo Merisi da Caravaggio, was Grand Master of the Hospitallers between 1601 and 1622. He undertook the construction of a number of coastal fortifications on the islands.

Although the Ottomans had nearly as many ships, the Christian vessels out-gunned the Turks by more than two to one, and, despite an initial tactical advantage, the Ottomans were soon facing the destruction of their central division. In an attempt to gain access to the Christians' rear line, the Viceroy of Algiers, Aluch Ali, attempted to manoeuvre between the right and centre divisions. Seeing three ships at the end of the centre division flying the red and white flag, he turned his full attention on the Hospitaller ships. Sir William Stirling Maxwell

in his biography of Don John of Austria, the overall commander of the fleet, tells of the Hospitallers' valour during the conflict:

'Wheeling round like a hawk, [Ali] bore down from behind the unhappy Prior [Giustiniana]. The three war-worn vessels of St. John were no match for seven stout Algerines which had not yet fired a shot. The knights and their men defended themselves with a valour worthy of their heroic Order. A youth named Bernardino de Heredia, son of the Count of Fuentes, signally distinguished himself; and a Zaragozan knight, Geronimo Ramirez, although riddled with arrows like another St. Sebastian, fought with such desperation that none of the Algerine boarders cared to approach him until they saw he was dead. A knight of Burgundy leaped alone into one of the enemy's galleys, killed four Turks, and defended himself until overpowered by numbers. On board the Prior's vessel, when he was taken, he himself, pierced with five arrow wounds, was the sole survivor, except two knights, a Spaniard and a Sicilian, who, being senseless from their wounds, were considered as dead. Having secured the banner of St. John, Aluch Ali took the Prior's ship in tow, and was making the best of his way out of a battle which his skilful eye soon discovered to be irretrievably lost. He had not, however, sailed far when he was in turn descried by the Marques of Santa Cruz, who, with his squadron of reserve, was moving about redressing the wrongs of Christian fortune. Aluch Ali had no mind for the fate of Giustiniana, and resolved to content himself with the banner of Malta. Cutting his prize adrift, he plied his oars and escaped, leaving the Prior, grievously wounded, to the care of his friends, and once more master not only of his own ship, but of the three hundred dead enemies who cumbered the deck, a few living Algerine mariners who were to navigate the vessel, and some Turkish soldiers, from whom he had purchased his life. The struggle cost the Order, in killed alone, upwards of thirty knights, amongst whom was the Grand Bailiff of Germany, Commander-in-Chief of its land forces.'

Although the Hospitallers faced some heavy losses through casualties and captures, only seventeen of the Christian ships were lost in

the five-hour naval battle. By contrast, the Ottomans lost 187 ships, fifty to the bottom of the sea, the remaining 137 towed home to Christian ports. The victory at Lepanto was celebrated throughout Europe with the same degree of enthusiasm that the repulsion of the Ottoman invaders had been celebrated after the siege of Malta, six years earlier. Malta had destroyed the myth of Ottoman invincibility, but the addition of Lepanto buried the spectre of Ottoman aggression, at least in the minds of hopeful Europeans who truly believed that the Ottoman defeat would end the sight of Turkish sails in the Mediterranean.

This was not to be the case. In 1574, Aluch Ali sailed down from Constantinople, through the Mediterranean and on to Tunis with a sizeable fleet of Ottoman ships, recapturing the port city that the Hospitallers and Spaniards had captured in 1535. Once again the waters of the Mediterranean were open to Ottoman aggression and once again the Hospitallers' principal duty was to patrol the waters to guard against Muslim aggression in the same fashion they and the Templars had performed that duty in the Holy Land. But while history does not record the countless skirmishes that went on over the years, it would not be the Muslims who would send the Hospitallers from Malta, never to return; it would be one of their co-religionists.

In 1797, Ferdinand Joseph Antoine Herman Louis von Hompesch was elected to the position of Grand Master of the Order. In addition to having the distinction of perhaps the longest name of all the Order's Grand Masters, von Hompesch's Mastership of the Order would be distinguished by an historical first and a last: he was the Order's first German Master and he would be the last to rule his Order from Malta. Although it was said that he reluctantly accepted the post, the fact remains that he spent large sums of his own money to campaign for the position.

The Hospitallers had come a long way from the days when Grand Masters were humbly elected by their brethren. Although they never failed in carrying on the mission started by the Blessed Gerard so many centuries earlier, the Order had veered far off the path that

Top: **Selmun Castle, built by the Hospitallers in the eighteenth century, is now a hotel.**
Bigstock/ Liam McCarthy

Above: **Monument to Napoleon Bonaparte in his birthplace of Ajaccio, Corsica.**
Bigstock/ Carsten Madsen

The Order's death knell, at least with respect to Malta, was rung on 23 April 1798 in the form of a written bill, but fell upon von Hompesch's deaf ears. On that day, the Order was declared an enemy of France for having assisted King Louis and for Grand Master Emmanuel de Rohan's subsequent refusal to accept the French Republic after the king was executed. The document's two resolutions ordered General Napoleon Bonaparte to seize the island of Malta, by force if necessary. Although news of the secret plan had reached von Hompesch's ears, he refused to heed all warnings and remained unmoved to prepare any defences.

On 6 June, Napoleon's fleet of eighteen sailing ships and seventy transport vessels appeared off the coast of Malta. The ships' commander, Commodore Sidoux, sent a request to allow some of the vessels to enter the Grand Harbour and permission was granted. Three days later Napoleon arrived with the rest of the fleet, fourteen ships of the line, thirty frigates and three hundred transports. Napoleon was onboard the *Orient*, a 5,000-tonne ship of the line that would have dwarfed the Hospitallers' great carrack, the *Santa Anna*. The French General sent word to von Hompesch that he wanted access to the harbour for his fleet and access to the shore for his men. The Grand Master, finally aware that the warning had been real, reminded Napoleon that the treaty signed between France, Spain, Naples and Malta thirty years previously allowed but four warships at a time into the harbour. Although not prepared to bend the rules, von Hompesch sent his assurance that the island's hospitals would see to as many of the sick as could be brought to the island. Porter quotes the letter that was sent to von Hompesch in reply to his refusal:

'9th June, 1798

Your Highness,
'Having been nominated to proceed on board the admiral's ship with the reply which your eminence made to my request for permission to the squadron to water in your harbour, the commander-in-chief Bonaparte is highly indignant that such permission should have been restricted to four vessels at a time, for how long would it take for 500 sail at this rate

Raymond du Puy laid down for his brethren in the 1130s. Brethren who once guarded one another's chastity were now just as likely to introduce one another to women and other worldly pursuits. Von Hompesch's Mastership came at the end of a century that had seen the Order go through a period of steady decline; the Age of Faith had long since passed and the Age of Reason was well under way. Even the Order's greatest enemy, the Ottoman Empire, was in a period of decline and had been for a century. In fact, by the time of von Hompesch's election in 1797, the Ottomans were trying to reform their military along European lines.

Although the Ottomans were no longer a credible threat, von Hompesch knew that a greater one existed in France. The execution of King Louis XVI in January of 1793 had marked not only an end to the French monarchy but also the end to any hopes that the Hospitallers would recover the property confiscated by the revolutionaries. In his attempt to hold on to the throne in 1789, Louis had appealed to all landowners for a donation. The Hospitallers had been among the first to come forward, offering the king's finance minister one third of their revenues. As things got worse, the French brethren offered a personal guarantee of 500,000 francs to help the troubled king escape. After his capture the Order was taxed the same as any French citizen, and in 1792, the Order's properties were seized, just as they had been in England three hundred and fifty years earlier.

to procure water and such other necessities as they are much in want of? This refusal has the more surprised General Bonaparte since he is not ignorant of the preference you have shewn to the English, and the proclamation issued by the predecessor of your eminence. General Bonaparte has determined to obtain by force what should have been granted to him of free will, in accordance with the principles of hospitality which form the basis of your Order. I have seen the stupendous armament which is under the command of General Bonaparte, and I foresee the impossibility of the Order making any resistance. It was to have been wished, therefore, that under such adverse circumstances your eminence, for the love of your Order, your knights, and the whole population of Malta, had proposed some measures of accommodation. The general has not permitted me to return to a town which he considers himself obliged to regard as hostile, and which has no hope save in his mercy. He has, however, given strict orders that the religion, the property, and the customs of the people shall not be interfered with.'

Napoleon wasted no time in sending his orders to his commanders to take to shore at key locations on the island, as well as Gozo in the early morning hours of 10 June. By noon 15,000 French troops had landed at eleven different points around the island. Von Hompesch remained impotent throughout the invasion, although there would have been little he could have done to mount any real counterattack. Of the 332 knights living on the island, fifty were too ill or old to fight. The Order's artillery was also equally incapable of rising to the challenge, its cannon having not been fired for more than a century, except for ceremonial purposes. But the Hospitallers deserved better than a Grand Master who sequestered himself in his palace in the company of a solitary aide-de-camp.

Without a strong leader like de Villaret, L'Isle Adam or la Valette, the commanders of the various posts made little effort to stand in the way of the French, and 36 hours later, Malta, which 233 years earlier had withstood the best the Ottoman Empire could hurl at its rocky shores, surrendered without Napoleon ever setting foot on the island before the

Referred to as the Red Tower, St Agatha's Tower was completed in 1649 overlooking Gozo and Comino.
Bigstock/ Francesca Rizzo

armistice was signed on 11 June. The next morning Napoleon entered Valletta relieved that he did not have to take it by force. The era of the crusades had begun on French soil on 27 November 1095 when Pope Urban II delivered his famed speech; it officially ended on 12 June 1798 when von Hompesch signed the articles of capitulation that gave Malta to Napoleon Bonaparte.

The articles of capitulation required the Order to surrender Malta, Gozo and Comino and all its forts to the French army, surrendering all property rights to the French Republic, although personal property was excluded. In exchange, von Hompesch was promised a principality equal to the one he gave up as well as an annual pension of 300,000 livres. French knights were permitted to return to France and their property in Malta would remain theirs. French knights over the age of 60 were to be provided with a pension of 700 livres per year. The native Maltese would be allowed the free exercise of their religion and were given the assurance that their new French masters would not impose excessive taxes on them and all civil acts passed by the Hospitallers would remain in effect.

On 18 June 1798, von Hompesch and his knights (those who had joined the French army) left Malta with the same relics they had left Rhodes with in 1522: a fragment of the True Cross, the icon of Our Lady of Philerimos and the right hand of their patron St John the Baptist. But where L'Isle Adam had left Rhodes with his head held high and

his knights united, von Hompesch left Malta with his head hanging in shame, his knights dispersed. The Grand Master settled briefly at Trieste in the northeast of Italy before moving on to Montpellier in southern France. The majority of the remaining knights took refuge in the Grand Priory of Russia where they gathered around Tsar Paul I who carried the title of Protector of the Order. Soon von Hompesch was considered deposed as Grand Master and Paul elected in his stead, even though he was not a member of the Order, or even Catholic.

Paul's Grand Mastership would prove every bit as short-lived as the French control of Malta. In 1800, the British under Rear Admiral Lord Horatio Nelson blockaded the island, after which the French garrison surrendered. Two years later the Treaty of Amiens ended the French Revolutionary Wars and was supposed to see the British leave Malta; however, they remained on the island and in 1814, at the conclusion of the wars between Britain and France, Malta officially became part of the British Empire and the Hospitallers would never return. As had been the case when they lost Rhodes, the remnants of the Order wandered around Europe for a number of years, starting at Messina; the central convent moved to Catania on the east coast of Sicily from 1803 until 1826, then briefly at Ferrera di Varese northwest of Milan before finally settling into its permanent home in Rome in 1834. It was here at Rome where the Order could finally rise like a phoenix from the ashes. After nearly 80 years of being led by a series of lieutenants elected by the brethren and approved by the church, Pope Leo XIII restored the Order's leadership with the title of Grand Master. The Order elected an Italian, Giovanni Battista (John Baptist) Ceschi a Santa Croce.

Since that time the Order, now known as the Sovereign Military Hospitaller Order of St John of Jerusalem of Rhodes and of Malta, has elected nine Grand Masters, the most recent being Matthew Festing, who is the third Englishman to be elected to the position of Grand Master. Festing's English predecessors were Hugues de Revel in 1258, a man who did much to reform the militarisation of the Hospitallers, and Andrew Bertie in 1988, who ensured that the Order remained true to the role set out for it by Brother Gerard in the eleventh century.

Today the Hospitallers continue that work by operating in 120 countries with 12,500 members and approximately 80,000 volunteers. After nearly a thousand years of continued existence, the Amalfian cross still represents the Hospitallers' mission to care for the sick and the poor.

HOSPITALLER CHRONOLOGY

325 Emperor Constantine I orders the construction of the Holy Sepulchre over the site of an old pagan temple dedicated to Aphrodite. It was during the excavation of the site that Constantine's mother, Helena, is alleged to have discovered the True Cross upon which Christ was crucified and the tomb in which he was buried. The discovery begins the practice of Christian pilgrimage to Jerusalem.

608/610 John Eleemon appointed Patriarch of Alexandria. It is this St John, rather than St John the Baptist, to whom the original hospital was dedicated.

870 Arabs take Malta from Byzantines.

969 The Fatimids capture Jerusalem.

1009 Caliph Al-Hākim orders the destruction of a number of Christian buildings, including the Church of the Holy Sepulchre and a hostel for pilgrims.

1050 Date often given for the construction of two hospitals in Jerusalem by Amalfian merchants.

1071 In August, Seljuk Turks defeat Byzantine Christians at the Battle of Manzikert. The weakened empire appeals to western Christianity for assistance.

1071 Seljuk Turks capture Jerusalem.

1080 Date which Blessed Brother Gerard is believed to have become involved with the hospital of Jerusalem. Gerard is universally recognised as the founder of the Hospitallers.

1095 On 27 November, Pope Urban II preaches a crusade to take Jerusalem from the Muslims.

1096 Several groups of Europeans ranging from peasants to princes depart to take up Urban's crusade. Most would never see Jerusalem; some would not even make it out of Europe.

1098 Baldwin of Bologne leaves the Jerusalem campaign to establish himself at Edessa.

1098 Bohemond of Taranto occupies Antioch after crusaders capture the fortified city.

1098 Fatimids regain control of Jerusalem from Seljuk Turks.

1099 On July 15, the crusaders capture the city of Jerusalem and it becomes the capital of the Kingdom of Jerusalem, one of several Crusader States that would exist in the Holy Land over the next two centuries. Godfrey de Bouillon becomes the first ruler; however, he refuses to accept the title of king, preferring the title of Defender of the Holy Sepulchre.

1113 On 15 March, Pope Paschal II officially recognises the Hospitallers and Brother Gerard as their leader. His bull of that day grants the new Order special privileges and protection within the Catholic Church.

1119 The Knights Templar are formed under Hugues de Payens and Geoffroi de St Omer, two French knights with the idea of creating a monastic and militant police force to protect Christian pilgrims visiting the Holy Land.

1120 Brother Gerard dies on 3 September and is succeeded by a French knight named Raymond du Puy.

1126 Mention is made of a Hospitaller constable, and for this reason some historians believe that the Hospitallers had taken on a military role at this time.

1128 Raymond du Puy is recorded as accompanying Baldwin II to Ascalon during a campaign, suggesting to some historians that the Hospitallers were engaging in military exploits by this early date.

1128 The Templars receive their rule of order at the Council of Troyes.

1130 Raymond du Puy creates a simple set of statutes of the Hospitallers.

1136 King Fulk of Jerusalem grants the Hospitallers his newly built castle at Beit Jibrin, roughly 20 kilometres north of Hebron in the Kingdom of Jerusalem's southern reaches. This gift strongly suggests that the Hospitallers were involved in military operations.

1136 Hugues de Payens, founder of the Knights Templar, dies and is replaced by Robert de Craon.

1142 Count Raymond II of Tripoli gives the Hospitallers the imposing castle Krak des Chevaliers, which would become a key fortress for the Hospitallers for more than a century. Krak was a particularly important gift because it offered the only real protection to a large undefended trading area from potential attacks from the Muslims' fortified city of Homs.

1144 Zengi, the Governor of Aleppo, recaptures Edessa from the Christians. The loss prompts Pope Eugenius III to call a new crusade.

1146 Zengi's son Nūr al-Dīn comes to power in Aleppo and begins attacks on Christian fortifications. When Count Joscelin tries to retake Edessa, Zengi kills the Christian inhabitants and destroys the city.

1148 Hospitallers take part in the siege of Damascus, a battle that effectively puts an end to the Second Crusade.

1153 Hospitallers take part in the siege of Ascalon and succeed in capturing the city after the Templars were killed.

1154 Nūr al-Dīn captures Damascus and adds it to Zengid territory.

1160 Death of Raymond du Puy.

1163 Egyptians invite King Amalric of Jerusalem to come to their aid against Nūr al-Dīn. Both the Hospitaller Grand Master Arnaud de Comps and the Templar Grand Master Bertrand de Blanchefort are enthusiastic supporters of the campaign and bring a number of their men.

1168 Belvoir Fortress, located 20 miles south of the Sea of Galilee, is sold to the Hospitallers by a French nobleman named Velos. The Hospitallers expand the existing fortress into a large concentric castle.

1168 Hospitallers take part in a failed military campaign in Egypt with King Amalric.

1169 Saladin becomes vizier of Egypt.

1170 Gilbert d'Aissailly resigns as Grand Master, largely due to the failure of the Egyptian campaign two years earlier.

1174 Nūr al-Dīn dies on 15 May.

1174 Amalric dies of dysentery in July and is replaced by his thirteen-year-old leper son who is crowned Baldwin IV.

1175 As Sultan of Egypt Saladin captures Homs, Hama and Baalbek.

1176 Saladin continues to expand his territory with the capture of

	Manbij and Azaz. His attempt to take Aleppo fails.
1176	Reynald de Châtillon is released from prison in Aleppo with a rabid hatred for Islam.
1177	Baldwin IV and the Templars defeat Saladin at the Battle of Montgisard.
1177	Roger de Moulins becomes Grand Master of the Hospitallers.
1179	Battles of Marj Ayyun and Jacob's Ford result in victories for the Christians.
1180	Baldwin IV's sister Sibylla marries Guy of Lusignan. The couple are married at Easter and Guy was given Ascalon and Jaffa as his fief.
1182	Battle of Belvoir Castle is a tactical draw.
1183	Battles of Al-Fule and Kerak in Outrejordain end in draws.
1185	Gerard de Ridefort becomes Grand Master of the Templars.
1185	Baldwin IV dies in March and is replaced by his seven-year-old nephew.
1186	Gerard de Ridefort and the Templars help Guy and Sibylla stage a coup in September to gain control of the Kingdom of Jerusalem. The Hospitallers support Raymond of Tripoli, the legitimate regent.
1186	Hospitallers purchase the castle of Marqab from a vassal of the Count of Tripoli.
1187	On 1 May, the Battle of Cresson Springs is fought, during which Roger de Moulins is killed. The only survivors are Gerard de Ridefort and three of his Templars.
1187	On 4 July, Hospitallers and Templars take part in the Battle of Hattin and suffer a monumental defeat which cripples the Christians' ability to resist Saladin's future attacks.
1187	Between July and September, Saladin captures Acre, Toron, Sidon, Gibelet, Beirut and Ascalon before turning his attention on Jerusalem.
1187	Saladin begins his siege of Jerusalem on 20 September and the city surrenders on 2 October.
1188	King Guy and Gerard de Ridefort are released by Saladin and after being refused entry into Tyre, Guy lays siege to Acre on 28 August. De Ridefort is killed in a skirmish soon after.
1189	The Hospitallers' Belvoir Castle is besieged and ultimately captured by

	Saladin who tears it down so that it cannot be used by the Christians.
1190	Garnier de Nablus elected Grand Master of the Hospitallers.
1191	On 12 May, King Richard I of England captures Cyprus en route to Acre.
1191	On 12 July, Acre surrenders to the crusaders. Thousands of Muslim captives are later executed when ransoms are not promptly paid.
1191	Battle of Arsuf on 7 September is a victory for the crusaders despite the Hospitallers breaking ranks and leading the charge before the call was given.
1191	Jaffa is captured by King Richard on 29 September.
1192	On 2 September, the Masters of the Hospitallers and the Templars, together with Henry of Champagne and Balian d'Ibelin, sign a peace treaty with Saladin on behalf of Richard I. The Christians once again have access to Jerusalem and the Third Crusade is brought to a close.
1193	Saladin dies on 4 March.
1199	King Richard I dies on 11 April.
1202	An earthquake causes considerable damage to Krak des Chevaliers. The Hospitallers enlarge the fortress at the same time as they make the repairs.
1204	Crusaders attack Constantinople during the Fourth Crusade, causing greater strain between the eastern and western churches.
1227	Frederick II goes on crusade.
1235	Pope Gregory IX intercedes in a dispute between the Hospitallers and Templars over each other's mills near Acre.
1236	Pope Gregory IX threatens the Templars and Hospitallers with excommunication to prevent them from co-operating with the Muslim Assassins sect against Bohemond V of Antioch.
1238	Pope Gregory IX accuses the Hospitallers of disregarding their vows of chastity, poverty and obedience.
1244	Jerusalem is captured by the Khwarezmian Tartars, allies of the sultan of Egypt, who moved south to escape the advancing Mongols two decades earlier.
1244	The Christians are defeated at Battle of La Forbie on 17 October. The Hospitallers lose all but twenty-seven of their men, and

	although Grand Master de Chateauneuf survived, he did so as a prisoner bound for Egypt.
1248	Hospitallers are finally permitted to wear wider surcoats instead of the tight-fitting monastic robes they had worn in battle since their beginnings. These wide surcoats are only permitted to be worn in areas where the threat of battle was most likely.
1250	Battle of Al Mansurah is fought from 8-11 February and results in another devastating loss for the Hospitallers and Templars.
1250	Chronicler Matthew de Paris suggests that the Hospitallers were then in possession of 19,000 manors while the Templars possessed 9,000.
1259	Pope Alexander IV orders the Hospitallers to create a distinction in dress between knights and sergeants, similar to what the other Military Orders had been doing for some time.
1263	After negotiations with the Templars and Hospitallers break down, the Mamluk Sultan Baibars marches into Christian territory, sacks Nazareth, destroys the Church of the Virgin and launches an attack on Acre. Although Baibars manages to sack the suburbs, he never actually lays siege to the city itself.
1271	Baibars takes Montfort Castle from the Teutonic Knights, Safita from the Templars, and Krak des Chevaliers from the Hospitallers.
1274	Council of Lyons discusses the idea of uniting the Military Orders.
1282	A change in statutes dictates that only knights of the Order could be elected Grand Master.
1285	Qalāwūn captures Marqab from the Hospitallers after a month-long siege.
1285	Philip IV becomes king of France.
1289	Templars receive advance warning of planned Mamluk attack on Tripoli.
1291	Mamluks begin siege of Acre on 5 April and capture the city on 18 May. Hospitallers and Templars take refuge on Cyprus with the rest of the Christian survivors.
1292	Pope Nicholas IV discusses the prospect of a new crusade. There is little interest. Also asks Hospitallers to increase their naval presence in the Mediterranean.

1293	Jacques de Molay elected Grand Master of the Templars. He will be their last.
1293	Jean de Villiers dies and is succeeded by Odo de Pins.
1294	Henry II of Cyprus imposes taxes on the Hospitallers and Templars, which causes Pope Boniface VIII to intercede. The Cypriot monarch also forbids the Order from owning any further property on the island.
1296	Odo de Pins is succeeded by Guillaume de Villaret.
1298	Templars involved in the Eperstone affair at Balantrodoch.
1300	Pope Boniface VIII recaps the original rule of Raymond du Puy lost at the fall of Acre in 1291 and sends it to the Hospitallers now stationed on Cyprus.
1302	Mamluks drive Templars from the island of Arwad back to the security of Cyprus.
1305	Foulques de Villaret succeeds his uncle Guillaume de Villaret as Grand Master of the Order.
1305	Bertrand de Got elected Pope. Takes the name Clement V.
1306	Templars assist King Henry II's brother Amaury in deposing his brother. The Hospitallers once again side with the rightful regent.
1306	De Villaret and de Molay are summoned by Pope Clement V to France. Only de Molay goes. De Villaret is busy beginning his moves against Rhodes.
1306	Hospitallers begin assault on Rhodes and by autumn capture the fortress of Faraklos and the hill of Filerimos at Trianda.
1307	De Villaret finally travels to Rome to visit Pope Clement V.
1307	Templars are arrested in France on 13 October under charges of heresy.
1309	Year given by modern historians for the capture of Rhodes by the Hospitallers.
1310	15 August is the date given by nineteenth-century historians for the conquest of Rhodes by de Villaret and the Hospitallers.
1311	Council of Vienne convenes on 16 October to try the Knights Templar.
1312	Pope Clement V issues the papal bull *Vox in excelso* on 2 May, officially dissolving the Templars for all time.
1312	Clement issues the bull *Ad providam*, turning the Templars' former properties over to the Hospitallers. The gift would prove

	to be more trouble than it was worth due to the difficulties in obtaining the land.
1314	Jacques de Molay, the last Grand Master of the Templars, is burned at the stake on 18 March.
1314	Hospitallers capture island of Lerro.
1315	Hospitallers capture island of Kos.
1317	Hospitallers build Castle Lindros on the acropolis.
1319	Turks capture the island of Lango from the Hospitallers.
1319	De Villaret is forced to resign as Grand Master and is succeeded by Hélion de Villeneuve.
1320	Villeneuve refines the system of Langues, assigning the *pilier*, head of each Langue, one of the Order's great offices: Provence provides the grand commander, Auvergne the Marshal, France the Hospitaller, England the turcopolier (commander of light cavalry), Italy the admiral, and Spain provided the Order's drapier; Germany played no special role at this stage of the organisational evolution.
1332	Dieudonné de Gozon is said to have slain a dragon on Rhodes. The legend would live long after he became Grand Master.
1334	Hospitallers under de Villeneuve destroy one hundred Turkish vessels.
1344	Hospitallers assist Papal League in capturing Smyrna (Izmir).
1346	Dieudonné de Gozon succeeds de Villeneuve as Grand Master.
1402	Hospitallers build Bodrum Castle in southwest Turkey.
1444	Mehmed II ascends to the Ottoman throne at the age of twelve.
1444	Mamluks attempt to take Rhodes.
1453	Sultan Mehmed II captures Constantinople for the Ottoman Empire ending more than a millennium of Byzantine rule.
1454	Pierre d'Aubusson is sent by Grand Master Jean de Lastic to Europe to secure arms and alms to prepare for a Turkish attack that de Lastic felt could come at any time.
1459	Mehmed II conquers Serbia.
1460	Mehmed II conquers the Peloponnese peninsula.
1460	Pierre d'Aubusson is appointed Castellan of Rhodes and soon after is elevated to the post of Captain General of the City. It is in this capacity that d'Aubusson personally oversees the upgrade to Rhodes' defences which include the erection of a seaward curtain wall and

	several new towers, the expansion of all landward ditches and the installation of a boom chain across the island's commercial harbour.
1465	Hospitallers build Fort of St Nicholas on the harbour at Rhodes.
1470	Mehmed II attacks Tilos, forcing islanders to take refuge on Rhodes.
1475	Mehmed II attacks Chalki. Residents evacuate to Rhodes.
1476	Pierre d'Aubusson replaces Giovanni Battista Orsini as Grand Master in June.
1480	Ottomans begin their invasion of Rhodes on 23 May and are defeated on 28 July.
1481	Mehmed II dies and his sons Cem and Bayezid fight over territory.
1482	Sultan Bayezid signs two peace treaties with the Hospitallers.
1485	Pierre d'Aubusson is made a cardinal in the Catholic Church.
1488	Orders of the Holy Sepulchre and St Lazarus are merged with the Hospitallers.
1495	Cem dies, virtually a prisoner of Pope Alexander VI.
1503	Pierre d'Aubusson dies and is succeeded by Emery d'Amboise.
1507	The Hospitallers capture the *Mogarbina*, part of the fleet of the Mamluk Sultan of Egypt, near Kos. They rechristen the carrack the *Santa Maria*.
1510	Hospitallers defeat Ottomans and Mamluks at Laiazzo (Yumurtalik).
1517	A German theologian named Martin Luther begins challenging Catholic beliefs and traditions with his *Ninety-Five Theses on the Power and Efficacy of Indulgences*, which he nails to the door of the Castle Church in Wittenberg, Germany, on All Saints' Eve.
1517	Ottomans defeat Mamluks.
1520	Suleiman becomes sultan of the Ottoman Empire at the age of 26.
1521	Grand Master Fabrizio del Carretto dies and is succeeded by Philippe Villiers de L'Isle Adam.
1521	Martin Luther is excommunicated by Pope Leo X and regarded as a criminal of the state by the Holy Roman Emperor Charles V.
1521	Sultan Suleiman captures Belgrade.
1521	France invades Navarre in the autumn.
1522	The Hospitallers are ejected from Rhodes by the Ottoman Sultan Suleiman after a six-month siege.
1523	Hospitallers arrive at Messina in the spring.

1523	Giulio de Medici, a former Hospitaller, is elected Pope Clement VII.
1524	Charles V offers the Hospitallers the islands of Malta and Gozo.
1525	Francis I taken prisoner by Charles V at the Battle of Pavia in Northern Italy, fought on 24 February.
1526	Francis I released from prison in Madrid.
1526	Suleiman defeats Hungarians at Mohács.
1527	Henry VIII threatens to seize Hospitaller property in England.
1527	Rome is sacked by mercenaries in the army of Charles V on 6 May and Pope Clement VII is forced to abandon the city after spending some time confined to his castle.
1529	Clement VII is able to return to Rome after truces are signed between Spain and France.
1529	Ottomans attack Vienna but are repelled.
1530	Charles officially coroneted Holy Roman Emperor by Clement VII at Bologna on 24 February.
1530	On 23 March, the Hospitallers are granted Malta, Gozo and Tripoli. Eight years of exile ends.
1531	Hospitallers assist Venetians in capturing Modon (Methoni) on the southwestern coast of Greece, but lose it shortly after.
1531	Henry VIII sends a ship to Malta with a number of cannon for the Hospitallers in lieu of the 20,000 crowns he had promised the Grand Master five years previously.
1532	Hospitallers assist Andrea Doria in capturing Coron (Koroni), southeast of Modon.
1533	Suleiman summons Khair al-Dīn from Algiers to aid him in building and running his fleet.
1533	Henry VIII divorces Catherine of Aragon and establishes his own Church after the backlash from Rome.
1534	Khair al-Dīn captures Tunis for the Ottomans on 16 August. L'Isle Adam dies three weeks after the capture and is replaced by Piero del Ponte.
1535	Hospitallers help Charles V capture Tunis from the Ottomans.
1535	Grand Master Piero del Ponte dies and is succeeded by Didier de Saint-Jaille.
1536	De Saint-Jaille dies and is succeeded by Juan de Homedes y Coscón.

1538	Francis I and Suleiman create a Franco-Ottoman alliance against Charles V.
1538	Henry VIII begins imposing conditions on the Hospitallers in England.
1540	Spanish abandon La Goletta.
1540	Henry VIII seizes Hospitaller assets and dissolves English Langue in April.
1540	Hospitallers decommission their great carrack, the *Santa Anna*.
1541	Christians defeated at Battle of Algiers.
1546	Khair al-Dīn dies at Constantinople and is replaced by Turgut Reis as admiral of the Ottoman fleet.
1550	Turgut Reis captures Mahdia, midway between Tunis and Tripoli. Hospitallers assist in recapturing it in the same year and the city is destroyed to prevent the Ottomans from using it in the future.
1551	Turgut Reis launches a failed attack on Malta. Succeeds in taking Tripoli instead.
1553	Juan de Homedes y Coscón dies and is succeeded by Claude de la Sengle.
1554	Jean Parisot de la Valette appointed admiral of the Hospitaller fleet.
1555	Hospitaller fleet damaged during a hurricane.
1556	Charles V abdicates the Spanish throne in favour of his son Philip.
1557	Claude de la Sengle dies and is succeeded by Jean Parisot de la Valette.
1556	Turks attack the Balearic islands of Majorca and Minorca and run coastal raids on the Spanish mainland.
1560	Philip II launches a failed campaign against Tripoli. Defeated at Battle of Djerba.
1564	Hospitallers under Romégas help capture Peñón de Vélez for Spain.
1564	Romégas captures a large galleon belonging to the Kızlar Ağası.
1565	Ottomans besiege Malta for nearly four months to be defeated by the Hospitallers.
1566	La Valette lays the cornerstone for Valletta on 28 March.
1566	Suleiman dies at Constantinople on 6 September.
1569	Grand Master la Valette dies on 21 August after suffering a stroke. He is succeeded by Pierre de Monte.
1570	Saint-Clement, the general of the Order, is tried for cowardice, imprisoned and expelled from the

	Order. He is executed after a public trial.
1571	Hospitallers take part in the Christian victory at the Battle of Lepanto.
1574	Aluch Ali recaptures Tunis.
1581	Romégas becomes a rival Grand Master.
1601	Alof de Wignacourt becomes Grand Master and undertakes a number of coastal fortifications on the islands.
1618	Marija Tower or St Mary's Tower on Comino is built to improve communication between the islands.
1649	Hospitallers complete St Agatha's Tower overlooking the islands of Gozo and Comino.
1670	Fort Ricasoli is built opposite Fort St Elmo in the Grand Harbour.
1792	Hospitaller properties are seized in France.
1793	King Louis XVI executed in France.
1797	Ferdinand Joseph Antoine Herman Louis von Hompesch elected Grand Master.
1798	Napoleon captures Malta on his way to Egypt.
1800	French surrender Malta to the British.
1803	Hospitallers move their central convent to Catania on the east coast of Sicily.
1814	Malta becomes part of the British Empire.
1834	Hospitallers relocate to Rome.
1869	Lutheran Church of the Redeemer is commenced over the Church of Santa Maria ad Latinos in Jerusalem. The church is completed by 1900.
1972	Sovereign Military Order of Malta erects a monument and garden in the Muristan at Jerusalem where the Order's hospital had once stood.

BIBLIOGRAPHY

Barber, Malcolm – *The New Knighthood: A History of the Order of the Temple* (New York: Cambridge UP, 1995)

Barber, Malcolm – *Trial of the Templars* (Cambridge: Cambridge UP, 1993)

Barber, Malcolm – *Battles of the Medieval World 1000-1500* (London: Amber Books, 2006)

Billings, Malcolm – *The Cross and the Crescent: A History of the Crusades* (New York: Sterling Pub Co Inc, 1990)

Boase, Thomas R. – *Kingdoms and Strongholds of the Crusades* (Indianapolis: Bobbs-Merrill Co, 1971)

Bosio, Giacomo – *Le Imagini Dei Beati e Santi Della Sacra Religione* (Rome: Decio Cirillo, 1860)

Bradford, Ernle – *Knights of the Order* (New York: Marboro Books, 1991)

Bronstein, Judith – *The Hospitallers and the Holy Land: Financing the Latin East, 1187-1274* (New York: Boydell, 2005)

Broun, Richard – *Synoptical Sketch of the Illustrious and Sovereign Order of Knights Hospitallers of St. John of Jerusalem and of the Venerable Langue of England* (London: Printed For the Order, 1857)

Bush, M. L. – *Renaissance, Reformation and the Outer World* (London: Copp Clark, 1967)

Caoursin, Guillaume – *The Siege of Rhodes Edition 1490* (London: Verbatim Reprints, 1870)

Comay, Joan – *The Temple of Jerusalem* (London: Weidenfeld and Nicolson, 1975)

Coulombe, Charles A. – *A History of the Popes* (New York: MJF Books, 2003)

Daftary, Farhad – *The Assassin Legends: Myths of the Isma'ilis* (London: I. B. Tauris, 1995)

De Boisgelin, Louis – *Ancient and Modern Malta* (Vol 1 Black Friars: Richard Phillips, 1805)

Dickens, A. G. – *European Emergence Time Frame AD 1500-1600* (Alexandria, Va: Time-Life Books, 1989)

Dickens, A. G. – *Reformation and Society in Sixteenth-Century Europe* (London: Thames and Hudson, 1971)

Ferguson, Wallace K. – *Europe in Transition 1300-1520* (Boston: Houghton Mifflin, 1962)

Forey, Alan – *The Military Orders* (Toronto: University of Toronto, 1992)

Francesco, Gabrieli – *Arab Historians of the Crusades* (New York: Dorset, 1989)

Froude, James A. – *The Divorce of Catherine of Aragon* (New York: Charles Scribener's Sons, 1891)

Ganshof, F. L. – *Feudalism* (New York: Harper Torchbooks, 1964)

Gies, Frances – *Knight in History* (New York: Harper & Row, 1984)

Hampson, Norman – *The Enlightenment* (New York: Penguin (Non-Classics), 1991)

Kagia, Betty – *Rhodes: An Ancient Medieval Modern Island of the Sun* (Grand Rapids: Mardin, 1997)

Karageorghis, Jacqueline – *Cyprus: There is an Island* (Nicosia, Cyprus: Philippides, 1987)

Keen, Maurice Hugh – *The Pelican History of Medieval Europe* (Harmondsworth: Penguin, 1969)

Kingsley, Rose Georgina – *The Order of St. John of Jerusalem* (past and present) (New York: AMS, 1978)

Larking, Lambert B., ed. – *The Knights Hospitallers in England* (London: Camden Society, 1858)

Lee, Stephen J. – *Aspects of European History* (Second ed. London: Routledge, 1984)

Lewis, Bernard – *The Assassins: A Radical Sect in Islam* (London: Phoenix, 2003)

Lord, Evelyn – *Knights Templar in Britain* (New York: Longman, 2004)

'Malta and its Knights' – *The Naval Magazine* (September 1837, pp413-19)

Nicholson, Helen, and David Nicolle – *God's Warriors: Knights Templar, Saracens and the Battle for Jerusalem* (Grand Rapids: Osprey, 2006)

Nicholson, Helen – *The Knights Hospitaller* (Woodbridge: Boydell & Brewer, 2006)

Nicolle, David – *Acre 1291: Bloody Sunset of the Crusader States* (Grand Rapids: Osprey, 2005)

Nicolle, David – *Knight Hospitaller (1): 1100-1306 (Warrior)* (Grand Rapids: Osprey, 2001)

Nicolle, David – *Knight Hospitaller (2): 1306-1565 (Warrior)* (Grand Rapids: Osprey, 2001)

Nicolle, David – *Knights of Jerusalem: The Crusading Order of Hospitallers 1100-1565 (World of the Warrior)* (Westminster: Osprey, 2008)

Ozment, Steven E. – *Protestants: The Birth of a Revolution* (New York: Doubleday, 1993)

Philips, Charles – *An Illustrated History of the Crusades and Crusader Knights: The History, Myth and Romance of the Medieval Knight on Crusade* (Lorenz Books, 2009)

Porter, Whitworth – *A History of the Fortress of Malta* (Valletta: P. Cumbo Army Printer, 1858)

Porter, Whitworth – *A History of the Knights of Malta or the Order of St John of Jerusalem* (London: Longmans, Green and Co, 1883)

Reston, James – *Defenders of the Faith* (New York: Penguin, 2009)

Reston, James Jr – *Warriors of God: Richard the Lionheart and Saladin in the Third Crusade* (New York: Anchor, 2002)

Riley-Smith, Jonathan – *The First Crusade and the Idea of Crusading* (Philadelphia: University of Pennsylvania, 1986)

Seward, Desmond – *The Monks of War: The Military Religious Orders* (London: Penguin Books, 1995)

Spitz, Lewis W. – *The Reformation: Material or Spiritual?* (Boston: DC Heath and Co, 1966)

Stearns, Peter N. – *European Society in Upheaval: Social History since 1750* (New York: Macmillan, 1975)
Stirling-Maxwell, William – *Don Juan of Austria. Vol 1.* (London: Longmans, Green and Co, 1873)

Sutherland, Alexander – *The Achievements of the Knights of Malta* (Vol 1. Edinburgh: Constable and Co, 1831)

Taaffe, John – *The History of the Holy, Military, Sovereign Order of St. John of Jerusalem V1: Or Knights Hospitallers, Knights Templars, Knights of Rhodes, Knights of Malta* (London: Hope and Co, 1852)

Taaffe, John – *The History of the Holy, Military, Sovereign Order of St. John of Jerusalem V3: Or Knights Hospitallers, Knights Templars, Knights of Rhodes, Knights of Malta* (London: Hope and Co, 1852)

Tyerman, Christopher – *God's War: A New History of the Crusades* (London: Allen Lane, 2006)

Vaughan, Richard, ed. – *The Illustrated Chronicles of Matthew Paris* (Cambridge: Corpus Christi College, 1993)

Vertot, René-Aubert – *The History of the Knights Hospitallers (Vol 1)* (Dublin: J. Christie, 1818.)

Vertot, René-Aubert – *The History of the Knights Hospitallers. (Vol 2)* (Dublin: J. Christie, 1818)

Vertot, René-Aubert – *The History of the Knights Hospitallers. (Vol 3)* (Dublin: J. Christie, 1818)

Wallen, William – *The History and Antiquities of the Round Church at Little Maplestead, Essex* (London: John Weal, 1836)

Windrow, Martin. – *Not One Step Back: History's Greatest Sieges* (London: Quercus, 2008)

Younge, Charlotte M. – *A Book of Golden Deeds of all Times and Lands* (London: MacMillan and Co, 1864)

INDEX